DISCOVERING OUR PAST

DISCOVERING OUR PAST

A Brief Introduction to Archaeology

SIXTH EDITION

Wendy Ashmore
University of California, Riverside

Robert J. Sharer
University of Pennsylvania

Connect
Learn
Succeed™

DISCOVERING OUR PAST: A BRIEF INTRODUCTION TO ARCHAEOLOGY,
SIXTH EDITION

Published by McGraw-Hill, a business unit of The McGraw-Hill Companies, Inc., 1221 Avenue
of the Americas, New York, NY, 10020. Copyright © 2014 by The McGraw-Hill Companies, Inc.
All rights reserved. Printed in the United States of America. Previous editions © 2012, 2010, 2006.
No part of this publication may be reproduced or distributed in any form or by any means, or
stored in a database or retrieval system, without the prior written consent of The McGraw-Hill
Companies, Inc., including, but not limited to, in any network or other electronic storage or
transmission, or broadcast for distance learning.

Some ancillaries, including electronic and print components, may not be available to customers
outside the United States.

This book is printed on acid-free paper.

1 2 3 4 5 6 7 8 9 0 DOC/DOC 1 0 9 8 7 6 5 4 3

ISBN   9780078034916
MHID   0078034914

Senior Vice President, Products & Markets:
   Kurt L. Strand
Vice President, General Manager, Products &
   Markets: *Michael Ryan*
Executive Director of Development: *Lisa Pinto*
Managing Director: *Gina Boedeker*
Brand Manager: *Courtney Austermehle*
Marketing Specialist: *Alexandra Schultz*

Managing Development Editor: *Penina Braffman*
Editorial Coordinator: *Adina Lonn*
Director, Content Production: *Terri Schiesl*
Senior Project Manager: *Lisa A. Bruflodt*
Buyer: *Nichole Birkenholz*
Media Project Manager: *Sridevi Palani*
Photo Research: *Editorial Image, LLC*
Cover Designer: *Studio Montage, St. Louis, MO.*

Cover Image: © Wendy Ashmore, 1991; © Orlando Sierra/AFP/Getty Images. Cover images
illustrate some of the research Robert J. Sharer conducted in the Copan Acropolis, the royal
precinct of that Classic Maya city.

Typeface: 10/12 Janson
Compositor: MPS Limited
Printer: R. R. Donnelley

Library of Congress Cataloging-in-Publication Data

Ashmore, Wendy, 1948–
   Discovering our past : a brief introduction to archaeology / Wendy
Ashmore, Robert J. Sharer.—Sixth edition.
     pages cm
   Includes bibliographical references and index.
   ISBN 978-0-07-803491-6 (acid-free paper) 1. Archaeology. I. Sharer,
Robert J. II. Title.
   CC75.A74 2013
   930.1—dc23

                   2012047506

The Internet addresses listed in the text were accurate at the time of publication. The
inclusion of a website does not indicate an endorsement by the authors or McGraw-Hill, and
McGraw-Hill does not guarantee the accuracy of the information presented at these sites.

www.mhhe.com

Contents

v

Preface

As CHILDREN, MANY OF us learn to associate archaeologists with adventurous exploits and searches for long-lost civilizations in exotic places. As adults, our associations of archaeology with adventure are often strengthened when we see and hear stories in the media about fantastic archaeological finds. But what is it that archaeologists actually *do* on a normal workday in the field? This book corrects some of the popular myths about archaeologists and archaeology and explains what archaeologists really do, and how they do it.

We begin with a brief overview of archaeology, how it grew over the past few centuries, and how archaeologists today use various means to attempt to discover the past. The remainder of the book is organized to follow the steps of actual archaeological research. Beginning with the formulation of questions that define the goals of each research effort, we then look at the methods used to gather and analyze archaeological evidence, how archaeologists interpret this evidence, and how they present results to other archaeologists and the public. The book closes with a discussion of the challenges faced by archaeologists—how to reconcile the needs of archaeologists and other concerned groups who have an interest in the past.

This book is written specifically for introductory archaeology courses, especially surveys of human prehistory that include an introduction to archaeological method and theory. It derives from our more comprehensive text, *Archaeology: Discovering Our Past* (Third Edition, McGraw-Hill 2003). Both texts follow the same basic organization and share the same underlying philosophy—that archaeology is part of the broader field of anthropology with its concern for investigating all aspects of the human experience. Both books are also based on the premise that the evidence sought by archaeologists in their study of the past represents a nonrenewable resource. This resource is fragile and especially precious, for archaeological evidence is the only means for us to discover most of our past.

This doesn't mean that there is only one way to view our past—often there are several ways to study the evidence from the past. Although hands-on exercises are beyond the scope of this volume, useful workbooks include *Archaeology to Delight and Instruct: Active Learning in the University Classroom* (Burke and Smith, 2007, for instructors) and *The Theory and Practice of Archaeology: A Workbook* (Patterson, 2005, for students and instructors). There is no single way for doing archaeology, and the best archaeology is that which uses the best methods available in each research situation.

NEW TO THE SIXTH EDITION

The text overall has been updated, bringing in more current examples. Many changes involve brief modifications to the text, but more new images and extensive verbal additions can be found in multiple chapters.

Everywhere in this edition, and particularly in Chapters 1, 4, and 10, we expand attention to cultural resource management, job opportunities, rising concern with global and local cultural heritage, and the relevance of archaeology in the modern world.

Throughout, we give new emphasis to the growing collaboration between descendent communities and archaeologists, and to the crucial importance of ethics and respect in all that archaeologists do.

Chapters 4 though 10 extend consideration of ecofacts and relations to the environment more generally. Chapter 5 highlights advances in remote sensing techniques for archaeological reconnaissance and survey. Chapter 6 discusses reconstructing life histories of ancient individuals though chemical isotope analysis of teeth and bones.

ACKNOWLEDGMENTS

Preparation of this new edition has once again benefited from the help of many people. Many improvements to this edition stemmed from the suggestions of colleagues who reviewed the manuscript, to whom we are immensely grateful for sharing their time and insights:

- Anthony Boldurian, University of Pittsburgh at Greensburg
- Douglas Sanford, University of Mary Washington
- William Doonan, Sacramento City College
- Royal Omar Ghazal, University of Chicago

- Michael Gregory, DePaul University
- Thomas Foster, Univ. of West Georgia

Many people at McGraw-Hill Higher Education have contributed to all stages of preparing this book. Nadia Bidwell, Development Editor, in particular provided motivation and enthusiastic encouragement. We also thank marketing specialist Alexandra Schultz, Managing Development Editor Penina Braffman, manuscript editor Kathryn DiBernardo, designer Studio Montage, St. Louis, MO., Photo Researcher Editorial Image, LLC and all of the folks "behind the scenes" who worked to make this book a reality.

Bob Sharer and I have collaborated on this textbook and all of its predecessors. We have been grateful throughout for support from our families, especially our spouses, Tom Patterson and Loa Traxler. As Bob and I were completing this edition, he fell ill and passed away before its submission for publication. It is with deep appreciation and fond collegial esteem that I dedicate this edition to him.

Wendy Ashmore

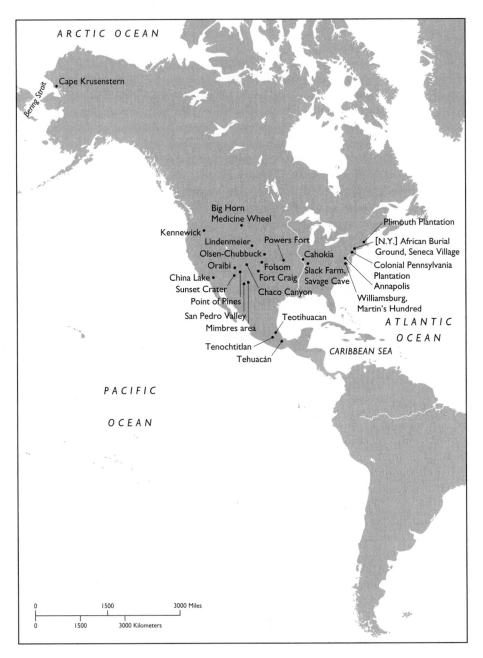

Places in North America and Central Mexico discussed in text.

Places in Central and South America discussed in text.

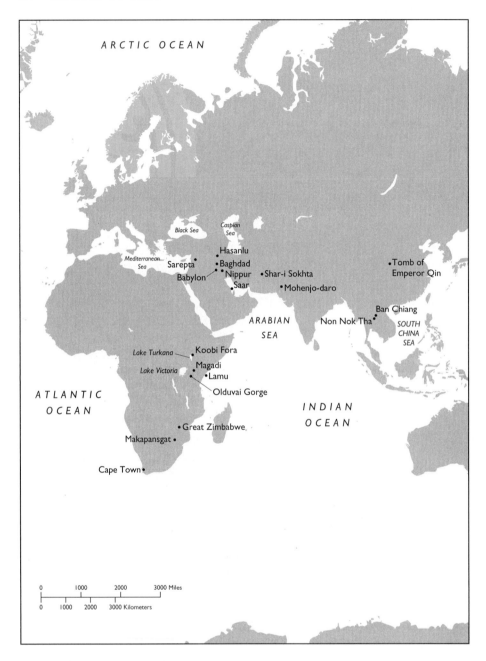

Places in Africa and Asia discussed in text.

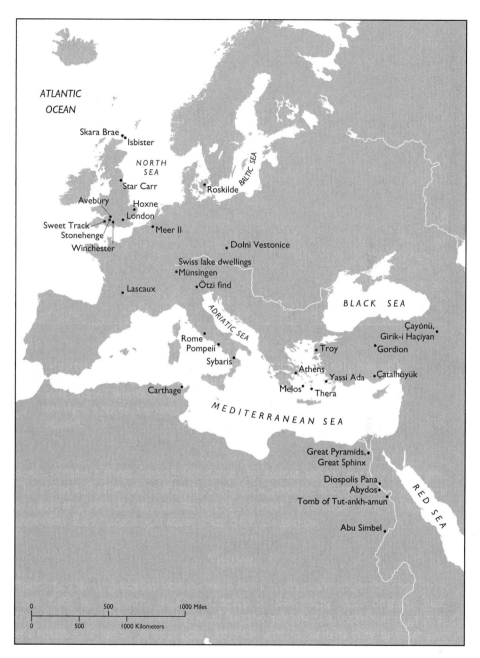

Places in Europe, northern Africa, and western Asia discussed in text.

For Robert J. Sharer (1940–2012)

1

Introduction

FOR MANY GENERATIONS THE Slack family worked their farm in Kentucky. But long before any European set foot in the Americas, this land had been the setting for a sizable Native American town. The name of this settlement has been lost, but we know that it was occupied for some two centuries, beginning about 1450. We also know that these Native Americans were part of a great tradition, now known as the Mississippian culture, that dominated southeastern North America from about A.D. 900 to the time these people (and all other Native Americans) were overwhelmed by European colonists.

In size, the settlement we now call the Slack Farm site was similar to other Mississippian towns, with a population estimated at 300–500. Like other towns of this culture, the settlement was composed of houses and other buildings used by its living inhabitants and places of burial for the dead. Most of the houses were occupied by farming families, but there were also large earthen platforms that supported the more elaborate houses of powerful families, those of the chiefs. Other earthen platforms supported the temples that housed the gods worshipped by these agricultural people.

We know these things about the Slack Farm site because of what archaeologists have learned from careful excavation of other Mississippian settlements. But although archaeologists had known for decades that the remains of this Native American town existed on Slack Farm, it had never been excavated. Thanks to the care of the Slack family, this site had been preserved. This preservation was all the more remarkable since most other Mississippian sites, along with those of other Native American cultures, have been badly damaged or destroyed. Some of this destruction has been accidental—mostly due to European colonization

1

FIGURE I.I

This aerial view of Slack Farm, Kentucky, illustrates dramatically the destruction wrought by looters: in just two months, ten men damaged this site significantly, leaving behind pottery fragments and shattered human remains.

and the expansion of modern society. But a great deal of destruction of Native American sites, and archaeological sites all over the world, is intentional. These sites are destroyed by **looters** who churn through the ground in their search for objects that have value—everything from souvenirs to treasure that can be sold for thousands or even hundreds of thousands of dollars.

The Slack Farm site was one of the largest known Mississippian sites to have escaped devastation by looters. All that changed in 1987, when the farm was sold out of the family. Its new owners immediately leased artifact-mining rights to a small group of looters, pocketing $10,000 from the deal. Within two months, the looters had transformed this preserved monument of Native American culture into a pockmarked wasteland. The site looked like a moonscape, littered with bits of pottery and human bone thrown out of more than 450 craters dug to find whatever few remains might prove valuable enough to repay the looters' investment (Fig. 1.1).

Once archaeologists learned of the destruction, they moved rapidly to salvage what they could (Fig. 1.2). But by that time much of the site had been demolished. Destroyed were the remains, once preserved beneath the ground,

FIGURE I.2

Archaeologists and volunteers from Kentucky and Indiana investigated
the looters' holes and dirt piles at Slack Farm to document damage and to
salvage information about this important habitation and mortuary site.

that could have told us about the lives of the people who lived there. True to
form, the looters wantonly desecrated the burials of the people who had once
lived there, destroying the human remains in at least 650 graves and callously
offending their living descendants. (Human burials are prized targets for looters
because they often contain objects with tremendous appeal to collectors of art
and antiquities.)

Neither the Slack Farm site nor any other archaeological site can tell us about
all aspects of an ancient society. Because peoples the world over have buried their
dead with objects reflecting their roles in life, burials offer invaluable insights into
the past. The Slack Farm tragedy and similar looting incidents have prompted
state-level legislation to protect such burial sites. But as we shall see in Chapters 6
and 10, the excavation of human burials also raises important ethical issues. Many
Native Americans do not want the remains of their ancestors disturbed in any way,
and under federal mandate, museums in the United States are returning previously
excavated human remains to their living descendants. Most archaeologists want to
work with Native Americans and other descendant communities to preserve the
remains of the past. In some cases this means ensuring that archaeological sites are
set aside as undisturbed cultural preserves. In other cases this means that archaeologists and descendant communities work together to create well-planned and careful
excavations to recover and preserve invaluable information about the past.

Looting takes place because there is a market for illegal antiquities. Looters and those who purchase looted antiquities are the real enemies of all people who want to preserve the past. All over the world, archaeologists who want to understand the human past are in a constant race with looters who destroy the past for personal gain. Why do people look for remains of the past at all, and once found, what is done with these materials? The objective for looters is obvious—to find valuable objects that can be sold for profit. The objectives for an **archaeologist** should be equally obvious—to preserve and to learn.

ARCHAEOLOGISTS AND ARCHAEOLOGY

Obviously, archaeologists are interested in the past, but their interest is defined by specific questions they seek to answer. These questions involve our origins as human beings, the origins of specific cultures, the way societies develop over time, and the relationship between the past and the present. Ultimately, archaeologists seek to better define who we are and understand why we behave as we do. What we are today, the way we behave, our customs, our beliefs, our entire civilization, are all the result of what happened in the past—an incredibly long and complex chain of human accomplishments that extends over millions of years. Thus, if we want to understand ourselves and our world today, we must try to understand our past.

The desire to understand ourselves motivates many people to pursue careers in fields such as psychology, sociology, economics, and other social sciences. These fields study different aspects of humanity, but they are all limited to the present—to today's behavior and today's society. Others seek knowledge about humanity in the biological sciences, medicine, molecular biology, and related fields, but these fields also study what we are today, in the present. To understand ourselves as fully as possible, we also must understand where we came from and how we developed over time. Of course, history also studies the past, but its scope is limited to the last few thousand years of our past—the era of written documents. Archaeology is the only field that explores and reveals the full extent of our past, from the most remote origins of human characteristics to the recent past. In this work archaeologists encounter both the greatest achievements and the greatest failures of human history.

The Lure of Archaeology

This book is about archaeology and how archaeologists conduct their work to better understand the past. Archaeology fascinates many people. Some people become archaeologists because of an interest that began when they were children. Certainly, to many children and adults alike, archaeology may seem to promise a life of adventure, travel to exotic lands, and discovery of lost civilizations. This romantic image can be found in books, on television, and in motion pictures—

FIGURE 1.3

Excavating the tomb of the "Lord of Sipán" required great care to recover
the well-preserved but fragile remains. Here archaeologists have just
removed the skeleton of this Moche lord, revealing lavish gold and feather
ornaments on which he had lain. Whereas looters would have been concerned only with profit from selling the sumptuous offerings, archaeologists
aim to recover the insights the tomb and its occupant, as well as the offerings, can give us about life and death in the Moche world.

best represented by the adventures of Indiana Jones. Fiction aside, this image of
archaeology is reinforced by the occasional reports of real discoveries, such as
the first unlooted Moche royal tomb in Peru (Fig. 1.3) or the spectacular ceramic
army of China's first emperor (Fig. 1.4). Even a discovery made almost a century
ago—Howard Carter's opening of the tomb of the Egyptian Pharaoh Tut-ankh-
amun (Fig. 1.5)—continues to excite the public imagination. Far less opulent
finds can likewise inspire worldwide fascination, as in the chance find in 1991 of
a single frozen mummy, now known as the "Iceman." When the body turned out
to be 5000 years old, an international team of experts embarked eagerly on study
of the mummy and the clothing and other possessions found with him (Fig. 1.6).
Ongoing study continues to reveal extraordinary details about this man, nicknamed "Ötzi" for the Ötztaler Alps where he was found—where and how he
lived, how he died, and what these facts tell us about his society.

FIGURE 1.4

Chinese archaeologists have cleared hundreds of clay soldiers, part of
the effigy army created to protect the tomb of Qin Shi Huang, the first
emperor of China, excavated from a collapsed underground vault near the
village of Xiyang, Shaanxi Province, China.

FIGURE 1.5

Archaeologist Howard Carter opens the inner doors of the tomb of
Tut-ankh-amun.

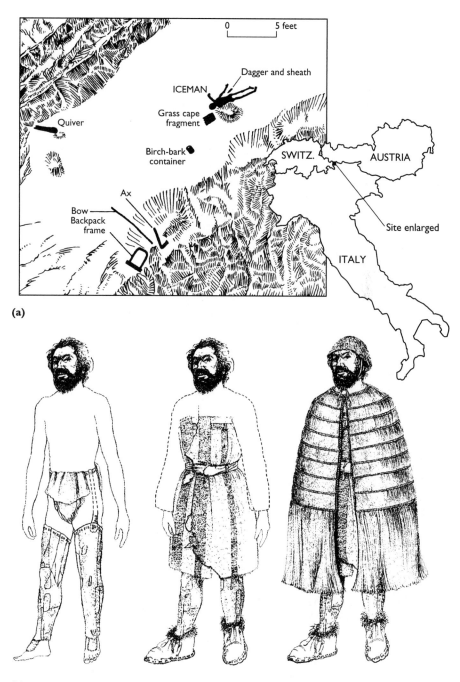

(a)

(b)

FIGURE 1.6

(a) In a remote area of the Alps, the frozen remains of a 5000-year-old man, nicknamed Ötzi after the place of his discovery, were found together with similarly frozen remains of his belongings. (b) Because of their state of preservation and their discovery together, the garments, the tools, and their owner permitted reconstruction of Ötzi's probable appearance.

In truth, discoveries such as these are very rare. Most archaeologists never find spectacular tombs or lost civilizations. It is far more typical for archaeologists to spend long periods of time doing spectacularly tedious research, apparently rewarded only by dramatically uncomfortable living conditions, bad food, pests, and diseases! Clearly, then, most archaeologists cannot be motivated by the prospect of a life of thrilling discovery or adventure. More important, they are not driven by the prospect of finding treasure or anything else for its monetary or aesthetic value. The actual motivation of archaeologists is far more mundane: to recover information that will increase our understanding of the past. Although finding that information may be tedious and uncomfortable at times, the rewards are great. Archaeologists have the privilege of being time travelers who can discover for themselves, and educate others about, parts of our past that otherwise would be lost forever.

Misuses of Archaeology

While looters destroy precious evidence before it can be used to understand the past, some individuals may misuse archaeological evidence for misleading or even harmful ends. Many of these people offer astonishing explanations for dramatic mysteries and baffling paradoxes supposedly revealed in the archaeological record. Their work is not archaeology; it is **pseudoarchaeology.** Other accounts are subtler and lead people into believing things about our past that not only are untrue but also can be harmful.

Pseudoarchaeologists claim to build their accounts from evidence, but in fact they do not. Examples include many of the accounts dealing with the supposed lost civilizations of Atlantis and Mu, imaginary continents inhabited by amazingly sophisticated peoples who supposedly gave rise to the known early civilizations throughout the world before disappearing beneath the waves of the Atlantic and Pacific oceans, respectively. Every so often, reported discoveries of lost hieroglyphs or symbols revive speculation about the mysterious origins of some famous civilization—usually with the added punch that, once again, all the so-called experts were wrong.

Money is the usual motive for pseudoarchaeology. Pitchmen peddling bogus accounts keep proving P. T. Barnum correct: there *is* a sucker born every minute. Many millions of dollars have gone into the pockets of unscrupulous authors who sell millions of pseudoarchaeology books in many languages all over the world. People eager to join this lucrative scheme have also created television programs, movies, and, in Europe, at least one theme park. Over the years the most successful of these pseudoarchaeological writers has been Erich von Däniken, who updated the old Atlantis and Mu stories by trying to show that the world's civilizations stem from ancient visits by space aliens. As one of his alleged proofs, von Däniken described the sculpted scene on the stone coffin lid from a famous tomb at the Maya site of Palenque, Mexico, as representing an ancient astronaut at the controls of a rocketship (Fig. 1.7). In making this claim, von Däniken ignored a

FIGURE 1.7

This sculpted stone coffin lid was found in the tomb beneath the Temple of the Inscriptions at Palenque, Mexico. It depicts the dead ruler surrounded by Maya supernatural symbols.

vast body of evidence from Maya art, symbolism, and inscriptions, all of which identify the sculpted figure as the ruler buried in the stone coffin, shown falling into the underworld at his death. In this and other examples of pseudoarchaeology, carefully selected items are used to support the case being made, while all other evidence is ignored. In this case a mere superficial resemblance between an astronaut's launch position and the carved portrait of a dead Maya ruler was treated as if it were positive evidence for the ancient space visitor theory.

One might argue that such fantasy is harmless, no matter how lucrative for its creators, but sometimes archaeological evidence is misused for political reasons, as when nationalistic or racist doctrines are supported by falsified reconstructions of the past. The most tragic such case occurred in Nazi Germany. The German prehistorian Gustav Kossinna (1858–1931) manipulated archaeological evidence to build a false and racist reconstruction of the past purporting to show the superiority of Germany to other nations. By exaggeration and falsification, he produced a prehistoric reconstruction in which everything of importance had begun in Germany before spreading to surrounding, allegedly inferior nations.

This slanted view of the past was used by Adolf Hitler in his book *Mein Kampf* to help justify the doctrine of German racial superiority. In this case, therefore, what began as a nationalistically biased reconstruction ended up as part of the rationale for Nazi German military expansion, leading to World War II and, ultimately, to the slaughter of millions of innocent people.

The terrible experience of Nazism provides a bitter lesson about the impact of racist doctrine. While the harmful effects of such blatantly racist descriptions are obvious, pseudoarchaeological accounts claiming that past civilizations were founded by survivors of Atlantis or by space aliens are a subtler but still insidious form of racism. Such pseudoarchaeology assumes that the actual builders of these civilizations could not have succeeded without outside help. Inherent in von Däniken's version of the past is the assumption that the ancient Egyptians, Maya, or Inca did not themselves possess the ability to build their great monuments. In fact, the accomplishments of these civilizations did not require superhuman skills or knowledge. Ancient Egyptians, and all other early civilizations, certainly were able to move huge stones from quarries to their building sites by either water or land.

The peoples of the past clearly were capable of more artistic, engineering, and intellectual achievements than the purveyors of pseudoarchaeology are willing to admit. Tales of extraterrestrial visits make for exciting science fiction, but we should keep these imaginative stories in the realm of fantasy where they belong. As a science seeking to understand the human past, archaeology has a responsibility to ensure that our ancestors get credit for their accomplishments.

Archaeology Defined

Archaeology is the study of the human past through its material remains. Over the past few hundred years, archaeology has grown from an amateur pastime to a scientifically based profession. In that time it has emerged as the field that uses recovered physical remains to order and describe ancient events, to explain the human behavior behind those events, and to understand the meaning of the past. To study the past, archaeologists have developed a series of methods by which they discover, recover, preserve, describe, and analyze these remains, referred to as the **archaeological record.** To make sense of this record, archaeologists are guided by a body of theory. Ultimately, theory provides the means to interpret archaeological evidence and allows description, explanation, and understanding of the past. This book will explore both the methods (Chapters 4–7) and the theories (Chapters 8 and 9) used by archaeologists.

Archaeology has four principal goals in studying the past, involving determination of form, function, process, and meaning. Form refers to the description and classification of the physical evidence that is recovered. The goal here is to outline the distribution of remains of ancient societies in both time and space. Function refers to the purposes of the objects found, determined from an analysis of the objects themselves and the interrelationships among different pieces of evidence. The goal here is to reconstruct past human activities. Process refers to the changes that occurred in past societies. The goal here is to determine how and why ancient cultures changed over time. Meaning refers to understanding past societies within their own cultural contexts. The goal here is to determine the attitudes and beliefs of ancient peoples and to learn things from the past that may be of use to us in the present.

Archaeology is also defined by strong ethical responsibilities. As we discuss at more length in Chapter 10, these include protecting the remains of the past, conducting research according to professional standards, making research results known to professional and public audiences, and having respect for people of the past and the present. Prominent among the latter are the communities that are descended from people whose lives archaeologists study; these communities are increasingly involved in shaping and conducting investigations of the past. Consistent with the ethical obligations to respect the rights of all peoples, many archaeologists throughout the world are working to repatriate archaeological materials to the living descendants of past societies. In the United States, repatriation of Native American materials is conducted under a federal law passed in 1990 (the Native American Graves Protection and Repatriation Act, or "NAGPRA"). This law created a process for museums and federal agencies to return Native American human remains, funerary objects, sacred objects, and objects of cultural patrimony to their descendants (discussed further in Chapter 10).

ARCHAEOLOGY AS A SCIENCE

Science is concerned with gaining knowledge about the natural world by observation. Science is not concerned with things that cannot be observed or examined; these are the subjects of theology, philosophy, the occult, or pseudoscience. To do its job, science systematically describes phenomena, classifies observations, and reaches conclusions. This often involves controlled and repeatable laboratory experiments, such as those in chemistry or psychology, but it may also consist of detailed observation *without* experimentation. Some fields cannot rely on experiments; these are called historical sciences—for example, geology, evolutionary biology, and archaeology. All deal with long-ago events that no longer can be directly observed, although the evidence left behind can be studied to reconstruct what took place.

Some scientists follow a uniform set of formal procedures in an effort to be as objective as possible. Many scholars, however, question whether any scientific study can be truly objective and unbiased, regardless of the procedures used. They argue that all scientists have inherent biases based on their own cultural and personal background and that these biases affect objectivity. For example, most archaeologists are the products of modern Western society and may perpetuate views of the past that are biased by that society's view of itself. This implies that there are many ways of viewing the past and that both our questions and our interpretations are shaped by our individual backgrounds.

To be as unbiased and objective as possible, science uses an approach to acquiring knowledge that is continuously self-correcting, so that the conclusions reached in earlier research are subject to repeated testing and refinement. This self-correcting set of procedures for gaining and testing our knowledge of the observable world is called the **scientific method.**

Science discovers facts about the natural world by observing objects or events. A scientist may draw conclusions by observing the real world and then test those conclusions by seeing if they hold true in other circumstances or cases. This involves starting from specific observations and proceeding to a generalization based on those observations. You can also do the opposite, deriving specific propositions from a generalization. For instance, if cell phones from the Whizbang Company frequently fail to work, you might generalize that Whizbang's products are unreliable. If the same company started making laptop computers, you might reason that the quality of these products is also suspect. You could then *test* your conclusion about Whizbang's general manufacturing quality standards by trying out some of the new products.

To see how these reasoning processes work within archaeology, let us look at an example. Julian Steward, an anthropologist of great importance to archaeology, conducted extensive fieldwork in the Great Basin of the western United States in the 1920s and 1930s, studying the Native American Shoshonean peoples living in the region. From this work with living groups, he developed a generalization to describe the distribution of earlier, prehistoric Shoshonean activities and campsites, relating their locations to the changing seasonal cycle of food procurement. That is, Steward presented his data as a **model,** a summary description of the patterns of and regularities in behavior of the ancient Shoshonean people as they moved from place to place to acquire food.

In the 1960s archaeologist David Hurst Thomas took Steward's model of shifting settlement in the Great Basin and derived from it a series of propositions or **hypotheses** (statements of relationships based on a set of assumptions). As Thomas phrased it, "if the late prehistoric Shoshoneans behaved in the fashion suggested by Steward, how would the artifacts have fallen on the ground?" (Thomas 1973). In other words, if Steward's model of shifting settlement and seasonal exploitation of food resources in different locations were true, Thomas could expect to find the tools associated with specific food activities in predictable locations. For example, more hunting tools and butchering knives should be found in the sagebrush zones where, according to the model, hunting was more important.

Thomas's archaeological research supported more than 75 percent of the hypotheses derived from Steward's model. As a result, the model was refined, and new hypotheses were generated, which in turn furthered our understanding of ancestral Shoshone. This sequence of generating and testing hypotheses can be continued indefinitely to refine and improve Thomas's results.

The contrast between this approach to understanding the past and pseudoarchaeology could not be stronger. Instead of systematically collecting and evaluating all available evidence and using it to develop and test hypotheses to produce the most reasonable reconstruction of the past, pseudoarchaeologists dismiss much of what has been learned about the past, choosing instead to select only those bits of information that can be made to fit their preconceived theories.

Note that the scientific method does not attempt to *prove* one hypothesis correct. Rather, in testing a series of contrasting hypotheses, one tries to eliminate those that are incorrect and isolate the single hypothesis that best fits the observed phenomena. Thus, there is no *proof* in science, only elimination or disproof of inadequate hypotheses. Science advances by disproof, promoting the most adequate propositions of the moment while recognizing that new data and better explanations will come along in the future. Scientists, therefore, often disagree with one another, presenting alternative interpretations for consideration.

Like other scientists, archaeologists apply the scientific method to a specified class of phenomena: the material remains of past human activity. Like other scientists, archaeologists attempt to isolate, classify, and explain the relationships among pieces of evidence—in this case among the variables of form, function, time, and space. Archaeologists can observe the variables of form and space directly to determine the composition, size, and shape of each piece of evidence and its location. The variables of function and time must be inferred, to determine the purpose and age of each piece of evidence. Once these relationships are established, archaeologists use the evidence to infer past human behavior and, by combining many such examples, begin to reconstruct past human societies.

Because of the sheer volume of the evidence that archaeologists deal with, as well as the need to quantify and statistically manipulate these data, computers have become virtually indispensable for archaeological research. Computers and statistics are tools to aid research, but these should not be equated with the scientific method. It is the underlying philosophy and procedures governing the search for knowledge that define the scientific method.

The scientific method requires that archaeologists carefully state the assumptions under which they work and clearly formulate the questions they attempt to answer about the past. To answer those questions, archaeologists present their data and hypotheses and explain how these hypotheses were tested. However, although archaeologists, like other scientists, try to be completely objective in their search for knowledge, they can never escape their cultural and personal experiences. Complete objectivity remains the goal, but all scientific research is shaped to some degree by cultural factors.

ARCHAEOLOGY AND HISTORY

Archaeology and history are related by their common concern with past human events. The major difference between the two disciplines is their sources of information. History works with written accounts and oral traditions about the past; archaeology works with material remains of the past. These material remains are mute; their significance depends entirely on the inferences made by trained archaeologists. In contrast, historical documents are direct communications from the past, although their significance is also subject to interpretation by trained historians. **Oral history,** as well, preserves extensive historical knowledge, especially among peoples who rely less exclusively on written information than does modern Western society.

By definition, **documentary history** focuses primarily on societies with writing. Moreover, because relatively more documents deal with the richest and most powerful people in those societies, history tends to emphasize the royal and priestly elite. Archaeology is less partial to rich or learned folk. Everyone eats, makes things, discards trash, and dies, so everyone contributes to the archaeological record. Archaeology, far more than history, deals with the whole range of humanity, regardless of social standing. Because of these contrasts, history and archaeology often complement each other, together providing a more comprehensive record of the past than either can furnish alone. While archaeology considers all aspects of the past, there are always some things that leave no material traces, and these activities may be described in historical documents. Archaeology, in turn, by finding evidence of the daily lives of common people in earlier societies, can enrich the views of historians.

For these reasons, archaeology and both documentary and oral history are closely allied fields in which the methods of one or more of these fields, as appropriate, are applied to the study of a particular era. For instance, the field of classical archaeology combines the methods of archaeology with the use of historical sources to document the classical civilizations of Greece and Rome. Classical archaeology is also allied to the field of art history, which provides another route—the analysis of art styles and themes—to understanding the past.

Most archaeologists, however, are concerned with aspects of the past that cannot be directly supplemented by historical studies. Oral histories of varied time depth are associated with a relatively restricted number of societies, and documentary history is limited to a relatively recent era of human development, beginning with the invention and use of writing systems. This era extends at most some 5000 years into the past, in Southwest Asia, the area with the earliest examples of writing. When compared with about 2.5 million years of human cultural development, the era of documentary history represents less than 1 percent of the total (Fig. 1.8). Historical studies are even more limited in time outside Southwest Asia, and they are not possible in areas where writing systems never developed.

The contrasts between history and archaeology distinguish **historical archaeology,** or archaeology combined with analysis of written records, from **prehistoric archaeology,** or research on societies and time periods that lack written records. The latter seeks to understand the full sweep of human development on earth, from its earliest traces to its most remote variations. For example, the Slack Farm site and the Mississippian culture represent a time period without written records in North America. Given the lack of historical accounts, our understanding the Mississippian era depends on prehistoric archaeology and the recovery

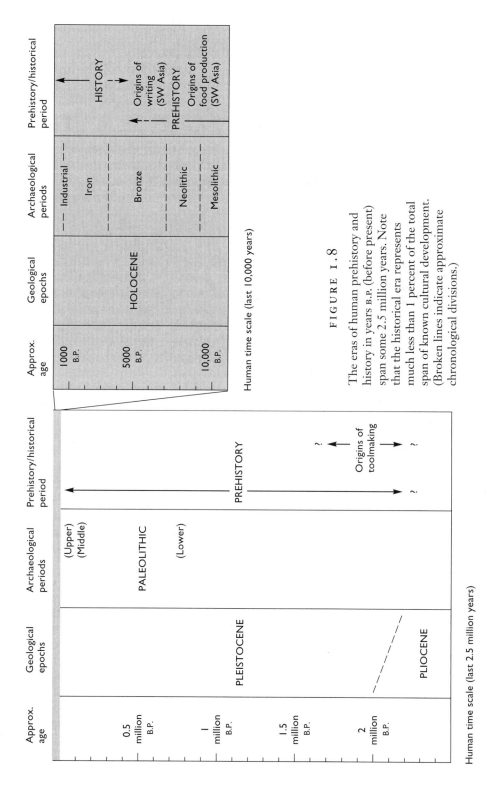

Human time scale (last 10,000 years)

FIGURE 1.8

The eras of human prehistory and history in years B.P. (before present) span some 2.5 million years. Note that the historical era represents much less than 1 percent of the total span of known cultural development. (Broken lines indicate approximate chronological divisions.)

Human time scale (last 2.5 million years)

of the fragmentary material remains from sites like Slack Farm. Of course, both historical and archaeological data are fragmentary; neither can provide a complete reconstruction of the past. Even when historical records are available, archaeological information can add to our understanding of that past era.

A good example in which history was illuminated by archaeology is the excavation of Martin's Hundred, where archaeologist Ivor Noël Hume and his associates unearthed the fragile remnants of one of the earliest British colonial settlements of Tidewater Virginia. Originally, the team had been seeking traces of the 18th-century Carter's Grove plantation. Illustrating that archaeology often discovers the unexpected, they found instead remains from the early 1600s, virtually all that was left of what historical records refer to as Wolstenholme Towne in a tract known as Martin's Hundred. The tract was established in 1619 by fewer than 200 English settlers, who faced disease, hunger, and an unfriendly environment. In 1622 the town was attacked and burned and some inhabitants killed by local Native Americans. Although Martin's Hundred was reoccupied, Wolstenholme Towne was subsequently all but forgotten.

Noël Hume's excavations in the 1970s rediscovered the settlement and documented the drama of the massacre. Ash and other traces of the fires were abundant, and several human skeletons attested to violent death (one bore evidence of scalping) and hasty burial. As dramatic as these findings are, however, the deeper impact of these excavations is what could be learned about daily life in early colonial Virginia. The products and discards of a resident potter reveal local manufacturing, while the imported helmets and other pieces of armor discovered are the earliest such pieces known in colonial America. The traces of a wooden fort, the oldest example of its kind yet recovered, testify to the well-founded insecurity of the settlers. Although the town was small, its sometimes poignant traces have yielded important glimpses of life and death in what Noël Hume calls "the teething years of American colonial history" (1979).

Both archaeology and history have contributed to our knowledge of Martin's Hundred. For most of the human past, however, archaeology lacks any sort of historical record to supplement its studies. Nevertheless, prehistoric archaeology can draw on the resources and results of allied fields, including history, historical archaeology, cultural anthropology, and geography. Both historical and prehistoric archaeology have usually allied themselves most closely to anthropology. Through the concept of culture, anthropology provides a variety of frameworks for archaeology to describe, explain, and better understand the past.

ARCHAEOLOGY AND ANTHROPOLOGY

In its broadest sense, **anthropology** is the comprehensive science of humankind—the study of human beings both as biological organisms and as culture-bearing creatures. It also studies human society from two perspectives: (1) a **diachronic** view

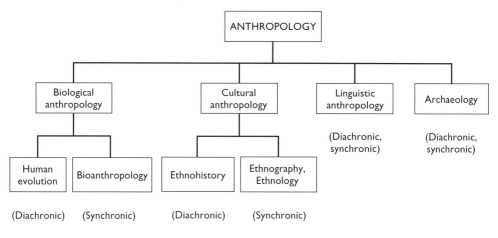

FIGURE I.9

The field of anthropology can be divided into several subfields.

that stresses development through time and (2) a **synchronic** view that emphasizes the contemporary state of human societies with little or no time depth.

Anthropology is divided into four major subdisciplines: biological (or physical) anthropology, cultural anthropology, linguistic anthropology, and archaeology (Fig. 1.9). Each of these subdisciplines incorporates numerous specialties. Biological anthropology studies the human species as a biological organism, including our evolution (a diachronic aspect) and our contemporary biological characteristics and variations (a synchronic aspect). Cultural anthropology studies the human species as a cultural organism, including two synchronic approaches to the study of living societies: (1) **ethnography,** which studies individual cultures throughout the world, and (2) **ethnology,** which uses a comparative and generalizing perspective to understand the way all cultures work. Ethnohistory takes a diachronic approach within cultural anthropology, using written records and oral history to reconstruct the past. Linguistic anthropology specializes in the study of human languages throughout the world, individually and comparatively (a synchronic aspect) and developmentally (how languages change and evolve through time, a diachronic aspect). The subject of our book, archaeology, studies the human past from a variety of perspectives. It often emphasizes a diachronic view, to describe and understand the development of societies over time, but archaeology may also emphasize a synchronic view, as in the study of a society at a particular moment in the past. As we have already seen, archaeology can be divided into the fields of historical and prehistoric archaeology.

This description of anthropology is a simplified view of a complex field. The pursuits of anthropological research must be as diverse as the varieties of human behavior and the complexities of culture. The concept of culture is what unifies all the subfields of anthropology. **Culture** has both a general and a specific meaning. In its general sense, culture refers to the uniquely human addition to the biological and social dimensions we share with other life-forms. It is in this general sense that we will be concerned with culture and will refine our definition shortly. But we must realize as well that the term may also be used in a specific sense to refer to the particular and unique cultural systems of individual human societies, as when we speak of the "culture of the Shoshone."

The concept of culture in the general sense is much too complex to define comprehensively in a few paragraphs, encompassing as it does some 2.5 million years of human evolution, as well as hundreds of unique and varied contemporary societies throughout the world. One of the most often cited definitions, formulated more than 125 years ago by Edward Tylor (1871), remains useful today:

> [Culture is] that complex whole which includes knowledge, belief, art, morals, law, custom, and any other capabilities and habits acquired by [a person] as a member of society.

Today many archaeologists prefer to emphasize culture as the primary means by which human societies adjust or adapt to their environment, in contrast to the genetic (biological) adaptations of our own and other life-forms. According to this view, culture comprises the cumulative resources of human societies, perpetuated by language, that provide the primary means for nongenetic adaptation to the environment by regulating behavior on three levels: (1) the technological (relationships with the environment), (2) the social (organizational systems), and (3) the ideational (belief systems). We will return to this concept later in this book, when we discuss the various views of culture that have developed along with the field of anthropology.

Archaeology has benefited as well from the contributions of many other fields. In pursuing their goals, archaeologists often make use of the expertise of specialists in the other subfields of anthropology, as well as those in disciplines such as art history, geography, history, biology, astronomy, physics, geology, and computer science. These fields enrich the mix of scientific and humanistic perspectives that characterize modern archaeology. They also contribute both to the refinement of archaeological methods and to the development of archaeological theory by which the evidence of the past is interpreted.

ARCHAEOLOGY AS A PROFESSION

Because archaeology is both fascinating and important—it is the only bridge to our entire past heritage—many people are interested in the prospects for a career in archaeology. As we have seen, archaeology is a diverse field, so there are many different career opportunities for all kinds of interests.

Formal academic training is not a requirement for participating in archaeo-logical research. Many people begin their experiences in discovering the past by joining an archaeological dig or by volunteering their time to help a museum pre-serve or study archaeological collections. Some individuals who are employed full-time in other jobs continue to follow their interest in archaeology as volunteers, working on weekends or during vacations. To one interested in pursuing archaeol-ogy as a profession, however, some sort of formal academic training is necessary.

Training in archaeology usually begins in the classroom, where methods and theory can be introduced by lectures and discussions, but archaeology cannot be learned solely in a traditional academic setting. Archaeological training must also include time spent in the field—participating in research at archaeological sites and in the field laboratory—so that coursework can be put into practice. In most cases archaeological field schools are where students learn the practical applica-tion of research methods. After such training students may take more advanced courses (in data analysis and theory, among other fields) leading to a degree. Most archaeological training in the United States is offered within anthropology programs, and the resulting degrees, both undergraduate and graduate, are in anthropology, not archaeology.

Most archaeologists subscribe to the definitions and goals outlined earlier in this chapter. Yet when it comes to the actual application of method and theory to meet these goals, a considerable diversity of approach becomes apparent. There is more variation than there should be in the standards by which archaeological sites are excavated and the results recorded. In some extreme cases, unfortu-nately, the lack of proper standards leads to an irreversible loss of information about the past, rather than to a gain in knowledge. For example, Kent Flannery describes the following scene at a site in Mexico:

> Four stalks of river cane, stuck loosely in the ground, defined a quadrilat-eral (though not necessarily rectangular) area in which two *peones* [laborers] picked and shoveled to varying depths, heaving the dirt to one side. On the backdirt pile stood the archeologist himself, armed with his most delicate tool—a three-pronged garden cultivator of the type used by elderly British ladies to weed rhododendrons. Combing through every shovelful of dirt, he carefully picked out each figurine head and placed it in a brown paper shopping bag nearby—the only other bit of equipment in evidence. This individual was armed with an excavation permit that had been granted because, in the honest words of one official, "he appeared to be no better or worse than any other archeologist who had worked in the area." When questioned, our colleague descended from the backdirt pile and revealed that his underlying research goal was to define the nature of the "Olmec presence" in that particular drainage basin; his initial results, he said, pre-dicted total success.
>
> As [we] rattled back along the highway in our jeep, each of us in his own way sat marveling at the elegance of a research strategy in which one

could define the nature of a foreign presence in a distant drainage basin from just seven fragmentary figurine heads in the bottom of a supermarket sack.

(FLANNERY 1976:1–2)

At first this case strikes us as humorous, until we realize that it is based on an actual incident and that, unfortunately, similar situations continue in the name of archaeology throughout the world. To establish archaeological standards, the Register of Professional Archaeologists (ROPA) is sponsored by the Society for American Archaeology, the Society for Historical Archaeology, the Archaeological Institute of America, and the ROPA membership. ROPA has defined as specifically as possible the professional standards for archaeologists. The online application includes the following criteria for education, training, and experience, as well as standards for research performance and ethics:

1. Education and Training
    a. A professional archaeologist must have received an advanced degree (such as an M.A., M.S., Ph.D., or D.Sc.) from an accredited institution in archaeology, anthropology, art history, classics, history, or another germane discipline with a specialization in archaeology.
    b. A professional archaeologist must have a minimum of one year's field and laboratory experience, which includes a minimum of 16 weeks in the field (of which at least 8 are in excavation), 16 weeks in the lab, and 20 weeks in a responsible supervisory capacity.
    c. A professional archaeologist must have designed and executed an archaeological study and have reported on that research in the form of a master's thesis, Ph.D. dissertation, or report (or several smaller reports that together are equivalent in scope and quality to a master's thesis or Ph.D. dissertation).

2. Experience

    A professional archaeologist must have at least one year of experience in field and laboratory situations under the supervision of a professional archaeologist, with a minimum of 6 months as a supervisor.

The most prominent national professional archaeological societies in the United States are listed in Table 1.1. Several of these have regular publication series, and the Archaeological Institute of America also publishes annual listings of field schools and excavation opportunities. There are also numerous regional and state archaeological societies throughout the country. Further information about these and other archaeological organizations in your area can be found by contacting the office of your state archaeologist or the State Historic Preservation Office (SHPO) in your state capital.

TABLE 1.1

Professional Archaeological Organizations

American Anthropological Association
2200 Wilson Blvd., Suite 600
Arlington, VA 22201
www.aaanet.org

Archaeological Institute of America
656 Beacon Street, 6th Floor
Boston, MA 02215–2206
www.archaeological.org

Register of Professional Archaeologists
5024-R Campbell Blvd.
Baltimore, MD 21236
www.rpanet.org

Society for American Archaeology
1111 14th Street, NE
Washington, DC 20005-5622
www.saa.org

Society for Historical Archaeology
9707 Key West Avenue, Suite 100
Rockville, MD 20850
www.sha.org

World Archaeological Congress
www.worldarchaeologicalcongress.org

Also listed in Table 1.1 is a prominent international organization, the World Archaeological Congress (WAC), which was formed in 1985 with the primary objectives of encouraging ethical archaeological research and academic dialogue throughout the world. Every four years WAC sponsors an international congress to meet these objectives and realize its commitment to archaeological training, research, public education, site conservation, and empowering indigenous peoples.

Traditionally, most archaeologists had academic appointments in universities or museums, where they taught archaeology and conducted fieldwork. Museums also house laboratories for analyzing field information and repairing and conserving fragile finds. Today, however, a majority of archaeologists are employed by private or governmental agencies, such as the National Park Service, where they engage in **cultural resource management** (or CRM). CRM is concerned with the identification and evaluation of archaeological sites to protect them from disturbance or destruction and the investigation of those that cannot be saved. CRM is the fastest-growing segment in archaeology and, according to some estimates, now accounts for as many as 80 percent of all professional archaeologists employed in the United States. In the same spirit, archaeologists express a steadily growing concern for protecting cultural heritage, worldwide, and find employment in **nongovernmental organizations** (NGOs) oriented to such protection, as we discuss in Chapter 10.

The growth of CRM and heritage protection is the result of an increasing concern over the destruction of archaeological sites in this country and throughout the world. In the United States, as in many other countries, legislation has been enacted to protect our cultural heritage. This development is part of the larger concern about the destruction of our environment (natural as well as cultural resources). Like many natural resources, past cultural remains are a nonrenewable resource. Unlike natural resources, however, each archaeological site is a fragile and unique representative of our human heritage. As we learned in the case of Slack Farm, once an archaeological site has been destroyed, that portion of our past is lost forever.

Two exciting developments are emerging the world over: **community-based archaeology** and the growth of **indigenous archaeologies.** The first involves partnerships between archaeologists and local communities, usually descendants of people whose lives are the subject of study. A recent example is the partnership between Cochiti Pueblo in New Mexico and the University of Pennsylvania Museum in studying the Pueblo Revolt of 1680. Working with the people of Cochiti, Robert Preucel examined the archaeological remains of Kotyiti, the hilltop refuge created during the revolt. The collaborative study has involved oral and documentary histories, as well as mapping of the architecture of Kotyiti. The result is valued by the people of Cochiti today, and it contributes to new perspectives on the revolt period, beyond those customarily written by non-Indian chroniclers. Community-based archaeology is also found at a growing number of other places in the United States, including Annapolis in Maryland and Little Rapids (*Inyan Cyaka Atonwan*) in Minnesota. As we will discuss at some length in Chapter 10, community-based archaeology can address real world issues such as homelessness, and played a key role in the later stages of inquiry at the African Burial Ground in New York City.

Indigenous archaeologies constitute archaeological research and interpretation conducted—or directed—by practitioners from non-Western societies. The form of inquiry used by archaeologists in this field addresses issues central to understanding the past among peoples once (or still) colonized by Western society, and for whom the questions of Western science alone are not sufficient. Such inquiry also selects methods and resources best suited to addressing the questions posed and increasingly makes use of oral tradition, as in Emory Sekaquaptewa and Dorothy Washburn's use of ritual song texts to study ancestral Hopi lifeways. In one review of developments, Joe Watkins cites creation of the Navajo Nation Cultural Resource Management Program in 1977 as "a watershed event in the history of American Indian archaeology" (Watkins 2003: 278), in which "professional anthropological expertise combined with regional archaeological experience and an understanding of Navajo customs" (Watkins, quoting Anthony Klesert).

SUMMARY

Archaeology is both a popular and a fascinating subject, and it often captures considerable public attention, especially when dramatic discoveries are made. Such discoveries, along with the appeal of exotic adventures, are certainly part of the reason for the popular fascination with archaeology. But a deeper attraction is generated by the substance of archaeology itself—the study of the past—and by the realization that knowledge about the past helps us better understand our own lives, now and in the future.

Archaeology is the one field that studies the full range of our human past. But this work is threatened by the alarming number of archaeological sites being destroyed by looting. In contrast to looters, who care only for objects with monetary value, archaeologists try to recover and analyze the full range of surviving material remains to reconstruct the past.

Archaeology has four main goals: (1) to describe the form of archaeological evidence and its distribution in time and space, (2) to determine the function of these remains and thereby reconstruct past behavior, (3) to define the processes of culture to determine how and why cultures change over time, and (4) to use the archaeological record to understand the meaning of culture in the past and its relevance to the present.

The purpose and goals of archaeology stand opposed to those of pseudo-archaeology—fanciful reconstructions of the past that ignore facts and instead cater to human desires for fantasy and mystery. Archaeology, like any scientific discipline, involves a search for knowledge based on making careful observations and following a logical and consistent method, all guided by a body of theory. Archaeology is allied to several other disciplines. These include history, the study of the past from the written record; and anthropology, the study of human society, past and present, from both cultural and biological perspectives. The span of history divides the realm of archaeology into historical and prehistoric archaeology. In the United States both historical and prehistoric archaeology are part of the broader discipline of anthropology. Anthropology, history, and related fields provide the theories that guide prehistoric archaeology in reconstructing the past from material remains.

The training of professional archaeologists usually combines classroom, laboratory, and field experiences at both the undergraduate and graduate levels. Professional standards for archaeological ethics and research have been defined, but some variation in their application still exists. Most U.S.-trained archaeologists are employed in cultural resource management and expanding numbers in global heritage and other NGOs. Community-based projects are also growing in frequency, and indigenous archaeologies are playing an increasingly prominent role.

VOLUME OVERVIEW

This book takes readers through the steps of archaeological research. After a brief consideration of archaeology's history (Chapter 2), we look at the theories shaping the questions archaeologists ask (Chapter 3). Then we define the kinds of material data archaeologists encounter, the factors determining preservation or fragmentation of those remains, and the ways archaeologists make plans for studying the remains (Chapter 4). We focus next on how archaeologists actually recover information, through survey and excavation (Chapter 5), and the kinds of analyses that yield useful insights about the material remains recovered (Chapter 6). We then highlight the ways archaeologists determine how old the recovered materials are (Chapter 7), and we outline how archaeologists use analogy to make inferences about technology, social systems, and ideology in ancient lives (Chapter 8). Chapter 9 links the reconstructed lifeways back to the theoretical frameworks of Chapter 3. We close with renewed emphasis on archaeology being firmly a part of the real world (Chapter 10).

FOR FURTHER READING

Following is a list of sources organized by chapter heading, followed by a more inclusive set of sources for further background reading ("Additional Sources"). A similar list can be found at the end of each chapter. Complete titles and publication information can be found in the Bibliography.

INTRODUCTION
Arden 1989; Bahn 1995; Barfield 1994; Cleere 1989; Fagan 1988; Fowler 2001; Smith and Ehrenhard 1991

ARCHAEOLOGISTS AND ARCHAEOLOGY
Alva and Donnan 1993; Arnold 1990; Feder 2010; Man 2008; Williams 1991

ARCHAEOLOGY AS A SCIENCE
Binford 1983, 1989; Flannery 1986; Kelley and Hanen 1988; Shennan 1988; Steward 1955; Thomas 1973; Watson, LeBlanc, and Redman 1984; Wylie 2002

ARCHAEOLOGY AND HISTORY
Andrén 1998; Deetz 1977; Kepecs and Kolb 1997; Little 2007; Noël Hume 1969, 1979; Paynter 2000

ARCHAEOLOGY AND ANTHROPOLOGY
Binford 1962; Gosden 1999; Hodder 1982b; Taylor (1948) 1967; Tylor 1871

ARCHAEOLOGY AS A PROFESSION
Altschul and Patterson 2010; Flannery 1976; Lanata and Drennan 2010; Pearce 1990; Preucel 2000, 2002; Sebastian 2010; Sebastian and Lipe 2010; Sekaquaptewa and Washburn 2004; Shackel and Chambers 2004; Silliman 2008; Silliman and Ferguson 2010; Spector 1993; Swidler et al. 1999; Ucko 1987; Watkins 2000, 2003, 2010; Wilcox 2010; www.nps.gov/history/nagpra/; www.saa.org; www.worldarchaeologicalcongress.org

ADDITIONAL SOURCES
Ashmore, Lippert, and Mills 2010; Bass 2005; Binford 1972, 1983; Bruchac, Hart, and Wobst 2010; Catsambis, Ford, and Hamilton 2011; Derry and Malloy 2003; Ellis 2000; Hardesty and Little 2000; King 2002; Lipe 1974, 1984; Little 2002, 2007; Little and Zimmerman 2010; Marshall 2002; Meltzer, Fowler, and Sabloff 1986; Miller 1980; Neumann and Sanford 2001; Sabloff 1982, 2008; Schliemann (1881) 1968; Wiseman 2001; Zimmerman et al. 2003

2

Archaeology's Past

THE DEVELOPMENT OF SCIENCE is one of the hallmarks of Western civilization. Although their origins can be traced back several thousand years, science and the scientific method have taken their modern form in the 500 years since the European Renaissance. Archaeology is a relative newcomer among sciences, emerging as a distinct field only in the 19th century, but it has followed a developmental course similar to that of other scientific disciplines.

Since modern scientific disciplines are a product of Western civilization, they reflect a view of the world that has been conditioned by Western culture. Every cultural tradition has its own ways of understanding the world, including the world of the past. Thus, while archaeology represents a scientific means of approaching and understanding the past, because it is derived from one particular cultural tradition, it is only one of many ways of viewing the past. The recognition that there are many ways of viewing the world has led some archaeologists to attempt to reconstruct the past of non-Western societies according to those societies' own cultural perspectives. As we will see in Chapter 3, the recognition of multiple perspectives on the past is an important distinction that sets some contemporary archaeological approaches apart. In this chapter, however, we will look at the development of archaeology from the Western cultural perspective.

Many scientific fields, including archaeology, originated with the work of amateur collectors. These individuals, often part-time hobbyists, pursued their interests because they valued the objects collected, often as things of beauty or curiosity. For example, the modern field of biology took root with European collectors of local plant and animal life, including many 17th- and 18th-century English country parsons and other gentlemen of leisure. Amassing a collection leads naturally to attempts to bring order to the assembled material. These often result in efforts at **classification,** dividing a collection into groups that share one or more characteristics. The earliest classifications were usually based on the most obvious traits, such as appearance or form. Today all classifications continue to be based on the observed characteristics of the material being categorized.

Attempts to classify collections often led to questions concerning the meaning of both similarities and differences in the things being studied. The desire to know more about a collection leads to questions about its origins and purpose, and about the relationship of one category in a classification to another. Such questions were often answered initially with pure speculation, but at times firmer conclusions emerged that were based on systematic observation. More often than not, however, the first answers to such questions have long since been replaced by more firmly grounded explanations.

In time, amateur collectors increasingly gave way to individuals committed to discovering the meaning behind the assembled facts. First, they sought to define and break down the full range of forms into classes. Later, individuals attempted to infer purpose from physical appearance and to discover the underlying organizing principles inherent in the classification. In other words, a concern with function and meaning replaced the concern with simple form. With this step the first professionals within any given discipline can often be discerned. Nonprofessionals in many fields continue to make important discoveries even today. But in every scientific discipline the emergence of true professionalism corresponds to the rise of full-time specialists interested in investigating and understanding, rather than merely collecting.

As attention shifts more to questions of function and explanation, it becomes obvious that descriptive classifications based solely on isolated traits cannot provide sophisticated answers about the origins and significance of a set of observable phenomena. The next step toward understanding any phenomenon is the attempt to comprehend the processes of its development—to explain the causes of change.

THE ORIGINS OF ARCHAEOLOGY

These trends of scientific development are visible in the emergence of archaeology as a professional discipline. Archaeology did not spring forth fully developed, but emerged gradually from diverse origins. As with other fields of inquiry, its roots lie in the work of amateur collectors and speculators; such individuals interested in the human past are often called **antiquarians.** But archaeology did not begin to develop as a separate discipline until its practitioners went beyond merely collecting ancient remains and developed the means to use these materials as evidence for a reasonable reconstruction of the past.

Countless individuals have encountered remains of the past, often accidentally or, in the case of looters, as the result of treasure seeking. As the number of discoveries accumulated, some individuals began to realize that these remains had an importance beyond curiosity or monetary value—they were, in fact, direct clues to the understanding of entire societies that had long since disappeared.

Examples of interest in the past can be found among the earliest known historical accounts, including those of China, India, and Egypt. For example, Thutmose IV, pharaoh of Egypt in the 15th century B.C., ordered the excavation of the Great Sphinx at Giza, then already centuries old and nearly buried by sand. He left a record of his work inscribed on a stone tablet between the paws of the sphinx. Nearly a thousand years later, in the mid-6th century B.C., the Babylonian king Nabonidus sponsored excavations in the ruined cities of his Sumerian predecessors and exhibited the artifacts that were found. These early examples of interest in the past illustrate several things that would eventually become part of archaeological research: excavating to reveal ancient remains, recording the work, and preserving the finds.

The later Romans were also interested in the past, but usually for personal gain. Wealthy Romans often systematically looted many sites in the Mediterranean region for sculpture and other works of art to decorate their palaces and gardens. However, they seemed to have little concern for using these finds to understand the past.

It wasn't until the Renaissance of the 14th–17th centuries, an era of reawakened interest in the arts, literature, science, and learning in general, that the study of the past began to flourish. Excavation and direct recovery of antiquities became increasingly popular in Italy as Roman ruins were probed in search of artifacts and art. In 1594 the construction of a water channel near Naples led accidentally to the most famous discovery of the period, that of the lost Roman city of Pompeii (Fig. 2.1). Archaeological excavation has continued at this site to the present day. Discoveries such as these stimulated a general frenzy of digging, often resembling looting more than archaeological inquiry, not only in Italy but also throughout the Mediterranean and beyond. Although this resulted in much destruction of important evidence, some knowledge was gained, monuments and works of art were saved, and excavation techniques began to improve.

Even as looting and destruction of antiquities became more common, some individuals stood out not only as notable collectors but also as people interested in learning about the past through classification and study of material remains. One of the earliest of these was William Camden. In 1587 he produced *Britannia*, the first compilation of all archaeological sites and artifacts then known in England, a work that marks the beginning of serious interest in British prehistory. Two other British antiquarians of the 17th and 18th centuries, John Aubrey and William Stukeley, are noteworthy for their pioneering, if speculative, attempts to interpret the purposes of the great stone enclosures of Avebury and Stonehenge (Fig. 2.2).

Elsewhere in Europe, other individuals were also beginning to probe their local prehistoric past. In 16th- and 17th-century Scandinavia, for example, royally commissioned antiquarians such as Ole Worm of Denmark and Johan Bure

FIGURE 2.1

Archaeologists have excavated and partially reconstructed a street in the ancient Roman city of Pompeii, Italy.

FIGURE 2.2

The ancient function of Stonehenge, located on the Salisbury Plain in England, remains a subject of popular speculation—regardless of the archaeological evidence.

FIGURE 2.3

Runic inscriptions were used as early as the 16th and 17th centuries to aid archaeological investigation in Scandinavia.

of Sweden were recording ancient runic inscriptions (Fig. 2.3), excavating early burial sites, and compiling inventories of national antiquities. Like other scholars of the time, they connected their findings with semilegendary accounts of ethnic or national origin in prehistoric times. Professional archaeology has its roots in the gradual discovery of the prehistoric era in Europe. While professional archaeology in the Americas also sprang from the search for prehistory, the development of archaeology in Europe and the New World followed somewhat separate courses, shaped by different concerns and perspectives.

The Search for European Prehistory

As archaeological evidence accumulated, speculative interpretation of European prehistory gradually gave way to firmer reconstructions. The first problem to be solved was the recognition of the earliest products of human activity, usually tools made of stone. William Dugdale, a 17th-century British prehistorian, identified ancient stone hand axes as "weapons used by the Britons before the art of making arms of brass or iron was known." This essentially correct interpretation represented a revolutionary advance over the prevailing view—that these artifacts were the work of elves or other mythical beings. Another two centuries would pass, however, before the implications of these discoveries for human prehistory would be generally accepted. The initial reaction to such discoveries was to ignore or reject them, because they conflicted with the dominant view, based on the version of the creation given in the Old Testament. This belief held that human existence was confined to a mere 6000 years since the earth's creation.

Once these earliest artifacts were recognized as products of human manufacture, determination of their true age became a pressing concern. The best indication of the antiquity of human presence in Europe came from a growing inventory of human bones and tools found associated with the bones of extinct animals. For example, in 1797 at the English site of Hoxne, John Frere described the discovery of chipped-flint artifacts in association with bones of extinct animals some 12 feet below the earth's surface, sealed in place by three higher and therefore, as he realized, later deposits. Frere concluded that these remains belonged "to a very remote period indeed; even beyond that of the present world." In the mid-19th century a French customs inspector named Boucher de Perthes found a group of stone handaxes and extinct animal bones among the gravels of the Somme River. By this time the fossilized remains of the earliest inhabitants of Europe had begun to appear, one of the first finds being the discovery in 1856 of bones from the Neander Valley in Germany. This find is now well known as an example of the ancient Neanderthal people; at the time, however, the ancient anatomical attributes of these bones were explained away as coming from a pathological modern individual.

After bitter and heated debate the tide of scientific opinion finally turned in the mid-19th century. By this time geologists such as Charles Lyell had demonstrated the considerable antiquity of the earth and proposed that the processes responsible for its current form were the same in the past as today—a position known as uniformitarianism. (The opposing view, catastrophism, held that the earth's features were shaped by violent cataclysmic events.) They had also shown that many of the human tools discovered with extinct animal bones were indeed so ancient that the literal interpretation of the Book of Genesis was clearly contradicted. In 1859 the publication of Charles Darwin's *On the Origin of Species* provided a systematic scientific theory to account for the evolution of all life that was in harmony with the geological evidence pointing to the earth's great antiquity. All in all, by the mid-19th century the combination of archaeological, geological, and biological evidence was able to challenge successfully the theological position regarding prehistoric human development in the Old World.

The Search for Prehistory in the Americas

While the origins of European archaeology developed out of an interest in discovering the connections between the prehistoric and historic eras of European society, this link between past and present did not concern most early prehistorians in the Americas. These New World scholars were of European extraction, and most looked upon Native Americans and their past as inconsequential when compared with the development of civilization in the Old World. Only recently have indigenous peoples, including Native American archaeologists, been able to assert their views on their own past. But in the 18th and 19th centuries a biased Eurocentric view prevailed in both popular and scholarly prehistoric accounts. This led to imaginary reconstructions that presented pre-Columbian civilizations

FIGURE 2.4

Publication of drawings by Frederick Catherwood sparked public interest in ancient New World civilizations in the mid-19th century.

in the New World as derivations from ancient voyages and settlements from the Old World. These speculative accounts credited the many ruined mounds, temples, sculptures, and tombs found in North, Central, and South America to Old World immigrants such as ancient Egyptians, Hebrews, Phoenicians, Hindus, Chinese, and even the mythical inhabitants of Atlantis and Mu. Native Americans were usually dismissed as incapable of such achievements. Even as sober a scientist as Benjamin Franklin attributed the construction of the monumental mounds of the Mississippi Valley to the early Spanish explorer Hernando de Soto!

Yet some scholars maintained that the prehistory of the Americas was produced by the ancestors of living Native Americans, and that the diversity and achievements of New World societies before 1492 owed nothing to Old World civilizations. The growing weight of archaeological data, including a pioneering excavation by Thomas Jefferson, eventually established rightful credit for the ancient New World sites. Jefferson's excavation of an earthen mound in Virginia established that it had been built by Native Americans. Jefferson was also a pioneer in systematic excavation, accurate recording, and the use of **stratigraphy** (see Chapter 5), by observing that the sequence of earthen layers (or **strata**) reflected the passage of time.

In 1841 and 1843 John Lloyd Stephens and Frederick Catherwood published their accounts of the discovery of spectacular ruins of the Maya civilization in the jungles of Mexico and Central America. Stephens and Catherwood's books revealed the wonders of ancient Maya culture to readers in England and the United States (Fig. 2.4). Publicity of this kind helped spur the often romantic

FIGURE 2.5

When Squier and Davis encountered Monk's Mound, Cahokia (Illinois), it
was crowned by a modern house (compare Fig. 8.16).

but destructive search for other so-called lost civilizations, not only in the New
World but in Africa and Asia as well. But Stephens's appraisal of the source of
Maya civilization stands in marked contrast to the speculations popular at the
time: "We are not warranted in going back to any ancient nation of the Old
World for the builders of these cities. . . . There are strong reasons to believe
them the creations of the same races who inhabited the country at the time of
the Spanish Conquest."

In 1848 E. G. Squier and E. H. Davis published the results of their research
into the mounds of the Mississippi and Ohio valleys, providing one of the first
classifications of burial mounds, temple platforms, and effigy mounds, inferring
that these different types of mounds served different functions (Fig. 2.5). But
in trying to identify the ancient occupants of these sites, they lapsed into pure
speculation, refusing to believe that Native Americans—or their ancestors—
could be the builders. In contrast, Samuel F. Haven's sober appraisal of Native
American prehistory—*Archaeology of the United States*, published in 1856—used

available archaeological evidence to dismiss many fantastic theories about the origins of the Native Americans and concluded that the prehistoric monuments in the United States were built by the ancestors of living tribal groups. Further research reinforced this conclusion, so that by the end of the 19th century, the weight of archaeological evidence required recognition of a complex past for Native American societies without the need to resort to pseudoarchaeological tales of Old World visits or other influences.

Archaeology and 19th-Century Colonialism

By this time, archaeology was gaining recognition as a separate field of endeavor and a legitimate scholarly pursuit in both the Old and New Worlds. Unfortunately, at the same time, other forces contributed to an increase in looting and the destruction of archaeological sites. In particular, as European and American colonial expansion moved more deeply into Asia, Africa, and Latin America, proprietary claims were staked over newly discovered areas, including archaeological sites, which were often mined like mineral deposits. For instance, from 1802 to 1821 Claudius Rich, a British consular agent in Baghdad, collected and removed thousands of antiquities and sent them to England. The extraordinary Italian Giovanni Belzoni, working for the British government, systematically looted Egyptian tombs and even used battering rams to enter the ancient burial chambers. And Thomas Bruce, the seventh earl of Elgin, spent several years at the beginning of the 19th century removing a series of sculptures, now called the Elgin Marbles, from the Parthenon in Athens to their present location in the British Museum, sparking a dispute that continues today.

As destructive as many of these activities were by today's standards, many important discoveries were made. Prominent among these was the unearthing of the Rosetta Stone in Egypt, which enabled Jean François Champollion to decipher Egyptian hieroglyphs in 1822. Similar discoveries of inscribed clay tablets in Mesopotamia led to the decipherment of cuneiform writing soon thereafter. As a result of these two breakthroughs, historical records from two of the world's earliest civilizations were suddenly available to scholars and the public alike.

THE EMERGENCE OF MODERN ARCHAEOLOGY

As the discoveries continued, archaeology gained recognition as a distinct professional discipline. Professional archaeology emerged in the 19th century as many of its practitioners became full-time specialists (rather than part-time hobbyists) and as interpretations of the past relied more on evidence than on speculation. By this time the impact of the accumulating evidence of the human past was impressive. And the increase in finds was accompanied by a gradual refinement of methods of recovery and classification, which served to make the record even stronger. But what did all this new information mean? How could it be interpreted?

The problem was immense. Depending on the particular circumstance, archaeologists usually have only scattered remnants of past cultures to work with. One way to visualize the problem is to imagine what might survive from our own civilization for archaeologists to ponder some 5000 or 10,000 years from now. What could they reconstruct of our way of life on the basis of scattered softdrink bottles, porcelain toilets, plastic containers, spark plugs, reinforced concrete structures, and other nonbiodegradable products of our civilization? In approaching the problem of interpreting the past, the archaeologist needs a framework to help in putting the puzzle together. Imagine an incredibly complex three-dimensional jigsaw puzzle. If we knew nothing about its size, form, or subject matter, the puzzle would be impossible to reconstruct. But if we proposed a scheme that accounted for the puzzle's size, form, and subject, we could use this scheme to attempt to put it together. If one scheme failed to work, we could propose another in its stead, until we succeeded.

Today, the interpretive frameworks used by professional archaeologists and other scientists are generally called **models.** A model is essentially a form of hypothesis that describes the subject of investigation in a simplified way; it is constructed and tested according to the scientific method (see Chapter 1). Models may suggest additional information that may not be obvious in the archaeological data.

Early Interpretations

The earliest archaeological interpretations were based on historical models. The first historical scheme widely used by archaeologists was the **three-age system,** based on changes in technology, which held that prehistoric societies in many different areas of the world developed progressively through ages of stone, bronze, and iron technology. While the idea behind this model can be traced to writings from several ancient civilizations, including those of Greece, Rome, and China, credit for promulgating the three-age sequence for European prehistory is generally given to two early-19th-century Danish scholars. Christian Thomsen organized the collections in the Danish National Museum of Antiquities according to this scheme, not only as a convenience but also because it seemed to reflect chronological stages of human progress. His colleague, Jens Worsaae, conducted excavations in burial mounds, thereby verifying that stone tools underlay (and were thus earlier than) those of bronze, which underlay the still later tools of iron.

With further research the sequence grew more detailed. In 1865 Sir John Lubbock distinguished an earlier technology in which stones were chipped to form edges and points (Paleolithic, or "Old Stone Age") from a later technology in which the stones were ground (Neolithic, or "New Stone Age"). In 1871

Heinrich Schliemann used a quasi-historical source—Homer's *Iliad*—to discover the site of Bronze Age Troy, thereby linking the study of prehistoric societies with the later classical civilizations known to history. Also in the 19th century, archaeological method was refined to near-modern precision in the work of the Englishman General A. L. Pitt-Rivers.

Thus, by the end of the 19th century, European archaeology was based on a well-developed chronological framework that followed a historical model. To this day many European archaeologists regard their discipline as allied more closely to history than to any other field.

By the early 20th century archaeologists in America were borrowing the excavation methods developed largely in the Old World but were taking a rather different path from their Old World counterparts in their attempts to interpret the past. The difference was due largely to contrasting circumstances. For one thing, the New World, unlike many areas of the Old World, appeared to lack historical records (a supposition later proved wrong). In addition, cultural development in the Americas did not seem to have the time depth found in the Old World; the earliest migration in the New World appeared to be relatively recent, taking place during the last glacial epoch. This meant that the historical (or historically based) schemes used in the Old World could not be meaningfully applied in the Americas.

Because the connection with history was not so immediately apparent in the New World, archaeologists turned to anthropology to interpret the remains that were being discovered. They compared contemporary Native American artifacts with those recovered archaeologically, using those artifacts of known use to infer uses for artifacts from the past. As a result, for New World archaeologists, anthropology, with its unifying concept of culture, ultimately became the main source of interpretive models, replacing history. Indeed, many anthropologists of this period, such as F. H. Cushing in the Pueblo area of the American Southwest, did archaeological as well as ethnographic and linguistic fieldwork.

In both Europe and America, several related interpretive currents fused into a broad interpretive model referred to as **cultural evolution.** The previously discussed three-age system was one contributing factor to the idea of cultural evolution. That is, cultural evolution defined a series of stages based on a broad set of technological criteria, along with additional social, economic, and other cultural factors. Cultural evolution was also based on a general belief that all cultural change, in technology and other customs, was progressive, from simple to complex and from primitive to civilized. Development of evolutionary theory in biology followed a parallel trend and supported acceptance of cultural evolution. These notions were coupled with the recognition of tremendous diversity among living societies, documented in the course of colonial expansion, and with the need to explain (and thereby justify) the political and economic dominance of 19th-century "European civilization" over many other societies. The result was a model of **unilinear cultural evolution.**

The unilinear theory of cultural evolution, as developed by Herbert Spencer, Lewis Henry Morgan, Edward B. Tylor, and others, was based on comparisons among societies. Data from any source—ethnographic, archaeological, or whatever—were accepted in assessing a society's evolutionary status. Above all, cultures were compared in order to determine their relative positions on a single scale of development or success. The assumption that all human cultures develop along a single or unilinear path is perhaps best expressed by Morgan's evolutionary stages: savagery, barbarism, and civilization. The inflexibility of this scheme stands out as both the principal hallmark and the greatest weakness of 19th-century cultural evolutionary theory.

The errors of the unilinear evolutionists are readily apparent to us, with the benefit of more than 100 years of hindsight. Above all, these 19th-century theorists were **ethnocentric**—that is, their assessment of the developmental stages of other societies was heavily biased by their assumption that contemporary Western culture represented the pinnacle of evolutionary achievement.

Of course, the idea that human behavior does change and that societies and cultures do evolve remains an important aspect of modern anthropological theory. But by the turn of the 20th century it was evident that the weaknesses in the unilinear view of cultural evolution outweighed its strong points. As a consequence, attempts to write a universal history of human culture were either cast aside or altered to remove the inherent problems of unilinear schemes.

The emergence of modern anthropology and archaeology took a somewhat different turn in America, through the influence of anthropologist Franz Boas and his students. These individuals rejected attempts to apply a universal developmental scheme via uncritical cultural comparisons. Instead, they saw a need for the accumulation of large amounts of well-controlled and documented empirical data—archaeological, ethnographic, and linguistic—for a single society. These data would then be used to reconstruct the unique cultural history of each society.

This Boasian emphasis on rigorous collection of data with a localized geographical focus dominated American archaeology until the middle of the 20th century. As a result, archaeological research was directed toward the establishment of specific cultural histories, usually concentrating on tracing form, style, and technological changes in particular artifacts, such as pottery. For the most part, however, cultural historians in America shied away from attempting broader comparative statements concerning developmental parallels and contrasts in the prehistoric record.

Beginning in the mid-20th century, comparative approaches regained popularity in American archaeology as part of a growing interest in understanding the processes of change and stability in prehistoric cultures. The study of artifact styles and the reconstruction of localized cultural historical sequences have remained useful, especially in previously unstudied regions. At the same time, more sophisticated questions are now being asked of archaeological data, such as how a given culture was organized internally—how it functioned—at particular points in time. Cultural evolution has again become an acceptable interpretive model, but now in a version recognizing that cultures do not develop according to some predetermined plan. Each society's development is conditioned by the natural ecological setting in which it occurs, the neighboring societies with which it interacts, and its own traditions. Therefore, the specific courses of evolutionary change must be expected to be **multilinear** rather than following a single universal or unilinear path. And as we shall see in Chapters 3 and 9, archaeology is going beyond evolutionary questions and exploring questions of meaning and behavior that can be gained from the archaeological record. Most important, in the 21st century archaeology has broken away from its 19th-century Eurocentric perspective and colonial origins. As discussed in Chapter 10, today there are professional archaeologists throughout the world, representing an array of different cultural and ethnic backgrounds, investigating topics and issues that enlighten all of us about the rich and diverse heritage of our human past. In many, but far from all, cases, as we noted in Chapter 1, this work is now carried out by CRM and NGO archaeologists.

SUMMARY

Like many other branches of science, archaeology has its roots in the work of amateur collectors of long ago. As the number of antiquities collected grew, attempts were made to bring order to collections by classification. This search for meaning led to the first attempts at understanding the prehistoric past, but such explanations were largely speculative. In the Old World prehistoric archaeology emerged from attempts to understand human origins and evolution, while in America the central issue was the antiquity of human populations in the New World.

The emergence of archaeology as a professional, scientific discipline was marked by the rise of full-time specialists committed to understanding the patterns and diversity in the physical remains from the past. This commitment to understanding required adopting models or interpretive frameworks that could be tested against the evidence. Models developed in the Old World, such as the three-age system, were initially derived mainly from history. In the New World, where most native cultures lacked written histories, archaeology became closely allied with anthropology. For both areas at the time the dominant framework was unilinear cultural evolution, whereby the same broad stages were defined for all societies. In the early 20th century the weaknesses in this scheme led to more rigorous descriptive approaches. More recently, multilinear evolutionary models have emerged, focusing research on the process of culture change and the respective developmental paths of each society. In the 21st century the questions and issues of concern to archaeology are as diverse as the backgrounds and interests of its practitioners.

FOR FURTHER READING

THE ORIGINS OF ARCHAEOLOGY
Christenson 1989; Daniel and Chippindale 1989; Trigger 2006; Willey and Sabloff 1993

THE EMERGENCE OF MODERN ARCHAEOLOGY
Brew 1968; Gosden 1999; Kehoe 1998; Patterson 1995, 2001; Trigger 2006; Willey and Sabloff 1993

ADDITIONAL SOURCES
Fagan 1985; Flannery 1967; Franklin and Paynter 2010; Haven 1856; Meltzer, Fowler, and Sabloff 1986; J. Sabloff 1998; Schliemann (1881) 1968; Snead and Sabloff 2010; Squier and Davis 1848; Stephens (1841) 1969, (1843) 1963; Trigger 1984; Willey 1974

3

Contemporary Approaches
to Archaeology

ARCHAEOLOGY IN THE 20TH CENTURY developed increasingly diverse and sophisticated approaches. This chapter reviews the most prominent ones—culture history, cultural process, and postprocessual approaches. It also explores emergent feminist, Marxist, behavioral, and evolutionary perspectives. The culture history approach, the earliest of the set, is based on a description of the archaeological record and the ordering of past events in time and space. The emphasis in culture history is *what, when,* and *where* events took place in the past. In the 1960s the cultural process, or processual, approach emerged, seeking to explain the events of the past and to identify the general processes of cultural change. Processualism focuses on *how* and *why* past events took place. Postprocessual approaches arose in the late 1980s as attempts to understand the meaning of the past. Postprocessual archaeologists also focus on the *why* of past events but emphasize the perspective of the ancient peoples involved—to gain an insider's understanding, rather than an outsider's explanation, of the past.

Of these three approaches, postprocessual archaeology is the newest and still the most diverse in outlook. In addition, other important perspectives have emerged and exist alongside the three dominant trends we define here. Some, such as Marxist or feminist approaches, are often treated as forms of postprocessual archaeology. Similarly, behavioral and evolutionary approaches are often linked to processualism. Although there is overlap, crucial distinctions remain. What is most important to recognize is that these and other perspectives ultimately enrich archaeology's search for understanding; disagreements among their advocates foster discussion and refinement of ideas. In this chapter we focus on the principal characteristics of the three most common approaches.

Taken together, these approaches address all four of the basic goals of archaeology outlined in Chapter 1—understanding the form, function, process, and meaning of the past. Thus, they all contribute to the field of archaeology as practiced today. But each approach also asks different questions and, in doing so, uses different definitions of culture, distinct ways of conducting research, and different frameworks for reconstructing the past. We will consider each of these topics separately, but we should remember that many archaeologists combine various aspects from all of these approaches to best suit their particular needs.

CULTURE HISTORY

The culture history approach dominated archaeology during the first half of the 20th century. Its emphasis on defining the sequence and spatial distribution of past events by studying patterns of material remains is still the foundation for most archaeology done today. Because this approach leads to an outline of the general trends of both cultural change and continuity, it often serves as the starting point for all other kinds of research.

The Normative Model of Culture

The **culture history approach** reconstructs the past by using a normative model of culture. The normative model holds that a culture is a set of rules or **norms** that govern behavior in a particular society. These rules are passed from one generation to the next; each new generation learns the norms of behavior within the family (parent to child), schools (teacher to student), occupations (master to apprentice), peer groups, and similar situations. Because the learning of rules of behavior is not perfect, a degree of change in the normative system is inevitable. Some behavior, of course, is idiosyncratic—unique to the individual—and may not be perpetuated. In any given culture a range of behaviors is tolerated for each situation; what the norms specify are the ranges and their limits.

The archaeologist often makes use of this model of culture to describe and reconstruct behavior in the past. Those who favor this approach assume that the material remains of ancient cultures reflect past behavioral norms. For instance, pottery is a good indicator of culturally controlled behavior. Although the methods for making and decorating pottery are many and varied, each society uses only a few of these techniques, learned by each potter as an apprentice. Departures from these manufacturing norms are usually discouraged by social and economic sanctions. Archaeologists, therefore, can infer the ancient rules governing pottery-making by studying shared characteristics in the surviving ceramics.

Within this conceptual framework the culture history approach emphasizes the goal of outlining the sequence (time dimension) and geographical distribution (space dimension) of past cultural norms. Once this is done, interpretation proceeds to apply descriptive models, usually drawn from ethnography and history, that describe the mechanisms most likely to have been involved in stability and change. The culmination of the interpretive process is thus a chronicle of events and general trends of cultural change and continuity in the prehistoric past. In fact, a culture history approach is well suited to outlining the temporal, spatial, and even functional dimensions of prehistory. It is less suitable, however, for analyzing the causal factors operating in cultural development and change.

Culture History Research

Typical culture history research begins with specific data from individual sites, combining these in increasing degrees of generalization and synthesis. The specific techniques used to collect, process, and analyze archaeological data will be discussed later. Here we will briefly describe how archaeological research leads to the application of culture history frameworks for reconstructing the past.

The choice of a location for archaeological research is made by weighing a variety of factors (discussed in Chapter 4). In most cases surface survey identifies archaeological sites and provides the initial round of data collection. The archaeologist selects the material cultural traits that seem most sensitive to temporal change and that will therefore best allow a collection to be arranged in a tentative chronological sequence. Depending on the kind of archaeological site being investigated, these chronologies may be based on traits seen in stone tools, pottery, architecture, or other remains.

Once the preliminary chronological scheme is proposed, excavations are undertaken to test the sequence and to provide further data to refine the sequences. Other goals may also be pursued in excavation, but the first goal in the culture history approach is usually the discovery and investigation of stratified deposits that enable the archaeologist to perfect or further document the tentative time scheme.

Culture History Frameworks

Culture history begins with chronology. By correlating all of the sequences of data, the archaeologist defines chronological **periods** or phases for the site as a whole. The next step in the procedure is to expand the chronology beyond the individual site to encompass wider geographical areas. This enlargement of scope is accomplished by investigating sites adjacent to those already studied. Newly acquired data can be compared to extant sequences. In this way, not only is the cultural chronology refined, but the archaeologist can also begin to plot the spatial distributions of data. As more and more sites are investigated and the number of known prehistoric cultural sequences grows, the temporal and spatial coverage expands over ever-widening areas. These larger temporal and spatial frameworks are called **time-space grids** (Fig. 3.1).

As a rule, the largest time-space unit used in culture history research is the **culture area,** a geographical region based on ethnographically defined cultural similarities (Fig. 3.2). Archaeologists working within a given culture area usually help their investigations by using common terminology and concepts to make

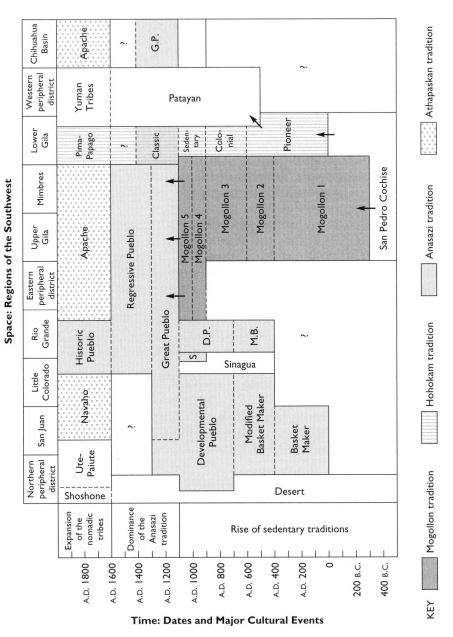

FIGURE 3.1

The culture history approach leads to the development of time-space grids, like this one for the southwestern United States, to summarize ancient developments and cultural relationships.

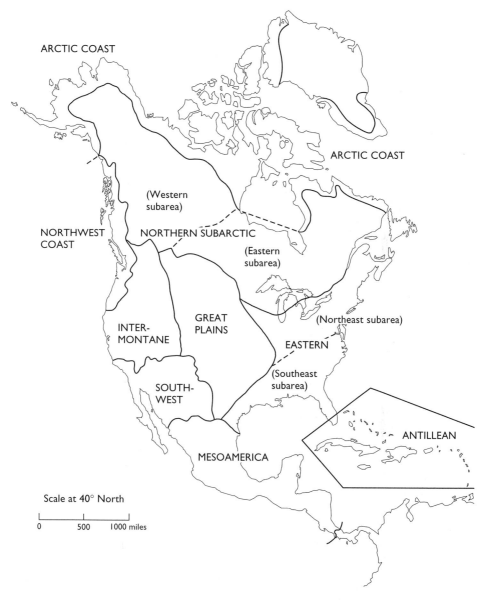

ARCTIC COAST

ARCTIC COAST

(Western
subarea)

NORTHWEST
COAST

NORTHERN SUBARCTIC

(Eastern
subarea)

(Northeast subarea)

INTER-
MONTANE

GREAT
PLAINS

EASTERN

(Southeast
subarea)

SOUTH-
WEST

ANTILLEAN

MESOAMERICA

Scale at 40° North

0   500   1000 miles

FIGURE 3.2

Cultural attributes combined with geographical factors are used to define
culture areas—in this case those of North America.

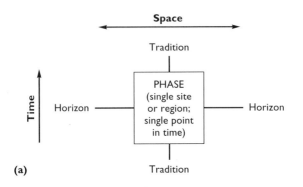

(a)

DEVELOPMENTAL STAGES	ATTRIBUTES		
	Technological	*Social*	*Ideological*
Postclassic	Metallurgy	Complex urbanism, militarism	Secularization of society
Classic	Craft specialization, beginnings of metallurgy	Large ceremonial centers, beginnings of urbanism	Developed theocracies
Formative	Pottery, weaving, developed food production	Permanent villages and towns; first ceremonial centers	Beginnings of priest class (theocracy)
Archaic	Diversified tools, ground stone utensils, beginnings of food production	Beginnings of permanent villages	?
Lithic (or Paleo-Indian)	Chipped-stone tools	Nonsettled hunters and gatherers	?

(b)

FIGURE 3.3

Willey and Phillips comprehensively outlined New World culture history by (a) integrating the dimensions of time and space through the concepts of tradition and horizon (a *phase* represents the form or content of a particular tradition on a particular horizon) and (b) summarizing the documented course of cultural development through five generalized stages.

information from different sites comparable. The first culture history synthesis of an entire culture area in the Americas was defined for the American Southwest. Since that time other prehistoric culture area syntheses have been worked out, both in the Old World and throughout the Americas.

As culture history research began to create broader and more general syntheses in the Americas, it became increasingly obvious that some kind of overriding interpretive model would be necessary. Such a framework was worked out in the mid-20th century; it represents a temporal-spatial synthesis for all the Americas (Fig. 3.3). The terminology is distinct from that used in the Old World, where such frameworks were usually based on unilinear cultural evolution (see Chapter 2). Yet the resulting framework in the Americas does suggest a course of cultural development from simple to complex that, although certainly not identical, was clearly parallel to the course of Old World prehistory.

The model for the Americas was developed by Gordon R. Willey and Philip Phillips based on the complementary concepts of tradition and horizon. **Tradition** refers to cultural continuity through time; **horizon** deals with ties and uniformity across space at a single point in time (see Fig. 3.3). Applying these concepts to data from all areas of the Americas, Willey and Phillips defined a series of five developmental stages or, as they have been more commonly treated, chronological periods. The exact temporal boundaries for each stage differ from area to area, but overall, Willey and Phillips's scheme represents a culture history synthesis for the entire New World that remains useful today.

CULTURAL PROCESS

The second major means for reconstructing the past involves a **cultural process approach.** Cultural process refers both to how the component parts of a culture function as a system at one point in time and to how cultures change over time. It seeks to explain the processes of culture by discovering the causes of change at both points—within the internal workings of specific cultures and from the broader perspectives of cross-cultural interaction in space and cultural change through time.

Ecological and Materialist Models of Culture

The cultural process (or simply *processual*) approach is based on two complementary models of culture: (1) the ecological model, which emphasizes a synchronic view of culture, and (2) the materialist model, which emphasizes a diachronic or evolutionary view of culture.

The ecological model portrays culture, and especially technology, as the primary means by which human societies adapt to their environment. Whereas the normative model emphasizes regularities and rules, the ecological model highlights the variation evident in cultural forms (for example, spear points used in hunting or horticultural implements used to cultivate different crops), seeing the range and variety as potential clues to how the society in question dealt with its environment as a whole. Change stems from alteration of this adaptive relationship between culture and environment, as reflected archaeologically in new forms or new frequencies of particular material remains.

The ecological model has an analog in biology, where scientists study how each species adapts to a set of environmental conditions, but archaeologists must take into account additional factors. Animal species adapt to both a physical environment (geography, climate, and so on) and a biological environment (other species of plant and animal life). Human societies adapt to these same environments but also to a cultural environment (neighboring groups or societies). Moreover, in biology physical and behavioral traits are transmitted genetically, from parent to offspring, which limits the ability of a species to adapt to environmental change. Human societies, however, also have culture as a mechanism for the transmission of behavior (see the discussion of the normative model of culture earlier in the chapter). Because culture is learned, changes need not wait for new generations to be born before they spread. This does not mean that all cultures are constantly undergoing rapid changes. But culture gives human societies the *potential* for speedy and flexible responses when a change in the environment occurs.

Note that this ecological model does not imply that the environment determines the form of a culture. Indeed, the contrary is true: through time and on a global scale, our physical and biological environments have become increasingly determined by human culture. We need only look around us to see the changes our culture has wrought—altering the landscape and the very composition of the water we drink, the food we eat, and the air we breathe.

In the ecological model the culture's mode of adapting to the environment is significant, though. The environment provides the opportunities for human exploitation, and each technology exploits a different part of the environment. Because each technology is different, the organizational and ideological aspects of each culture, which follow the technological adaptation, will also be unique. Furthermore, certain environments offer more alternatives—and more fruitful choices—than others. Finally, in another parallel with biology, societies that are less specialized in their environmental adaptations tend to be less vulnerable to changes in their environment than are more specialized societies.

One benefit of the processual approach is an increased understanding of causality. By viewing the archaeological record from an ecological perspective, the archaeologist may detect shifts in adaptation that suggest causes and consequences of change, rather than merely describing changes in norms.

As mentioned, the processual approach also relies on a materialist model of culture. Cultural materialism holds that there are biological and psychological needs common to all humans, such as hunger, sex, and shelter. How these shared needs are met in different societies provides a means for evaluating each society's adaptive efficiency by measuring input, output, costs, and benefits. Human needs are satisfied most directly by a culture's infrastructure, composed of technology, economy, and demography (the size and composition of its human population). The infrastructure is the main focus of change as it responds to changing human needs and environmental conditions by optimizing benefits relative to costs for each society. Changes in the infrastructure also foster change in the culture's social, political, and ideological systems.

These factors are illustrated in one of the most basic materialist models, advanced by anthropologist Leslie White and his students. The model focuses on increases in harnessing energy and organizing human labor as the keys to the relative efficiency of evolving human societies. Critical changes occurred when people increased their productive potential by increasing their energy output, at first by using animals to serve as beasts of burden. This allowed the same number of people to do more work and increase production while using less time. Other transitions took place with the advent of water, steam, and oil as energy sources.

Evolutionary Archaeology

A neo-Darwinian approach to archaeology emerged in the final decades of the 20th century. According to this approach, culture change is a product of evolutionary processes that are analogous to those that drive biological evolution. The combination of ecology, evolution, and society yields within each culture a series of unique cultural lineages, each produced by a process of selection and change through time. Evolutionary archaeologists are concerned with how this selective process works in the transmission, replication, and use of artifacts. The work of Robert Dunnell is the basis for much of the **evolutionary archaeology** conducted in the United States. This work is noted for its adherence to scientific methodology and a Darwinian perspective applied to human culture.

Dunnell introduced the concept of waste to give a neo-Darwinian explanation for societies that invested in energy-consuming activities that did not directly benefit the reproductive success of the individual or the population. This kind of cultural waste would include the construction of monumental structures and energies expended in the trade of luxury goods—both of which benefit only a small, elite minority. Examples from Peru, Egypt, and the eastern United States suggest that periods with increasingly wasteful behavior correlate with growing conflicts over resources, and that lavish expenditures increased evolutionary fitness of society as a whole by causing a decrease in the reproductive rate of individuals. Waste of this kind can thus be considered something like "bet hedging," in that by bearing fewer offspring and investing more energy in their sustenance, a society can offset environmental (resource) limitations and keep the population from outstripping its resource base. Although evolutionary archaeology is not equivalent to processual archaeology, both emphasize the use of scientific methodology, especially hypothesis testing of the sort described in the paragraphs below.

Processual Research

How does the processual approach attempt to identify the causes of change and thereby explain cultural processes? It begins with hypotheses that specify, at the outset of research, the working model of change (or interaction) and the kinds of data that will support or refute each hypothesis. Competing hypotheses are then tested against the archaeological data in order to eliminate those not supported by the evidence. Hypotheses that are supported in the first test are retested and refined by further research in order to isolate the factors involved in a given situation of prehistoric cultural change. An example of this is David Hurst Thomas's tests of Steward's model of Great Basin (Shoshonean) culture, discussed in Chapter 1. In the processual approach, then, interpretation refers to the selection and refinement of hypotheses that best delineate cultural processes.

Of course, the processual approach is rooted, either directly or indirectly, in culture history reconstructions. A direct link may be apparent when the hypotheses have been derived from culture history research. In an indirect way, however, *all* processual interpretation is built on a culture history foundation, because culture history provides the temporal and spatial frameworks of prehistory. These frameworks furnish the foundations without which cultural processes cannot be discerned.

For example, in studying the ancient society of the Ulua Valley around Santa Bárbara, in west-central Honduras, initial culture history research suggested that two adjacent valley pockets—Gualjoquito and Tencoa—had quite different developmental sequences. Gualjoquito supported a small local capital between about A.D. 200 and 900 but seemed to lack earlier or later evidence of localized leaders. Tencoa yielded a comparable center, but one that pertained to an earlier period, probably 400 B.C.–A.D. 200. Tencoa has better agricultural resources, but Gualjoquito occupies an obvious crossroad position (which Tencoa does not). Also, Gualjoquito's period of peak development seemed to coincide with the flourishing of the major Maya city of Copán, to the southwest along one of the routes linked by the crossroads.

From these data several models were proposed to be tested against new data. One linked Gualjoquito's rise and fall to the importance of external alliances—specifically, to ties with Copán. Because the valley pockets are small, the model included the further hypothesis that when the crossroads was not in active use, the pocket with more natural subsistence resources (Tencoa) would be the seat of local power. If the model were correct, further survey should reveal no further elite centers in the two periods cited and should yield evidence of a return to power in Tencoa with the decline of Copán by A.D. 900. Survey and excavation should also turn up more imports, especially those likely to be owned by society's leaders, in Gualjoquito, and the homes and possessions of those same leaders should show strong links with the culture and styles of Copán.

The next step in the processual approach involves assembling all the data relevant to rigorous testing of hypotheses under consideration. Hypothesis testing in archaeology, as in any scientific discipline, must follow an explicit, fully documented procedure. As discussed in Chapter 1, many sciences test hypotheses by conducting controlled and repeatable experiments. For example, the hypothesis that explains how a barometer works holds that the weight of the earth's atmosphere—atmospheric pressure—supports the column of mercury. An experiment to test this hypothesis would involve moving one barometer to a new altitude while a second remained at the first altitude, as a check against any change in weather conditions. This experiment is controlled, in that it rules out interference by other factors (in this case weather). It is also repeatable: it can be performed any number of times.

In some cases, as in the experimental archaeology examples discussed in Chapter 8, archaeologists do use controlled experiments to test specific findings. But archaeologists generally cannot rely upon controlled, repeatable experiments to test hypotheses. The archaeological record already exists, and those who study it cannot return to the past to manipulate situations to test their reconstructions. This observation highlights a fundamental distinction between the physical sciences (such as physics and chemistry) and the historical sciences (evolutionary biology, geology, and archaeology). In the words of Stephen Jay Gould, "historical sciences are different, not lesser. Their methods are comparative, not always experimental; they explain, but do not usually try to predict; they recognize the irreducible quirkiness that history entails" (1985:18). Archaeologists and other historical scientists can, however, test their reconstructions by explicitly and clearly stating the conditions and expectations of their hypotheses and then collecting and analyzing the data specified by the expectations.

The testing procedure for archaeological hypotheses actually begins at the outset of research, with the formulation of multiple hypotheses that make mutually exclusive predictions about the data. The use of **multiple working hypotheses** means that as many explanatory alternatives as possible are considered. This minimizes the opportunity for explanatory bias on the part of the investigator and maximizes the chance of finding the best available explanation. In the example cited earlier, archaeologists working in the Santa Bárbara area set forth at least two mutually exclusive hypotheses: (1) if Copán and the crossroads were the key to Gualjoquito's prosperity, the predictions outlined above should be met; (2) if, however, other resources underlay its leaders' successes, the data would match predictions from models other than the one described here. Three years of subsequent data collection and analysis supported the link to Copán.

In this and other situations the goal is to invalidate all but one hypothesis. The surviving hypothesis may then be advanced, not as proven, but as the best possible explanation given the present state of knowledge. All science involves the assumption that contemporary explanations will eventually be modified or replaced as new data become available.

Cultural Process Frameworks

Two interrelated frameworks underlie most process research: (1) cultural systems and (2) multilinear cultural evolution. Following from the ecological model, cultural process research is concerned with reconstructing past societies as integrated cultural systems. A **system** is a complex entity made up of interrelated components, and the relationships among these components are as important as the components themselves. Each human society is actually composed of many

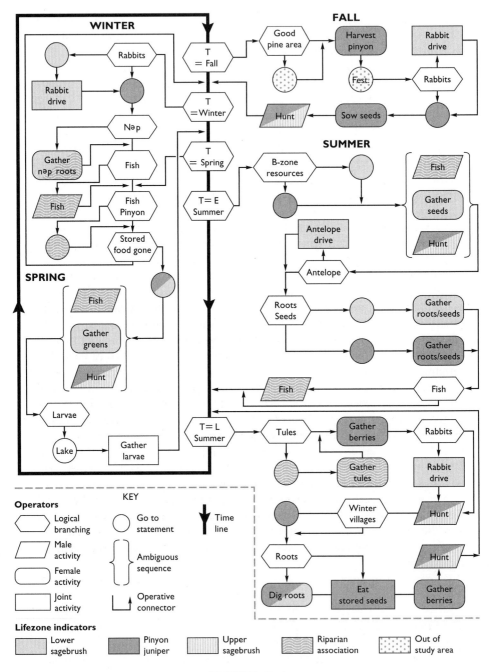

FIGURE 3.4

An example of a cultural system is shown in the related activities (components) of food acquisition used by the Shoshonean peoples of the Great Basin in the western United States.

subsystems that function together. For example, all societies have a means for acquiring food (Fig. 3.4), a subsystem composed of all the activities involved in ensuring that society members have enough to eat. The components of this subsystem include the ways of collecting or growing food and of processing, storing, distributing, and preparing food. Changes in one component would create changes in other components because all are interrelated. As a result of one change, therefore, the entire system would change.

Archaeologists use the ecological model of culture to identify as many components of a past cultural system as possible. If the system can be reconstructed and a change in one of its components identified, then the consequences of that change for other components can be traced. For instance, a change in weapons technology may lead to successes against enemy societies, increased wealth, and perhaps an increase in population. This might then change the economic and political system, perhaps resulting in a more authoritarian power structure. Eventually, changes in the belief system could follow, such as increased importance of worship of deities for war and political authority.

By viewing the archaeological record this way, the archaeologist can move from a well-established synchronic base to a diachronic perspective. Thus, the ecological culture model and a systems framework lead together to finding the causes and consequences of change, instead of merely describing the appearance of new weapons, new status goods, and new images of deities. In other words, rather than merely describing what has changed, the archaeologist begins to unravel the process of change.

This brings us to the second framework of processual archaeology, multilinear cultural evolution. This framework is actually based on both ecological and cultural materialist models of culture. The ecological model shows that cultural systems do not evolve according to a single uniform sequence. Rather, cultural evolution is a many-channeled process, governed by each society's ecological adaptation within its own environmental setting. The materialist model holds that each human society adapts to its environment primarily via its technology and secondarily through its organizational and ideational subsystems. When viewed over the long term, changes in each individual culture result from the accumulation of all of its specific adaptive responses. What suits one society to one environment will not necessarily be adaptive elsewhere.

Beyond the particular instances of adaptation and change stressed by the ecological model, multilinear evolution emphasizes the degree of success or efficiency of each system from a materialist perspective. This leads to the measurement of the efficiency of cultural development by how it survives over time or, if appropriate, how it becomes extinct. A particular society may be well adapted to its environment so that it achieves a stable balance or equilibrium, in which change is minimal and survival is the measure of adaptive efficiency. In other cases human societies become involved in growth cycles. For example, changes originating either from the environment or from within the society may trigger changes in the technological system—and as a result in the organizational and ideational systems. If these technological changes result in increases in food production and if the organizational and ideational changes allow for increases in population size, a process of growth may begin. Continued growth will eventually place new strains on technology (the amount of food produced), organization (management of people), and ideology (beliefs justifying the other two systems). This pressure may trigger further changes in the society—technological innovations to increase food production or new forms of social and political organization to mobilize the population—and the cycle may continue. Such a growth spiral is evident in the archaeological record of the development of civilization in both the Old and New Worlds.

The frameworks of cultural systems and multilinear evolution allow prehistoric archaeologists to explore the patterns and dynamics of growth within human societies. Whereas culture history reconstruction emphasizes identification of cultural interaction and change through description of a sequence of events, cultural process reconstruction is concerned with discovering the causes of interactions and change. That is, the processual approach seeks not only to identify and describe similarities and differences across time and space but also to explain the observed distributions.

EMERGENT APPROACHES

Three kinds of archaeology have emerged most prominently as responses to processual archaeology: Marxist, feminist, and postprocessual perspectives.

Marxist Perspectives

In the late 19th century, Karl Marx wrote widely and critically on the human condition. Australian archaeologist V. Gordon Childe, one of the most influential archaeologists of the mid-20th century, applied Marx's ideas effectively in interpreting social and cultural change in the past. There are several strands of Marxist thinking. Common to many is the view that society everywhere is based on conflict, not consensus, and that social life is subject to constant change, struggle, and resistance among social classes. Not surprisingly, Marxist archaeologists call for identifying processes of class formation, and of the gender, ethnic, and racial hierarchies they promote. Philip Kohl and Thomas Patterson, for example, found that such an approach could explain ancient societies and cultures in Southwest Asia and Peru, respectively, better than could the processual approach, which emphasized adaptation and system equilibrium. William Marquardt, on the other hand, has advocated *combining* processual and Marxist perspectives in his study of foragers of the Shell Mound Archaic in western Kentucky, between ca. 2500 and 1000 B.C.

Feminist Perspectives

In 1984, Margaret Conkey and Janet Spector published a critique of archaeology as perpetuating male-centered stereotypes of past lives, which portrayed men as active and powerful, while women were cast consistently as passive, powerless, or simply absent. Looking for evidence of women in the archaeological record and correcting male-centered bias are important parts of the challenge posed by a gendered archaeology. But feminist theory informs a more extensive overhaul of archaeology, not only toward the examination of men's and women's activities, but also toward rephrasing research questions and findings, in which "women" need not always be the focus of inquiry.

From this standpoint, Elizabeth Brumfiel challenges the ecosystem approach of processualism, arguing forcefully that the texture and active nature of people's lives are lost in processual analysis. In its place, she advocates greater recognition of gender, as well as class and faction, as means through which members of society interact with one another. She has pursued such recognition through her own research on Aztec society, illustrating how women's *and* men's lives were changed by expansion of the Aztec empire. For example, she has shown how men were conscripted to work farther from home and how, to feed them, women made fewer tamales and greater quantities of more portable tortillas (Fig. 3.5).

FIGURE 3.5

Aztec mother teaching her daughter to make tortillas.

Postprocessual Perspectives

Postprocessual archaeology emerged from the perceived shortcomings of processual archaeology. Whereas processual archaeologists treat culture as adaptation and portray cultural change as a response to shifts in one or another aspect of the environment, some archaeologists began to argue for a more humanistic approach that would recognize the importance of nonmaterial factors in people's lives. These archaeologists contend that changes in behavior have to be understood in the context of each culture's particular values, attitudes, and other beliefs that give the world meaning.

All these emergent approaches complement culture history and cultural process in at least four ways. First, believing that the normative, ecological, and materialist cultural models present people as passive, these archaeologists call for a more active or dynamic model of culture. This model focuses on the human ability to adjust learned customs deliberately, in response to changing social conditions. Second, rather than dealing with time in large, undivided blocks, these archaeologists treat time more like the continuous flow in which people actually live their lives. Third, whereas both culture history and cultural process are concerned with collective behavior at the level of entire societies, emergent approaches attempt to get at the smallest-scale behaviors, such as those of the individual, family, or ethnic group. Fourth, whereas culture history and cultural process interpret the archaeological record from an external, scientific point of view, emergent approaches emphasize insiders' perspectives, seeing people's actions as efforts to make sense of or even reshape their lives. For this reason, feminist, Marxist, and postprocessual archaeologists view the past as dependent on the specific conditions and perspectives of the society being investigated, from its members' points of view.

This goal of achieving an internal perspective reflects changes in studies of human culture, a cycle alternating between knowledge gained from formal objective science and that gained from subjective insight. For processual archaeologists the goal is objective scientific explanation—specifying components, relationships, and points of change within past cultural systems. In emergent approaches, the goal is understanding the meaning of past events within their own cultural contexts. This has brought the fourth goal of archaeology, the determination of meaning (see Chapter 1), to the forefront.

The Practice Model of Culture

As we have seen, the models for culture used in the culture history and cultural process approaches emphasize people as collective and passive participants rather than individual and active agents. In contrast, feminist, Marxist, and postprocessual archaeologists assert that people are indeed active agents, constantly choosing how best to relate to those around them. In this view, social diversity, social interactions, and individual choices are central; social relations are always being negotiated. The practice model of culture is appropriate here: it sees culture as perpetually changing, while individuals and groups adjust learned customs to fit the contexts of their lives, especially in response to the people with whom they interact. The changes in day-to-day practice may be either deliberate or unconscious, molded by individual or group interests. Because culture is seen as perpetually changing, even on a short-term basis, this model of culture is diachronic. Postprocessual archaeologists try to address spans of time between the moment and the long term, which they feel earlier archaeologists have ignored.

Let us contrast how the three most prominent approaches view pottery, one of the most commonly encountered remains of past activity. Culture historians see pottery decorations as idealized traits that allow identification of cultures and their variations in time or space. Processual archaeologists see the same decorations as a means of defining social groups and as changing over time in response to shifts in their boundaries. Archaeologists taking emergent approaches look at who likely made the vessels, for whom, and under what circumstances. For example, pottery-making is often done by one gender, frequently women. Such gender roles should not be simply presumed, however. And whatever their gender, potters can work in varied contexts, from individual households to community-wide settings to government-controlled workshops.

Feminist, Marxist, and Postprocessual Research

As we have mentioned, a central tenet in these emergent approaches is to gain meaning from the archaeological record by using material culture to reconstruct an internal view of an ancient symbol system. Ethnographers may interact with living people of other cultures to gain this insider's view, but doing so with an extinct prehistoric society is obviously much more difficult. Under some circumstances historical or ethnohistoric documentation may provide clues. In fact, in U.S. historical archaeology, written records often detail insiders' views, offering details of everyday life and tighter interpretive and chronological control than in prehistoric archaeology.

The means for generating and testing propositions via these emergent approaches differ little from those used by other archaeologists. For example, the archaeological record is examined for regularities and patterns, and these patterns are interpreted on the basis of propositions that can be tested by data from subsequent research.

Archaeologists schooled in the hypothesis-testing procedures of the scientific method wonder how to derive and test a proposition describing points of view that once existed in the minds of long-dead people. Feminist, Marxist, and postprocessual archaeologists do not deny the difficulty of using formal scientific method to this end; rather, they conclude that traditional science is simply inappropriate for the task, because it represents a perspective inherently bound to a Western cultural tradition. Instead, when archaeological data are linked by cultural continuity to specific and known ethnic groups, meanings of specific cultural values, gained from ethnographic or ethno-historical accounts, may be used as the basis for understanding similar patterns in past situations. With growing commitment to community-based and indigenous archaeologies (see Chapter 1), living descendants play ever more central roles in understanding archaeological traces of past lives.

Particularly for cases without documented links between past and present, Ian Hodder and others have advanced a **reflexive method.** Based on the premise that evidence does not exist apart from interpretation and theory, a reflexive method emphasizes constant and continuous interpretation and reinterpretation, and encourages diverse observers to contribute to the interpretive stream. A single interpretation is not the goal. In Hodder's research at Çatalhöyük, Turkey, varied, sophisticated, and often intricate data-gathering techniques yield a complex array of evidence that is subject to interpretation by all members of the research team—plus visitors and other observers on the field site, at the project's website, and in any other communicative context. It is not true that "anything goes," however, for as Alison Wylie and others have argued, archaeological evidence permits only so much latitude in inference.

Feminist, Marxist, and Postprocessual Frameworks

Central to emergent approaches is recognition that because past societies were composed of individuals with differing goals and views the archaeological record should be viewed as similarly complicated. Although the multiple original dimensions may be difficult to reconstruct, frameworks for understanding should make it possible to study as many aspects of human behavior as possible.

Shifts in goals and views can be seen in specific artifacts and features known from the archaeological record. For example, an implement such as the atlatl, or spear thrower, is usually seen as a weapon, but it also has social and ideological meanings in native North American societies. In North America the atlatl was replaced by a more efficient weapon, the bow and arrow, by about A.D. 500. Instead of disappearing, however, the ancient atlatl was transformed over time into the calumet or "peace pipe," thus becoming an important social and religious symbol (Fig. 3.6). Socially, it became an emblem for kin groups, such as clans. Ritually, it became a symbol of peace or friendship celebrated between adversaries. In this way a former weapon developed into a symbol used in meetings between potential enemies, much as our handshake derives from a gesture to demonstrate that no weapon is being held in the hand.

Historical archaeology has produced some of the best examples of how meanings varied for different members of society. Mark Leone and his colleagues combined archaeology with written and oral histories to explore life in Annapolis, Maryland, from the 18th century forward. In partnership with today's diverse Annapolis residents, the team documented distinct cultures within the city. Although members of different races and classes shared belief in the right to personal freedom and liberty, options to express those values were often

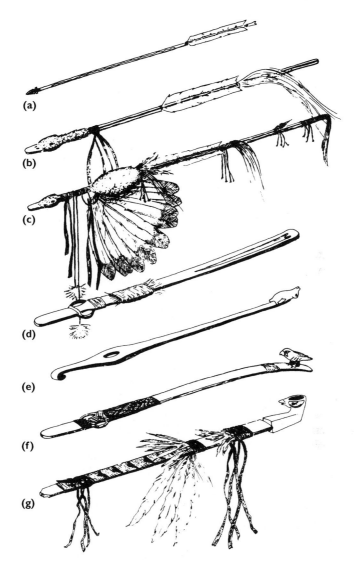

FIGURE 3.6

Historical (b–d, g) and prehistoric (e, f) materials illustrate similarities
in form between spear throwers (d, e) and calumets and other Native
American pipes (b, c, g), as well as their co-occurrence sometimes in the
same item (f). The arrow (a) is shown for scale.

dramatically unequal. Elaborately landscaped homes identified the wealthiest Euroamerican residents, including men prominent in the American Revolution. In some of the same homes, crystals and other cached items attest that enslaved individuals drew on African spiritual traditions for protection from the violence in their lives. In the same centuries, free African American families staunchly resisted racist constraints, building economic independence and often affluence. Clearly, members of Annapolis society have led diverse lives.

As these examples show, feminist, Marxist, and postprocessual archaeology has to be tied to specific cultural traditions to be able to reach levels of meaning not even attempted by other archaeological approaches. But this requirement could make it less useful for the more general view of the past, beyond the confines of a particular cultural tradition. Indeed, most archaeologists in the United States continue to take a processual approach. Emergent approaches, however, increasingly address issues (such as the role of gender in ancient life) raised by critics dissatisfied with the limitations of processual archaeology. It is already clear that the ultimate impact of emergent approaches will include recognition that the archaeological record represents many levels of meaning and that the diversity and patterns in that record represent how past peoples actively used and interpreted their world—a world that was often very different from our own.

SUMMARY

Archaeology today has a variety of means to reconstruct the past by applying a series of useful cultural models and interpretive frameworks. Following the general tenets of the scientific method, the culture history approach gathers data and tests propositions, primarily to order the past into ever-larger temporal and spatial frameworks. Its descriptions are usually broad and general, founded in a normative concept of culture. The results of culture history archaeology usually provide the essential foundations for the other two major approaches.

The second major approach emphasizes identification and explanation of cultural processes—how cultures operate at any one point in time and why they change over time, sometimes relatively rapidly and other times almost imperceptibly. Multiple-hypothesis-testing research is used to reveal the causal factors operating in specific cases. The approach is based on two complementary cultural models. The ecological model stresses synchronic study of human culture as a means of adaptation with the physical, biological, and cultural environment. This model contributes to a cultural systems framework, which views past societies as dynamic interactions between component parts. The materialist model emphasizes the role of the technological core of culture as it responds to changing human needs and environmental conditions by optimizing benefits relative to costs for society. Both models contribute to a multilinear cultural evolution framework to establish general cross-cultural trends of human prehistory, with technology usually seen as playing the leading role. Evolutionary archaeology shares hypothesis testing with processualism but is distinguished from it through its consideration of cultural change as analogous to biological evolution.

Emergent approaches include Marxist and feminist perspectives, as well as postprocessual archaeology. All three focus on understanding the past by using a more active or dynamic model of culture, studying a more human time scale, and focusing on individual, family, or ethnic group behavior. In contrast to other cultural models, the practice model of culture portrays people as active participants in shaping how they live their lives and defines culture as constantly in flux. Whereas culture history and processual approaches use the archaeological record in the context of objective science, postprocessual approaches attempt subjective insight, seeking to reconstruct the point of view of the people who produced that record. Historical accounts may help investigators identify this perspective, but doing so is far more difficult in the case of an extinct prehistoric society. Emergent approaches point to the need for multiple interpretations of the archaeological record and for a greater understanding of the meaning of that record, both for ancient societies and for our own.

Although archaeologists have debated the relative merits of these approaches, it seems clear that all contribute importantly to the most complete understanding of the past.

FOR FURTHER READING

CULTURE HISTORY
Kelley and Hanen 1988; Kidder (1924) 1962; Lyman, O'Brien, and Dunnell 1997; Rouse 1962; Taylor (1948) 1967; Trigger 2006; Willey and Phillips 1958; Willey and Sabloff 1993

CULTURAL PROCESS
General: Binford 1962, 1972; P. Sabloff 1998; Trigger 2006; Watson, LeBlanc, and Redman 1984; Willey and Sabloff 1993
Cultural ecology: Crumley 1994; Hardesty and Fowler 2001; Kelly 2000; Steward 1955
Evolutionary archaeology: O'Brien 1996; Preucel 1999; Shennan 2008

EMERGENT APPROACHES
Marxist perspectives: Kohl 1981; Leone 2005; McGuire 1992; Patterson 2003, 2004; Patterson and Orser 2004
Feminist perspectives: Battle-Baptiste 2011; Brumfiel 1992, 2006; Conkey and Gero 1997; Conkey and Spector 1984; Conkey and Wylie 2007; Franklin and Paynter 2010; Gero and Conkey 1991: Nelson 2006
Postprocessual perspectives: Funari, Zarankin, and Stovel 2005; Hall 1977; Hodder 1985, 1999; Hodder and Hutson 2003; Preucel 1995; Wylie 1992

ADDITIONAL SOURCES
Binford 1962, 2001; Funari, Zarankin, and Stovel 2005; R. A. Gould 1980; S. J. Gould 1985; Liebmann and Rizvi 2008; Little 2002, 2007; La Motta and Schiffer 2001; Lucas 2012; Meltzer, Fowler, and Sabloff 1986; O'Brien, Lyman, and Schiffer 2005; Pauketat and Meskell 2010; Schortman et al. 1986; Van Pool and Van Pool 2003

4

How Archaeology Works

IN THIS CHAPTER WE will examine the information archaeologists work with and the ways it is acquired. You may have read about archaeologists piecing together the past by studying ancient pottery, arrowheads, or other artifacts found by excavation. These artifacts represent only one of several categories of evidence that archaeologists work with, and excavation is only one of several means of collecting information about the past.

ARCHAEOLOGICAL DATA

The archaeological record is composed of surviving and retrievable material remains of past human activity, from the microscopic debris produced by chipping stone tools to the most massive architectural construction. These residues of past activity become data when the archaeologist recognizes their significance as evidence and collects and records them. Here we are concerned with the three basic classes of archaeological data—artifacts, features, and ecofacts—and how they cluster into larger units. These categories are not inflexible, as there is some overlap among them, but together they illustrate the variety and range of information available.

Artifacts

Artifacts are portable objects whose form is modified or wholly created by human activity (Fig. 4.1). Stone hammers or pottery vessels are artifacts because they are either natural objects modified for or by human use, such as a hammer

FIGURE 4.1

Artifacts are portable objects whose form is modified or wholly created by human activity, while ecofacts are nonartifactual remains that nonetheless have cultural relevance. Here a projectile point (an artifact) lies embedded among the bones (ecofacts) of an extinct form of bison at Folsom, New Mexico.

stone, or new objects formed completely by human action, such as a clay pot. The shape and other traits of artifacts are not altered by removal from their place of discovery; both the hammer stone and the vessel retain their form and appearance after the archaeologist takes them from the ground.

Features

Features are nonportable human-made remains that cannot be removed from their place of discovery without altering or destroying their original form (Fig. 4.2). Some common examples of features are hearths, burials, storage pits, and roads. It is useful to distinguish between simple features such as these and composite features such as buildings and other remains with multiple parts. It is also useful to differentiate features that have been deliberately constructed—such as the examples just given—from others, such as trash heaps, that have grown by simple accumulation. Features usually define an area where one or more activities once took place.

FIGURE 4.2

Features are artifacts that are not portable—in this case a partially excavated cremation burial pit.

Ecofacts

Ecofacts are nonartifactual natural remains that nonetheless have cultural relevance (see Fig. 4.1). Some are significantly modified by human activity, such as
remains of domesticated plants and animals; others are unmodified by human
action, such as remains of undomesticated plants and animals or soils. But any
natural material that provides information about past human behavior can be
considered an ecofact. Examples include bones, seeds, pollen, and soils, all of
which contribute to our understanding of the past because they reflect ancient
environmental conditions, diets, and resource exploitation patterns.

The line between ecofacts and artifacts is often blurred. For example, bones
with cut marks from butchering might be considered both artifacts (reflecting
human technology) and ecofacts (yielding clues to ancient environment and
subsistence).

Sites

Sites are spatial clusters of artifacts, features, and ecofacts (Fig. 4.3). Some sites
may consist solely of one form of data—a surface scatter of artifacts, for example.
Others consist of combinations of all three forms of archaeological data. Site
boundaries are sometimes well defined, especially if features such as walls or
moats are present. Usually, however, a decline in density or frequency of the
material remains is all that marks the limits of a site. However boundaries are
defined, the site is usually a basic working unit of investigation.

FIGURE 4.3

Sites are spatial clusterings of archaeological remains. Stonehenge is an example of a site with well-defined boundaries.

Sites can be described and categorized in a variety of ways, depending on the characteristics one wants to note. For instance, location—in open valleys or in caves, on the coast or on mountaintops—may reflect past environmental conditions, concern for defense, or the relative value placed on natural resources found in different areas. Sites may be distinguished by one or more functions that they served in the past. For example, one can speak of habitation sites, trading centers, hunting (or kill) sites, ceremonial centers, burial areas, and so on. Sites may also be described in terms of their cultural affiliation or chronological position. For instance, sites in the American Southwest may be described as belonging to the Anasazi or Chacoan tradition, or a Mesoamerican site may be identified as Late Formative (ca. 400 B.C.–A.D. 100).

The nature and depth of cultural deposits at a site can reveal the time span of activities, indicating whether occupation was brief or extended. At some sites occupation and deposition of artifacts are continuous. Other sites have had multiple occupations, with periods of abandonment marked by naturally deposited layers called nonartifactual or sterile. Depth of accumulation is not an automatic indicator of length of occupation, however; a great deal of material can be

FIGURE 4.4

This archaeologist is conducting an underwater excavation of the Roman shipwreck at Yassi Ada, off the coast of Turkey.

deposited very rapidly at one spot while elsewhere a relatively thin deposit of trash might represent layers laid down intermittently over hundreds or thousands of years. Whether thick or thin, the remains of sites may be visible on the ground surface or completely buried and thus invisible to the naked eye.

Some sites that are not visible lie not underground but underwater, the most common being sunken ships (Fig. 4.4). However, sites that were once on dry land may also become submerged because of changes in water level (sometimes resulting from human activity such as dam building) or land subsidence. A famous example of the latter is Port Royal, Jamaica, a coastal city that sank beneath the sea after an earthquake in 1692.

Regions

Regions are the largest and most flexible spatial clusters of archaeological data. The region is basically a geographical concept: a definable area bounded by topographic features such as mountains and bodies of water (Fig. 4.5). But the definition of an archaeological region is also often based on ecological and cultural factors. For instance, a region may be defined as the area used by a prehistoric population to provide its food and water. By considering whole regions, the archaeologist can reconstruct aspects of a past society that may not be well represented by a single site.

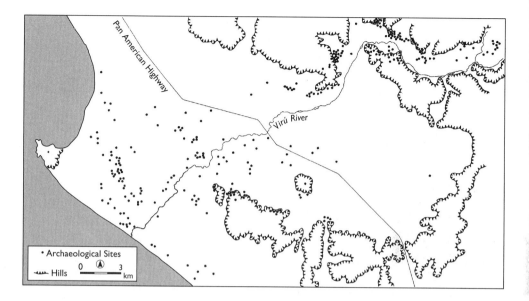

FIGURE 4.5

An archaeological region is often defined by topographic features. In this case hilly areas and seacoast define the limits of the Virú Valley in Peru.

The definition and scope of an archaeological region vary according to the degree of complexity of the society and its means of subsistence. Part of the archaeologist's task is to identify the factors that define a particular region under study, as well as to show how these factors changed over time. The archaeologist usually works with a convenient natural region defined beforehand by geographical boundaries and then seeks to determine that region's ancient ecological and cultural boundaries as well.

DEPOSITION AND TRANSFORMATION

Archaeological data are the result of two factors: (1) behavioral processes and (2) transformational processes. We will describe them in the order of their involvement with archaeological data.

All archaeological sites are the products of human activity. While some human behavior, such as storytelling, may leave no tangible trace, many activities produce material remains. The activities responsible for these remains are **behavioral processes,** usually comprising four consecutive stages: **acquisition, manufacture, use,** and **deposition** (Fig. 4.6). Artifacts such as tools are made from acquired raw materials, used for one or more specific purposes, and then discarded when broken or worn. Features such as houses are built from gathered

ACQUISITION   MANUFACTURE   USE   DEPOSITION

FIGURE 4.6

Archaeological data represent at least one behavioral cycle, as exemplified
by the acquisition of clay, the manufacture and use of a pottery vessel, and
deposition of its broken fragments.

materials and then occupied, abandoned, and destroyed or left to ruin. Ecofacts
such as food animals are hunted, butchered, cooked, eaten, and passed as waste
products. The complex aggregate of these activities delineates similar stages in
the life span of entire sites as well.

Some remains may pass through all four stages; others enter the archaeological record at intermediate points, as in a tool broken and discarded during
manufacture. Still other items may pass through more than one behavioral cycle,
as in an old tool that is modified for new uses.

All forms of archaeological data, individually and collectively, are used
to reconstruct the acquisition, manufacture, use, and deposition stages of
ancient behavior. Clues to all four kinds of ancient behavior may be found in
characteristics of the data themselves and in the circumstances of their deposition (Fig. 4.7).

These behavioral processes represent the first stage in the formation of
archaeological data. The second stage, **transformational processes,** begins
after material remains have been deposited. These processes include all conditions and events that affect material remains from the time of deposition to the
time the archaeologist recognizes and acquires them as data. Transformational
processes include (1) changes by natural agents, such as organic decay, disturbances by animal activity, or burial by volcanic deposits, and (2) changes caused
by humans, such as disturbances by plowing or looting. When the remains are
plants or animals, the archaeologist draws on the field of **taphonomy**—the study
of what happens to plants and animals after they die.

The tangible products of ancient human behavior are never completely
indestructible, but some survive better than others. As a result, the archaeological
record is never a perfect reflection of behavioral processes but is always biased by
the effects of transformational processes (see Fig. 4.7). To gauge these effects, it is

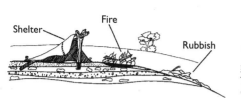

2000 years ago: Hunting camp (acquisition, manufacture, use, and deposition behavior)

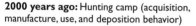

1800 years ago: Flood covers remains of camp with silt (transformational process)

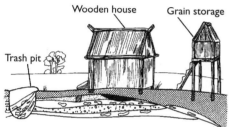

1500 years ago: Farming village built on silt (new cycle of acquisition, manufacture, use, and deposition behavior)

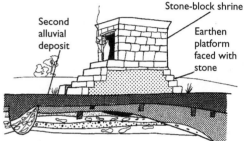

1000 years ago: New flood destroys farming village (transformational process); stone shrine built on new ground surface (new cycle of acquisition, manufacture, use, and deposition behavior)

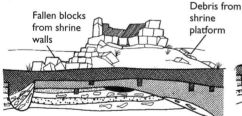

500 years ago: Shrine is abandoned and begins to disintegrate, forming mound (depositional and natural transformational processes)

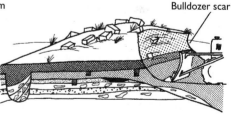

Today: Mound is mined for fill to be used in highway construction (cultural transformational process)

FIGURE 4.7

The characteristics of archaeological data and their deposition reflect both behavioral and transformational processes.

FIGURE 4.8

This corpse, known as the Tollund man, was preserved for some 2000 years in a Danish bog.

crucial to determine the processes that have been at work in each archaeological situation. Natural and human events can either accelerate or retard destruction.

Natural agents are usually the most basic influences acting on the archaeological record. Temperature and humidity are generally the most critical: extremely dry, wet, or cold conditions preserve fragile organic materials, such as textiles and wooden tools, as well as perishable remains, such as human corpses (Fig. 4.8). Organic remains have been preserved under these circumstances along the dry coast of Peru, in the wet bogs of Scandinavia, and in the frozen steppes of Siberia. Ötzi, the "Iceman" described in Chapter 1, was preserved by the extreme cold of the high Alps.

Natural destructive processes, such as oxidation and decay, and catastrophic events, such as earthquakes and volcanic eruptions, also have profound effects on the remains of the past. Underwater remains may be broken up and scattered by tidal action, currents, or waves. Catastrophes such as volcanic eruptions either preserve or destroy archaeological sites; often the same event may have a multitude of effects. For example, in the 17th century B.C. an earthquake and a volcanic eruption struck the island of Thera in the Aegean Sea near Greece (Fig. 4.9). Part of the island disappeared in the explosion while the rest was immediately buried under a blanket of ash. The local population abandoned the island, but some settlement remains were sealed beneath the ash.

FIGURE 4.9

In the 17th century B.C., a blanket of volcanic ash sealed and preserved the remains of a large Bronze Age settlement on Thera. Here we see two views inside excavated buildings with pottery vessels and other artifacts in primary context.

Excavations have disclosed well-preserved buildings, some intact to the third story—a rarity in more exposed sites—as well as beautiful wall paintings and traces of fragile baskets.

At some point activities ceased at all sites and they were abandoned, upon which their remains entered the archaeological record. Archaeologists use recovered evidence to determine how sites were abandoned. Was it gradual, as at most sites, or was it sudden, as at Pompeii and Thera? Although catastrophes often cause rapid abandonment, sometimes these events preserve remains that would otherwise not survive, providing a unique window into the past. The best example of this from pre-Columbian America comes from excavations at Cerén, El Salvador, directed by Payson Sheets from the University of Colorado. As at Pompeii, ash from a sudden volcanic eruption about A.D. 600 preserved Cerén's buildings, household items, even nearby gardens and fields. But unlike urban Pompeii, Cerén was a small village, and its hundred or so inhabitants apparently escaped burial by the ash fall. Excavations indicate a relatively prosperous life style, with access to a wide variety of tools and other possessions, including rather fancy imported polychrome wares. Cerén residents produced diverse and plentiful foods, attested by remains of crops and stored food. Their buildings were flexible, earthquake-resistant structures constructed of interwoven sticks plastered with adobe and pole-and-thatch roofs. The roofs burned and collapsed from the ash fall, but the walls and contents survived. The village had about a dozen households and buildings for community gatherings and religious ceremonies. One excavated household contained a two-room sleeping house, with separate one-room kitchen, storage building, and structure used for craft manufacture. Another also had a domed steam bath. Each household tended adjacent gardens and surrounding agricultural fields, their crops preserved by the ash. When the plants decayed they left voids in the ash deposit; once archaeologists filled the voids with dental plaster, casts of agave, cacao, maize, manioc, and other plants were easily recognizable. Additional plants found in household storage included achiote, common beans, lima beans, cotton, and squash.

One of the most decisive factors in transformation is subsequent human activity. People who later reoccupy an archaeological site may destroy all traces of previous occupation. Earlier buildings are often leveled to make way for new construction or to provide construction materials. In other cases, later activity may actually preserve older sites by building over and sealing earlier remains (see Fig. 4.7). Of course, large-scale human events such as war usually destroy archaeological evidence. One of the worst agents of destruction is the looting of archaeological sites, encouraged by a flourishing market in antiquities.

Obviously, the archaeologist must determine what conditions and events have transformed the archaeological record before reconstructing past human behavior. The specific behavioral and transformational processes differ from site to site, so each site must be evaluated individually. The archaeologist begins to reconstruct these processes from the circumstances under which the data are recovered, including their matrix, provenience, and association.

FIGURE 4.10

This small kiln for firing ceramics has been partially separated by excavation from its surrounding matrix. The kiln is from the site of Harappa, Pakistan, and dates to the early third millennium B.C.

Matrix refers to the physical medium that surrounds, holds, and supports archaeological data (Fig. 4.10). Most frequently, it consists of combinations of soil, sand, gravel, or rock. The matrix provides important clues to understanding the artifacts, features, or ecofacts it contains. For instance, artifacts recovered from an alluvial matrix (deposited by running water) may have been deposited by the natural action of a river. A matrix may also be produced by human activity, such as the deposition of immense amounts of soil to construct an earthen platform. In this case the soil is not only a matrix for any artifacts or ecofacts it contains but also a constructed feature.

Provenience simply refers to a three-dimensional location of any kind of archaeological data within the matrix. Horizontal provenience is usually recorded relative to a geographical grid system using known reference points. Vertical provenience is usually recorded as elevation above or below sea level. Provenience information allows the archaeologist to record (and later to reconstruct) association and context.

Association refers to two or more artifacts (or any other kind of data) occurring together in the same matrix (Fig. 4.11). The associations of various kinds of data are crucial to the interpretation of past events (see Fig. 4.1). For instance, the artifacts found in association with a human burial, such as hunting weapons, may be clues to the individual's gender, status, and livelihood.

Context is an evaluation of archaeological data based on both behavioral and transformational processes. By considering the significance of provenience, association, and matrix for artifacts and ecofacts, the archaeologist identifies the

FIGURE 4.11

This group of stone figurines was found in association as a result of intentional ritual deposition (a *cache* in primary context). This indicates they were used together as part of an ancient ceremony.

transformational processes that have acted on these items and then reconstructs the original human behavior they represent. There are two basic kinds of archaeological contexts: primary and secondary.

Primary context refers to conditions in which both provenience and matrix have remained undisturbed since the original deposition. Intact archaeological features are always in primary context, although later disturbance can remove portions of such features from primary context.

Primary contexts may be subdivided into two categories: use-related and transposed. Artifacts recovered from the place where they were acquired, made, or used are in use-related primary context. Artifacts that have been deposited by human activity outside of the places where they were acquired, made, or used are in transposed primary context.

The occurrence of two or more associated artifacts in use-related primary context ideally means that they were used and deposited at the same time. Such an occurrence then allows the reconstruction of the ancient activity of which the artifacts were a part. Undisturbed archaeological contexts are rare, for the archaeological record is always altered to some degree by natural transformational processes. But the behavioral significance will be preserved if the original associations and matrix have not been disturbed.

Use-related primary contexts are dependent both on the original behavior and on transformational processes that tend to preserve rather than destroy. Discoveries of chipped-stone projectile points in clear association with the bones of animals of prey have been important keys to the reconstruction of early human activities. Discoveries at Folsom, New Mexico, revealed such points in undisturbed use-related contexts associated with bones of a species of bison that has been extinct for at least 10,000 years (see Fig. 4.1). The dates have been supplied by paleontological study, but archaeological association and context were critical in establishing the cultural meaning of these finds. In fact, the Folsom discovery was a turning point in American archaeology, because it led scientists to accept, for the first time, that people had lived in the Americas at such an early date.

In some cases the preservation of use-related primary contexts is intentional. One of the best examples of this is the preparation of burials and caches (see Fig. 4.11). In many areas of the world, elaborate funerary customs included the placement of offerings and other grave goods with the deceased. The resultant burials, when found undisturbed, provide opportunities to reconstruct ancient ritual activity and belief systems. Other examples of use-related primary context have been preserved by natural events. The deposition of soil by wind and water has buried countless sites under deep layers of earth, while far rarer events have covered and preserved the sites of Cerén, Pompeii, and Thera under volcanic ash.

The second kind of primary context, transposed primary context, refers to the deposition of artifacts and ecofacts after being moved from where they were acquired, manufactured, or used. This often happens when items are lost or discarded, as when a tool is thrown away after being damaged or worn out. Some discard activity produces **middens,** specialized areas for rubbish disposal apart from other activity areas. If used over long periods of time, middens may become stratified or layered, with each layer corresponding to a period of rubbish deposition. Middens are thus in primary context, but because of the way they were deposited, the only past behavior directly reflected by this context is the practice of rubbish accumulation and disposal. If a midden is used over a long period of time, then relative position within the deposit (or within a particular layer of the midden) can be used to assess relative chronological position (Fig. 4.12).

Secondary context refers to alterations of provenience, association, and matrix by transformational processes caused by either human or natural activity. Many archaeological sites have been disturbed by subsequent human activity, by accident or design (as in the looting of archaeological remains). It is critical

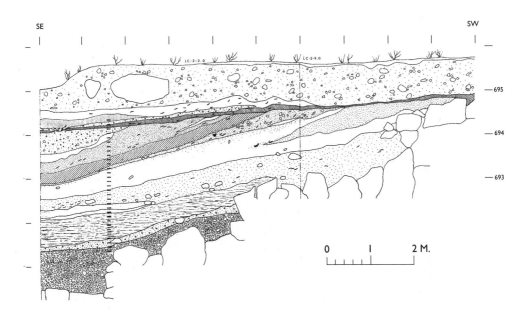

—695

—694

—693

0   1   2 M.

FIGURE 4.12

This cross-section drawing shows a stratified midden representing nearly 2000 years of accumulation at Chalchuapa, El Salvador. One of the characteristics of transposed primary context, such as this midden, is that the artifacts from a given layer are contemporaneous but cannot be assumed to represent the same set of ancient activities.

to distinguish undisturbed archaeological remains from those altered by subsequent human activity; otherwise, misleading interpretation can result. For example, the contents of a heavily disturbed tomb might include not only some portion of the original furnishings but also tools and containers brought in and left behind by the looters. During the excavation of the tomb of the Egyptian pharaoh Tut-ankh-amun, ancient looting was evidenced by two openings and reclosings of the entry; the final sealings of the disturbed areas were marked by different motifs from those on the undisturbed portions. If the disturbance had not been recognized, the associations and arrangements of recovered artifacts might have been wrongly interpreted as reflecting original burial customs.

Secondary contexts often result from disturbance by nonhuman agents, such as animal activity, tree roots, erosion, decay, volcanism, and earthquakes. For example, burrowing animals may place later artifacts in apparent association with earlier features and thereby make interpretation difficult. At Ban Chiang in northern Thailand, ancient burials are juxtaposed in a very complex fashion, with later pits intruding into and overlapping earlier ones. The job of segregating originally distinct units was made even more difficult by numerous animal burrows crisscrossing the units, so that tracing pit lines required exacting and intricate work.

The archaeologist uses archaeological data to reconstruct both behavior and the cultural systems that produced it. As the first step in linking the data to a past cultural system, the archaeologist must assess how the kinds of ancient behavior that produced the evidence (behavioral processes) and the natural or human events that have acted on the evidence from the time of deposition to the moment of archaeological recovery (transformational processes) have affected the data.

The types of archaeological context and the importance of accurately determining context can be illustrated by an example. As we have seen, any artifact may be modified to be reused for different purposes over its use span. Thus, a single pottery vessel may be manufactured for the transport of water but later modified for use to store food or other substances and then (when inverted) to serve as a mold for the shaping of new pottery vessels. If this vessel were abandoned during, or immediately after, any of these activities—say, during its use as a pottery mold—and if it remained within an undisturbed matrix together with its associated artifacts, ecofacts, and features, then its archaeological context would be primary (undisturbed) and use-related (part of pottery-making). Knowing the provenience, associations, and context—in this case by finding an inverted vessel surrounded by other vessels in various stages of manufacture along with clay-working tools and so forth—the archaeologist is able to reconstruct both the type of activity and many specific techniques used in this instance of pottery-making. But note that any prior uses, such as food storage, would not be detected.

On the other hand, if our vessel had been broken during use and its fragments swept with other debris into a rubbish pit, its context upon discovery would be primary (undisturbed) and transposed (the result of trash disposal). Because it was transposed, we could not assume the vessel was used for cooking or other culinary activity even if the pottery fragments were found associated with animal bones and food residues. We could conclude only that all these materials were deposited at the same time as a result of trash disposal activity.

Let us return to the original example of the vessel deposited during its use as a pottery mold together with its associated artifacts, ecofacts, and features. Suppose that river erosion washed away this deposit, and the vessel was redeposited on a sandbar downstream next to the remains of a drowned animal. Suppose further that, many years later, archaeologists excavated the vessel from this spot, far removed from its original associations that reflected its use. It is now in natural secondary context: the vessel's provenience and its association with animal bones reflect only the natural forces of river deposition and not human behavior.

Finally, we have to recognize that any kind of excavation, by archaeologists or anyone else, *destroys* matrix, association, context, and, therefore, information. The only way to preserve the information these factors convey is to record it by digital or photographic images, scaled drawings, and written records during excavation. Without them even the most painstakingly controlled excavation is no more justifiable or useful than a looter's pit.

RESEARCH DESIGN

Whether conducting a CRM (culture resource management) investigation in advance of a major construction project or long-term research within a remote region, archaeologists use **research design** to plan the ways they gather and evaluate evidence of past human activity. Carefully planning how archaeological research will be conducted is essential to ensuring that archaeological data are used to the maximum degree possible to understand ancient behavior and to meet both the specific objectives of research and the general goals of archaeology (see Chapter 1). Increasingly, research design is a collaborative endeavor, bringing together archaeologists, other scientific specialists, and descendent communities.

Data Sampling

Realization of these objectives requires discovering as much as possible about the archaeological record. Archaeologists seek to recover the full range of variation in the data relevant to their research questions. What was the range of activities carried on at a site? What was the range of places chosen for settlement? What was the range of forms and styles of artifacts? To the extent that such variation is not known, the picture of ancient life is incomplete, and any inferences drawn may be wrong. In a sense archaeological data are always unrepresentative; not all behavior produces tangible evidence, and even for that which does, not all the remains will survive. So the ideal goal of recovering the full range of variation is seldom realized. But understanding the processes that affected the production and preservation of the evidence can compensate to some extent for the unevenness in data availability. We need to consider how the archaeologist chooses data-gathering strategies in order to maximize the usefulness of the evidence that *is* available.

The first step in data gathering is defining the region under investigation in both time and space. This will impose a practical limit on the amount of evidence to be collected. A bounded research area defines a **data universe**. Thus, an investigator may define a data universe as a single site, or even a portion of a site. In research into a region, the research area corresponds to a much larger universe, such as an entire valley or coastal area containing many sites. The archaeologist may also draw temporal boundaries. One investigator may seek data from a relatively short era, such as the Pueblo II period of the American Southwest (ca. A.D. 900–1100); another might be interested in a much longer span, such as a period of several thousand years defining an interglacial period of the Pleistocene (Ice Age).

The data universe is subdivided into **sample units.** A sample unit is the unit of investigation, defined by either arbitrary or nonarbitrary criteria. **Nonarbitrary sample units** correspond either to natural areas, such as microenvironments, or to cultural entities, such as rooms, houses, or sites (Fig. 4.13). **Arbitrary sample units** are spatial divisions with no inherent natural or cultural relevance (Fig. 4.14), such as a grid system (equal-size squares). *Sample units should not be confused with data*. If an archaeologist is looking for sites, the sample

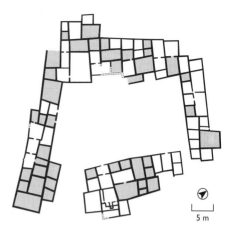

FIGURE 4.13

This diagram shows a universe
with nonarbitrary units—in
this case rooms in a prehistoric
southwestern pueblo. The
shaded rooms were the ones
excavated.

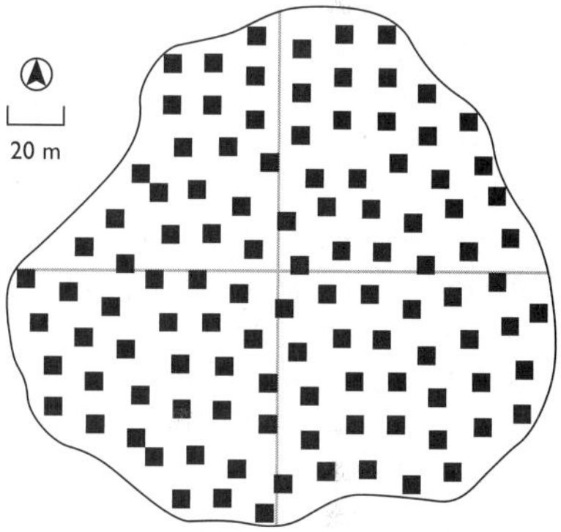

5 m

20 m

FIGURE 4.14

This diagram shows a universe with
arbitrary units at the mound site of
Girik-i-Haciyan, Turkey. The black
squares represent the units investigated.

units will be geographical areas where sites might be located. If the data universe
is a site, sample units are defined areas within that site; the data are the artifacts,
ecofacts, and features within each sample unit.

The choice between arbitrary and nonarbitrary sample units is based on
research objectives and the characteristics of the data and sites. But all sample
units are (or are assumed to be) comparable. Arbitrarily defined units are comparable because they are always regular in size or shape. Even nonarbitrarily
defined units of different sizes are assumed to yield similar or complementary
information about ancient behavior. For example, if sites are the sample units,
it is assumed that one cemetery site will give information similar to that from
another cemetery site and complementary to that from habitation sites and other
sample units within the data universe.

The aggregate of all sample units is the **population.** Note that when the
universe is a region and the sample units correspond to all known sites, the population will not include unknown sites or locations without sites, even though

these areas are part of the universe. Nevertheless, conclusions drawn about the population are often inferred to be true of the research universe as well.

Total data gathering involves investigation of all units in the population. Of course, the archaeologist never succeeds in gathering every shred of evidence from a given data universe; new techniques of recovery and analysis are constantly being developed that broaden the definition of archaeological data. A change in the research problem also alters the definition of what are considered appropriate data. But it is nonetheless important to distinguish between collecting all available evidence (by investigation of all sample units) and collecting only a portion of the available data. Something approaching total data gathering, in this sense, is often attempted in salvage situations, as when a site or region is threatened with immediate destruction by construction of a new highway or dam.

Sample data gathering refers to acquiring only a portion or sample of the data from a given data universe. The limits to the sample recovered are often influenced by economic constraints—the archaeologist seldom has the funds to study all potential units. Nor is research time unlimited: seasonal weather conditions, scheduling commitments, and other factors often limit the time available to gather evidence. Access to archaeological data may be restricted, as when travel is hampered by natural barriers or lack of roads or areas are closed due to lack of permission from property owners. Even when there are no restrictions, however, it is still desirable to collect only a sample of the available archaeological data. Except in situations of threatened site destruction, most archaeologists recommend that a portion of every site be left untouched for future scientists to investigate using techniques more sophisticated than today's. In this way, future research can check and refine the results obtained using current methods.

Probabilistic sampling is used to specify mathematically how a sample relates to a larger population. Three statistical sampling methods used by archaeologists are random, systematic, and stratified sampling. These methods can maximize the probability that a sample is fully representative of the whole population. **Simple random sampling** ensures that each sample unit has an equal chance for selection. To investigate a sample of five sites within a region containing twenty sites (numbered 1–20), five sites may be selected by a computer program that generates random numbers (or a published table of random numbers). **Systematic sampling** is a variation of simple random sampling that selects the first sample unit randomly (from a computer program or table of random numbers), while the remainder are selected by a predetermined, equal interval from the first (such as every third or ninth unit). This tends to spread the sample units more evenly throughout the data universe. Note that both methods treat all sample units as equivalent, but in most archaeological situations there are significant variations within the population. **Stratified sampling** is used to ensure the sample will represent these variations. For example, if sites are located in three different environmental zones, the population is divided (or *stratified*) into three sampling strata, one for each zone, and a sample is drawn separately from each, usually by either simple random or systematic sampling methods.

When it is not necessary or feasible to mathematically specify how a sample relates to the total population, archaeologists use **nonprobabilistic sampling.** This allows the archaeologist to apply his or her expertise to select the sample most relevant to the research being conducted. In other cases it may be necessary to restrict data collection to the most accessible sites, or portions of a site, or to sites most threatened with destruction in salvage situations. While it yields results as valid as any other investigation, there is no way to determine how representative nonprobabilistic sampling data are relative to the entire data universe.

Research Stages

Regardless of the type of data gathering, research must be planned carefully to ensure that its goals will be met. This is true for CRM investigations conducted by government agencies or private consulting firms and for academic research sponsored by museums and universities. Traditionally, most archaeological research was site-oriented. The major goal was to excavate a particular site, often with the aim of collecting spectacular remains. This site-oriented approach is still used, especially when a particular site must be assessed or salvaged by a CRM investigation. But when time and funding constraints allow, more comprehensive studies are the norm. These involve regional and problem-oriented investigations. This kind of research aims at solving specific problems or testing one or more hypotheses by using controlled and representative samples of data. Whatever the focus, the best designs incorporate input from all parties involved, including archaeologists, other scientific specialists, and descendent communities.

Archaeological research design includes a sequence of stages that guide an investigation (Fig. 4.15) to ensure the validity of results and make efficient use of time, money, and effort. Each stage has one or more specific purposes. Although portrayed as a series of steps, the process is flexible in practice. Aspects of two or more stages may be carried out simultaneously or in a different order, depending on particular circumstances. Furthermore, because each research situation is unique, this generalized research design must be capable of adapting to a wide variety of specific applications, including both CRM and academic research.

Formulation involves defining the research problem, performing background investigations, and conducting feasibility studies. This crucial first step often defines the major problem to be investigated, and it establishes the principal goals of the research. The research problem and goals may be influenced by a variety of factors—the archaeologist's personal interests, local concerns, and in a CRM situation, a government contract. The goals of most CRM projects focus on archaeological assessments to evaluate the importance of a site. These assessments may determine whether a site is salvaged, buried to preserve it for future study, or even developed for tourism. In an academic setting, the research may investigate a long-standing problem. For example, previous research may

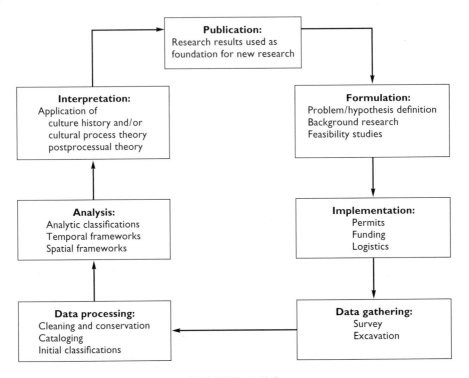

FIGURE 4.15

This diagram shows the stages of archaeological research. Note that when an investigation is completed by publication, its results may generate the formulation of a new investigation.

indicate that initial agricultural settlements appeared within a specific environmental zone. A new project might investigate a broader sample of sites within the indicated zone and in adjacent zones to refute or support the earlier conclusions.

Decisions regarding the problem to be investigated and the geographical area of study both limit and guide further work. Once these choices are made, the archaeologist conducts background research to locate and study previous work relevant to the investigation. Useful information at this point may include geographical, geological, climatological, ecological, and anthropological studies. Such data may be found in publications, archives, and laboratories and through consultation with individual experts. A feasibility study involving a trip to the region or sites to be investigated is usually necessary. Even after local communities have had input to the research design, an evaluation of the archaeological situation and local conditions, such as accessibility and availability of supplies, will probably be required.

Thorough background investigations facilitate research by refining the problem under investigation and defining research goals. The goals of most archaeological research include testing one or more specific hypotheses. In some cases these derive from previously proposed models; in others they arise during the formulation of the basic research problem. As the research progresses, new hypotheses may be generated and tested. It is important to remember, however, that the initial formulation of research problems leads the archaeologist to look for particular kinds of data and thus sets the course for the entire study.

Implementation involves completing all the arrangements necessary to the planned fieldwork. These arrangements may be complex, especially if the research is to be done in a foreign country. The first step may be securing the necessary permits for conducting the research, usually from government agencies responsible for overseeing archaeological work. The owners of the land on which the work will take place must also grant permission before investigations can proceed. The laws governing archaeological work vary from country to country, and from state to state within the United States, so the archaeologist must be aware of the relevant regulations and customs.

The archaeologist must also find funds to finance the research. In some cases this involves submitting a research proposal to either private or government agencies that support archaeological investigations. In many CRM situations, the agency issuing the contract provides the funding for the research.

When funding and permits have been secured, the archaeologist can turn to logistical arrangements. Research equipment and supplies must be acquired. In most cases field facilities must be rented or built for the safekeeping of equipment and for laboratory processing and storage of artifacts and field records. Many projects require a staff that must be recruited, transported, housed, and fed, and these arrangements must be completed before work can begin.

Data gathering involves two basic procedures: survey and excavation. We will treat these only briefly here because they will be considered in detail in Chapter 5. Survey is undertaken to gather as much data as possible about the archaeological record without excavation, including the identification and location of sites (sometimes called reconnaissance), mapping, use of remote sensors, and collection of samples of surface artifacts. Excavation exposes the buried characteristics of archaeological sites, using a variety of techniques to both retrieve and record data. Because artifacts recovered from the ground surface are almost always heavily disturbed, they are usually less reliable for assessing the full range of data buried beneath the ground. Thus, results gained from surface artifact collections should be tested by excavation whenever possible and appropriate.

Data processing involves the manipulation of raw data (artifacts and ecofacts) and the creation and manipulation of records. Portable remains are usually processed in a field laboratory to ensure that they are recorded, preserved, and stored so as to be available for further analysis. Records of these data (descriptions, photographs, and scaled drawings) are also completed to be accessible for later use. Some of the conservation efforts noted in Chapter 1 often begin in the field lab.

Analysis extracts information about each data category used in archaeological interpretations. For example, analysis of artifacts includes classification, determination of age, and varied technical studies designed to identify sources of raw materials, methods of manufacture, and uses. Some of these procedures can be done in the field laboratory, but more technical or complex analyses are usually undertaken at specially equipped permanent scientific facilities.

Interpretation synthesizes the results of data collection, processing, and analysis to meet the original goals of the investigation. The use of the scientific method in these procedures is characteristic of modern professional archaeology. A variety of models are tested in the interpretive process, including both specific and general historical and anthropological frameworks.

Publication completes the research cycle by making the findings fully accessible so that they can be used and retested by fellow archaeologists, other scholars, and all other interested individuals. Archaeological publications usually include preliminary and final research reports aimed at professionals, as well as more popular accounts (magazine articles, websites, and so on) aimed at a broader audience. These ensure that all research contributes to the broadest objectives of archaeology and science.

ARCHAEOLOGICAL RESEARCH PROJECTS

Scientific archaeology demands a broad range of expertise. Today's archaeologist must be a teacher, a theoretical scientist, a methodologist, a technician, and an administrator. Because it is nearly impossible for one individual to do everything necessary for a particular research project, archaeologists usually bring together specialists from a variety of disciplines. They must also ensure that descendent communities' concerns are met. This requires the coordination of many individuals, each of whom focuses on a particular aspect of the research. By depending on scientific teams of botanists, ecologists, geologists, and other specialists, archaeologists can ensure that data are collected and utilized to the maximum degree possible. In some cases most of the required support is housed under one roof, as in the larger museums and research institutions in many parts of the world (Fig. 4.16). In the United States, the Smithsonian Institution provides the most complete support facilities for archaeology.

The size and scale of archaeological projects vary considerably, depending on the problem and goals of the investigation. The rapid increase in CRM projects means that most archaeological research in the United States is conducted by CRM archaeologists working for government agencies or private consulting firms. Some CRM projects are large-scale undertakings limited by contracts to only a few weeks or months to complete their investigations. More traditional academic research can range from a small surface survey conducted by a single investigator to a multinational project staffed by a dozen or more professional archaeologists, specialists from a variety of disciplines, several dozen students and volunteers, and a labor/support force of a hundred or more people. Large-scale projects typically extend over several years, or even several decades.

FIGURE 4.16

Conservation specialists are seen here restoring pottery artifacts excavated from the site of Copán, Honduras, in the field laboratory adjacent to the site. Since 1976, Copán has been the subject of multiple research projects sponsored by many universities from many nations.

Both CRM projects and traditional archaeological research are limited by the availability of time and money. CRM archaeology is generally supported by a sponsoring agency, but funding for archaeology is typically only a tiny fraction of the overall budget devoted to the construction project that sponsors the archaeological assessment. In a few cases, such as sites excavated and consolidated for major touristic development, governments and international development agencies may allocate many millions of dollars for archaeology. But these kinds of nationalistic or economic development opportunities are not common; most academic archaeologists have to spend considerable time and effort to secure research grants and donations to support their research.

A far greater problem, one that threatens the very existence of archaeological research, is the increasing pace of destruction wrought by looting and the many modifications of our rapidly expanding world. The destruction of archaeological remains has reached such proportions that we may well ask, "Does the past have a future?" We will consider the problem of the destruction of our archaeological heritage in the final chapter of this book.

SUMMARY

Material remains from the past become archaeological data once they are recognized, collected, and recorded. The direct products of past human activity are either artifacts (portable remains) or features (nonportable remains). Indirect products of past human activity are called ecofacts. Archaeologists usually examine distributions of these data within sites (clusters of data) or within regions (clusters of sites). Further information is gleaned from recording the specific locations (proveniences), associations, and matrix that surrounds these classes of data. The context of these data—their depositional significance—is inferred by evaluating all of these factors. Understanding this context—and discriminating among the various kinds of context—is the crucial link that allows the archaeologist to reconstruct the kinds of ancient behavior the recovered data represent.

Ideally, the material record reflects four major categories of human activity—acquisition, manufacture, use, and deposition—which together constitute behavioral processes. But archaeologists can never recover data representing all kinds of past behavior. Some activity leaves no tangible trace. The evidence of other behaviors may be altered over time by transformational processes, both human and natural in origin. These processes act selectively either to preserve or to destroy archaeological evidence. Thus, the data available to the archaeologist constitute a sample determined first by ancient human activity (behavioral processes) and then by human or natural forces acting after the remains are deposited (transformational processes).

The resulting data form the base that the archaeologist attempts to recover, either totally (by collection of all available evidence) or partially (by sampling methods). Whatever collection method is used, the archaeologist seeks data that represent, insofar as possible, the full range of ancient human activity. With very few exceptions (such as cases in which a site is about to be destroyed), it is generally practical and desirable to collect only a sample of the data. Specific research goals and field conditions usually require a flexible mix of sampling schemes to enable the archaeologist to learn as much as possible about the past.

Archaeological research is conducted by both CRM (cultural resource management) and traditional academic archaeologists. CRM work usually involves archaeological assessments to determine the fate of sites threatened with destruction. Academic research is usually aimed at solving specific problems or testing specific hypotheses. To guide both types of investigations, archaeologists follow a research design that begins with formulation of the research problem and goals, based on background and feasibility studies, followed by implementation, involving fund-raising, securing of permits, and making logistical arrangements. The next stage is data gathering, often including survey (locating unknown sites, mapping, and collecting surface data) and excavation (removal of matrix to reveal buried data). This is followed by data processing and analysis, leading to interpretation (reconstruction of the past to address the specific research goals) and publication of the research. The next five chapters explore data gathering and processing (Chapter 5), data analysis (Chapters 6 and 7), and interpretation (Chapters 8 and 9).

To be successful researchers, archaeologists must command a broad range of expertise. They must master field methods, theory, administration, and a range of technical skills. Seldom can one individual perform all the tasks of archaeological investigation, so in most cases archaeologists call on teams of specialists for assistance. The scale of archaeological research varies from that conducted by a single person in a few weeks to that performed by large research teams over several years or decades. The practical limits to such research are usually determined by time and money, but the most severe threat to furthering our understanding of the past is posed by the destruction of archaeological data by looting and the growth of our modern world.

FOR FURTHER READING

ARCHAEOLOGICAL DATA
Binford 1964; Buikstra and Beck 2006; Deetz 1967; Erickson 2000; Fish and Kowalewski 1990; Flannery 1976; Willey 1953

DEPOSITION AND TRANSFORMATION
Binford 1982, 2001; Glob 1969; Lucas 2012; Schiffer 1976, 1987; Sheets 2006; Weiner 2010; Woolley 1934

RESEARCH DESIGN
Appelbaum 2011; Binford 1964; Black and Jolly 2003; Carroll 2001; Clarke 1972; Gero and Conkey 1991; Hill 1970; Hodder 1999, 2000; Redman and Watson 1970; J. Sabloff 1998; Silliman 2008; Silliman and Ferguson 2010; Sullivan and Childs 2003; Taylor (1948) 1967; Zeder, Buikstra, and van der Leeuw 2010; Zimmerman 2003

ARCHAEOLOGICAL RESEARCH PROJECTS
Agurcia 1986; Hodder 1997, 1999, 2000; Lanata and Drennan 2010; Noël Hume 1979; Rapp and Hill 1998; Silliman 2008; Spector 1993; Sullivan and Childs 2003; Tringham 1991; Wheeler 1954; Willey 1974

ADDITIONAL SOURCES
Allen and Joyce 2010; Bass 2005; Binford 1972, 1981; Brain 1981; Fagan 2010; Frink 1984; Stein and Farrand 2001; Villa 1982

5

Fieldwork

WITH A WELL-DESIGNED research plan in hand, the next consideration is the gathering and processing of archaeological data, the focus of this chapter. Archaeological data gathering is conducted in the field, and data processing usually takes place in a field lab. Both are part of research projects that are guided by a particular research design (see Chapter 4). Since archaeological fieldwork requires a broad range of expertise, it is usually a multidisciplinary team effort, conducted by many specialists. A project director leads the research team and works to meet the goals established by the research plan.

There are two major means of collecting evidence about the past, archaeological survey and excavation, each of which entails several methods of data collection. Although excavation dominates the popular image of what archaeologists do, surveys are also crucial to archaeological research, as are data processing and classification. The actual field methods used to collect archaeological data are often dependent on the specific goals of each research project, along with practical considerations, such as the amount of time and funding available for fieldwork.

ARCHAEOLOGICAL SURVEY

Archaeological survey refers to methods archaeologists use to acquire data from sites or regions without excavation. The overall objective of archaeological surveys is to determine as much as possible about a given site or region based on both observing surface remains and detecting subsurface features through remote means. The methods used for conducting archaeological surveys are noninvasive, or minimally so, as opposed to the invasive methods of archaeological excavation.

The choice of survey methods depends on the characteristics of the site or region being studied and the kind of data being sought. In conducting surveys, archaeologists attempt to detect and record all surface features. Traces of many ancient remains, such as ruined buildings, walls, roads, and canals, exist on the ground, where they can still be observed and recorded by mapping. On the other hand, buried features may not be directly detectable from the surface. In some cases these buried remains can be located and mapped by one or more of the remote sensing methods described later.

Archaeological surveys also include detection and recording of artifacts and ecofacts. When these are found on the surface, their provenience is recorded. Because they are portable, they may be collected and taken to the field laboratory for further study. The detection of buried artifacts and ecofacts is usually difficult. In some cases, as noted later in the chapter, augers, corers, and shovels can be used to determine the presence or absence of artifacts below ground, but recovery of buried artifacts and ecofacts must usually await excavation.

Time transforms the sites of past human activity in a variety of ways. Some sites, such as Stonehenge (see Fig. 4.3), may remain obvious to any observer. Others may be nearly destroyed or completely buried; in such cases the task of identification may be extremely difficult. Archaeological survey often begins with systematic attempts to identify sites, a procedure that is also sometimes called archaeological reconnaissance. Identification includes both the discovery of sites and the precise determination of their geographical location. Survey data can be used to formulate or refine hypotheses to be tested in later research stages. This is especially true when the work is taking place in geographical areas with no prior archaeological information or as part of a feasibility study for a larger project.

Archaeological survey yields data about the form (size and internal arrangement) of sites, as well as their total number and spatial distribution within a region. This distribution may reveal patterns in the placement of sites in relation to one another and to the natural environment, such as topography; plant, animal, and mineral resources; and water. Sometimes these findings may be used to define the region for later, more intensive study. For the Tehuacán Project, archaeological survey helped to define the study region by indicating the correlation between the limits of the arid Tehuacán Valley (Fig. 5.1) and the distribution limits of two pottery styles.

This example emphasizes the need for studies of a region's environmental resources, either as part of background research or in conjunction with the site identification process. Defining ecological zones within a study area can guide the archaeologist in searching for sites if site location can be correlated with the distribution of different environmental variables. The archaeologist may thereby gain an initial understanding of possible ecological relationships between past peoples and their environment.

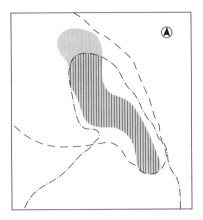

KEY

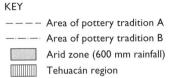

– – – – Area of pottery tradition A

–·–·– Area of pottery tradition B

Arid zone (600 mm rainfall)

Tehuacán region

FIGURE 5.1

Definition of the Tehuacán region of Mexico was based on both cultural and ecological criteria revealed by archaeological survey.

Discovering Archaeological Sites

Not all sites are found by survey. Some archaeological remains are never lost to history. In areas with long literate traditions, such as the Mediterranean basin, the locations and identities of many ancient cities have never been forgotten; Athens and Rome are obvious examples. Most sites, however—even many documented by history—have not fared so well. Many once-recorded sites have been lost, either razed by later conquerors or ravaged by natural processes of collapse and decay. Ancient Carthage, for example, was systematically destroyed by its Roman conquerors in 146 B.C. Only with archaeological research was it rediscovered near Tunis.

Sometimes histories and legends provide the clues that lead to the discovery of lost cities. The most famous quest of this sort was Heinrich Schliemann's successful search for the legendary city of Troy. As a child Schliemann became fascinated with the story of Troy and decided that someday he would find that lost city. By age 30 he had become a successful international merchant and had amassed the fortune needed for his archaeological quest. He learned more than half a dozen languages, whetting his appetite for Troy by reading Homer's tales of the Trojan War in the original Greek. Textual descriptions of the location of the ancient city convinced him that it was to be found at Hissarlik in western Turkey. Accordingly, in 1870 he began excavations that ultimately identified Priam's fabled city. Later it was found that the burned remains Schliemann had called Troy were really an earlier settlement and that in his determined digging he had cut right through the Trojan layers! Nonetheless, Schliemann is credited with the discovery of Troy, and his persistence gave great impetus to the search for the origins of Greek civilization.

Perhaps as many archaeological sites come to light by accident as by any other means. The forces of nature—wind and water erosion, natural catastrophes, and so forth—have uncovered many long-buried traces of past human activity. The deposits of Tanzania's Olduvai Gorge, from which Mary and Louis

Leakey recovered remains of early human ancestors, were exposed by thousands of years of riverine bed-cutting action. The famous Neolithic lake dwellings of Switzerland were discovered when extremely low water levels during the dry winter of 1853–54 exposed the preserved remains of the wooden pilings that once supported houses.

Chance discoveries of ancient sites occur all the time. For example, it was French schoolboys who in 1940 first happened on the Paleolithic paintings of Lascaux cave: the boys' dog fell through an opening into the cave, and when they went after their pet, they discovered the cavern walls covered with ancient paintings. As the world's population increases and the pace of new construction accelerates, more and more ancient remains are being uncovered. More often than not, new sites are first found by farmers, ranchers, outdoor enthusiasts, and explorers rather than archaeologists. Unfortunately, and often despite the best intentions, many are destroyed before they can be recorded.

When archaeologists set out to discover and identify sites, the techniques and procedures used depend on the kinds of sites being sought. The methods used to locate surface sites differ from those intended to discover deeply buried sites. In most cases limitations of time and money prevent the archaeologist from covering every square meter of the research area. Accordingly, selected sampling procedures are used to maximize the chance that the number and location of sites in searched areas are representative of the universe under study.

Some environments are more conducive to discovery than others. Dry climates and sparse vegetation offer near ideal conditions for both visual detection of sites and ease of movement across reconnoitered terrain (Fig. 5.2). Such environments have greatly aided archaeologists in discovering sites in Southwest Asia, coastal Peru, highland Mexico, the southwestern United States, and similar areas.

High-quality maps are essential for survey. Maps are often supplemented by aerial photos. Maps are used first to plot the grid squares or other boundaries for sample units and then to plot the location of discovered sites. Plotting of sample unit boundaries enables the archaeologist to indicate which areas have been covered and which have not. Sampling adequacy can then be assessed, and, depending on the results, the possible distribution of sites in nonreconnoitered areas can be posited. Plotting of new sites is necessary for distributional studies within the sampled area and for subsequent research at the sites.

Methods of Discovery

Three basic methods are used for discovering sites: (1) surface survey, (2) aerial survey, and (3) subsurface survey. Each requires specialized techniques, and each is effective in identifying sites under different conditions. These same three methods are also used to gather data from sites prior to excavation, or are sometimes used without subsequent excavation.

(a)

(b)

FIGURE 5.2

Present environmental conditions have a great influence on archaeological survey. (a) Tropical rain forest greatly reduces visibility, while (b) arid landscapes are often conducive to detection of surface sites.

Surface survey is used to detect and record archaeological evidence present on the ground by direct inspection of the terrain. This is the oldest and most common method of archaeological survey. It has been used since the days of antiquarian interest, when exploration by individuals such as William Camden in England and Stephens and Catherwood in Central America led to the discovery of countless sites. This approach is illustrated in recent years by numerous large-scale surveys in the United States and elsewhere. An example is the work in the Great Basin discussed in Chapter 1.

Most surface survey is still conducted by walking—the slowest method, but the most thorough. The efficiency of survey on foot is increased by using teams

FIGURE 5.3

Surface survey revealed traces of a building visible on the surface of Shahr-i Sokhta, Iran.

to cover extensive areas. Attention to changing ground conditions is also useful; for example, in farming areas, plowing may bring shallowly buried items to the surface. Many archaeologists increase the speed of large-scale surface survey by using horses, mules, or even motorized transport (four-wheel-drive vehicles are frequently necessary).

How does the archaeologist recognize archaeological sites on the ground? Some sites, of course, are identified by their prominence. Many ancient settlements in Southwest Asia are called *tell* or *tepe*—both meaning "hill"—because they stand out as large mounds against a relatively flat plain. In other cases a slight rise or fall in the landscape may indicate a buried ancient wall or other feature. Many sites are identified by concentrations of surface artifacts such as pottery sherds and stone tools. Shahr-i Sokhta in eastern Iran was found because of its densely littered surface. Another sign of this site was differential absorption of salt, which made the tops of the buried mud-brick walls stand out as white against the rest of the surface (Fig. 5.3). Many sites, however, lack obvious surface traces and require more than surface observation for their discovery.

There are several methods for discovering sites in which the observer is not in direct contact with the archaeological remains. A variety of these **remote sensing** techniques are used to conduct aerial and subsurface survey.

Aerial survey is used to detect and record archaeological evidence present on or beneath the ground by airborne sensing methods. These methods include a variety of established and experimental techniques, the most common being aerial photography. Although the most common platform for aerial photography is the airplane, less expensive options include balloons and kites equipped with remote-controlled cameras (Fig. 5.4).

FIGURE 5.4

This aerial photograph, shot by remote control from a balloon, reveals the site of Sarepta, Lebanon.

Aerial photography is useful in several ways. It provides data for preliminary analysis of the local environment and its resources, and it yields information on site location. Aerial photography can reveal sites from their surface characteristics or prominence, and often it can even detect buried sites. Low-growing vegetation, such as grass, grain, and other ground covers, grows better where ancient human activity, such as the construction of canals, deposition of middens, or burials, has improved soil moisture and fertility. In contrast, solid construction features, such as walls or roads immediately below the surface, will often impede vegetation growth (Fig. 5.5). Either way, buried remains are revealed by patterns visible on aerial photos.

Infrared film can detect patterns invisible to normal light-sensitive cameras. Nonphotographic aerial images such as radar and thermography are also used. Radar effectively penetrates cloud cover, and LiDar (Light Detection and Ranging) can also "see through" vegetation particularly well, even dense rain forest in Central America. As Arlen and Diane Chase and their colleagues report, a few weeks of LiDar recording and analysis at the Maya site of Caracol, Belize, yielded mapped results superior to those from more than 25 years of extensive reconnaissance and survey at ground level (Fig. 5.5). Thermography records differences in the absorption and reflection of heat and can detect archaeological features such as buried ditches and prehistoric fields.

Satellite scanners record the intensity of reflected light and infrared radiation. The satellite data are converted electronically to photograph-like images that can be built up, in a mosaic, to form a very accurate map revealing extensive features such as ancient road networks (Fig. 5.6).

FIGURE 5.5

LiDar 2-D image of central Caracol, Belize. Square elements are ancient buildings, the "bumps" are the hilly ground surface, and wavy lines are ancient agricultural terraces.

FIGURE 5.6

This satellite image shows the Great Pyramids of Giza, next to the expanding city of Cairo, Egypt.

Geographic information systems (GIS) combine computerized data from multiple sources, such as satellite imagery, historical maps, and ground survey. The result is a data base on landforms, vegetation, water systems, and cultural features for a specified region. Using a computer screen or a hard-copy printout, the archaeologist can view selected aspects of the landscape, highlighting individual elements, such as terrain or geological composition. At the same time, the digitized data can be subjected to statistical analysis, such as looking for the co-occurrence of cultural and natural features to analyze potential resources available to ancient settlements. GIS data allow archaeologists to locate and study areas in which new sites are likely to occur. Searches of such signature areas can then test hypotheses about site distribution.

As with data from all remote sensing techniques, aerial survey results require knowledge of the corresponding **ground truth** for reliable interpretation. This involves checking at ground level to determine what the various contrasting patterns and features visible on aerial imagery represent.

Subsurface survey is used to detect and record archaeological evidence beneath the surface by ground-based remote sensing methods. These methods range from the rather simple to those requiring exotic and expensive equipment. Most of these techniques provide limited coverage and are time-consuming and costly. For these reasons they are usually used only for subsurface identification of specific features within archaeological sites. Sometimes, however, they may be the only means available for locating buried sites.

The most direct and simple methods are **augering, coring,** and **shovel testing.** An auger is a large drill run by human or machine power. It is used to find the depth of deposits such as topsoil or middens. Corers are hollow tubes that are driven into the ground. When removed, they yield a narrow core of matrix, providing a quick and relatively inexpensive cross section of subsurface layers or construction. Together with ground survey, shallow probes with shovels or posthole diggers are the most common site discovery technique in eastern North America and similar regions, where many sites lie just below ground level.

The **magnetometer** is an instrument that discerns minor variations in the magnetism present in many materials. Unlike the compass, which measures the direction of the earth's magnetic field, magnetometers measure that field's intensity. These instruments have been applied successfully to archaeological survey because some remains create anomalies in the magnetic field. For example, iron tools and ceramic kilns are especially easy to find with this instrument. Buried walls made of volcanic stone, ditches filled with humus, and even burned surfaces may be detected by the magnetometer (Fig. 5.7).

A notable early use of the magnetometer was in the search for the Greek city of Sybaris. Founded in 710 B.C., Sybaris had a history and a reputation but no tangible existence. Notorious for the self-indulgence of its inhabitants (*sybarite* means "voluptuary" or "sensualist"), it was destroyed in 520 B.C. It was known to be located somewhere on the plain of the River Crati in the instep of Italy's boot,

(a)

(b)

FIGURE 5.7

Magnetometers are important aids in subsurface detection. The magnetic
values are read (a) as they are received from the detector carried by the
person in the foreground (b).

but all attempts at locating the ancient city had been unsuccessful. In the 1960s,
however, a joint Italian-American expedition succeeded in locating Sybaris
(Fig. 5.8). The investigators used a variety of approaches, including coring, but
the magnetometer was the instrument that located this elusive site.

The **resistivity detector** (Fig. 5.9) measures differences in the ability of subsurface features to conduct electrical current. Moisture content gives most soils a
low resistance to an electrical current; solid features, such as walls or floors, can raise
resistance considerably. Another instrument, **ground-penetrating radar,** sends
electromagnetic waves into the earth to be reflected as echoes by subsurface discon-
tinuities, such as soil strata and constructed features.

Locating Archaeological Sites

Once sites have been discovered, their exact location must be determined and
recorded. The central purpose of recording is to relate the newly found sites to
their spatial setting in order to place the previously unknown into the realm of
the known. Usually, this involves plotting the site location on a map or aerial
image. Sometimes base maps have to be specially drawn to record the results of
the survey. Other times, archaeological sites may already be indicated in some
way on a map or visible on an aerial photo. Although this may lessen the job
of the archaeologist, it does not remove the need for checking ground truth to
ensure that a site actually exists at the indicated location.

FIGURE 5.8

Excavations at Sybaris, Italy, following discovery by magnetometer, expose Roman construction superimposed on the remains of the earlier Greek colony.

FIGURE 5.9

These investigators search for subsurface features using a resistivity detector at a historical site in Pennsylvania.

The global positioning system (GPS) has been of tremendous help in accurately and quickly locating archaeological sites. Handheld GPS receivers can calculate the user's location very accurately by triangulation from a series of satellites in orbit 11,000 miles above the earth.

Archaeologists give each new site a designation for identification. Numbers are often the easiest labels. The system commonly used in the United States combines a number designation for the state, a letter code for the county, and a number for each site. Thus, site 28 MO 35 refers to the 35th site designated in Monmouth County, New Jersey. Names are also used, for they can be easier to remember, although they can be more cumbersome. Regardless, each site must have a unique designation so that all relevant information—descriptions, surface collections, maps, photographs, and so on—can be linked to it.

Surveying Sites

After archaeological sites have been discovered and located, the next step is to gain as much information as possible from the surface. To do this, both surface survey methods and remote sensors are used. Each of these will be considered in a little more detail before we turn to the results of surface survey.

Surface survey involves walking over the site under investigation to gather or record surface artifacts, ecofacts, or features. Surface features are recorded by making topographic or planimetric maps. The former depicts elevation differences by contour lines, while the latter uses symbolic representations of features (Fig. 5.10). Surface artifacts and ecofacts can be mapped as well, especially if their spatial distribution reflects ancient activity areas or patterns. In many cases, however, the remains are too disturbed and numerous for mapping to be practical. In such situations, after keying provenience to mapped sample areas, surface artifacts and ecofacts are simply collected for field laboratory analysis. In many cases surface collections provide indications of what may lie beneath the surface, but whenever possible the subsurface situation is verified by excavation.

Remote sensing is often used to detect and record buried features and sometimes to find artifacts. The techniques used are the same as described earlier in this chapter: (1) aerial sensors such as cameras and radar; (2) ground-based sensors, including magnetometers and ground-penetrating radar; and (3) mechanical devices such as corers and shovels. Although the techniques are the same, in surveying sites they involve different objectives. Instead of being used to discover unrecorded archaeological sites, they are used to detect and record internal components of sites as part of data gathering. For example, aerial photography can reveal the form and extent of features such as building foundations and road networks whether they are observable on the surface or detectable underground as crop marks.

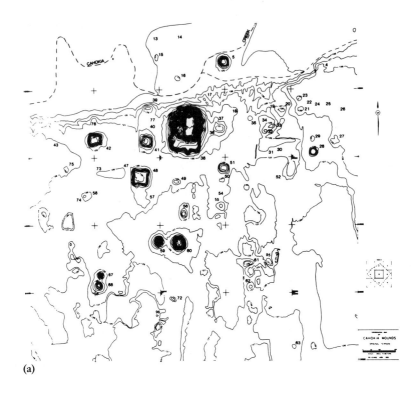

(a)

PALEOLITHIC

(b)

0   500

N

FIGURE 5.10

Information can be compared using (a) topographic and (b) planimetric
archaeological maps of the same site—in this case Cahokia, Illinois.

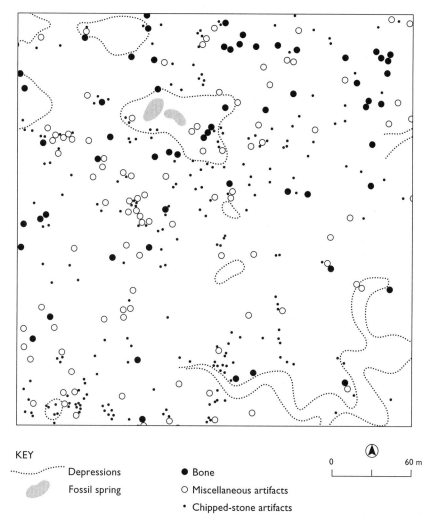

KEY

················· Depressions   ● Bone

▨ Fossil spring   ○ Miscellaneous artifacts

· Chipped-stone artifacts

0   60 m

FIGURE 5.11

This map shows surface finds at China Lake, California.

Preliminary Site Definition

A well-executed archaeological survey using one or more of these methods provides the archaeologist with a preliminary definition of the study universe, whether it consists of a single site or a region containing many sites. The preliminary definition should also include data bearing on the form, density, and structure of archaeological remains within the universe. The range in the forms of features may be assessed by both surface survey and remote sensing; the

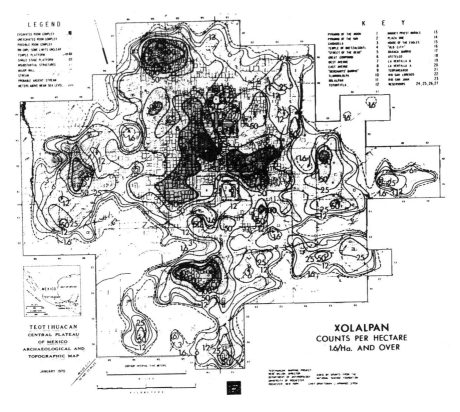

FIGURE 5.12

This map shows densities of potsherds recovered by surface collection at Teotihuacan, Mexico, ca. A.D. 450–650.

ranges in forms of artifacts and ecofacts are assessed from surface collections. Surface survey information may then be used to determine the relative density of each form, together with the forms' interrelationships (their structure). By plotting the spatial distribution of one artifact class—say, grinding stones—the investigator may find areas in which these artifacts cluster. Furthermore, it may be possible to relate these relative densities to the distribution of other classes of artifacts, ecofacts, and features. Surface survey data of this kind are often presented as maps to show the distribution and density of artifacts, ecofacts, and features within a site. From these maps the archaeologist may be able to formulate working hypotheses to account for the distributional patterns. For example, in the China Lake Valley of California, artifact and ecofact distributions were used to infer that two different stone tool types represented different parts of one tool kit rather than occupation by distinct human groups (Fig. 5.11). At Teotihuacan, in central Mexico, surface potsherd density was plotted for different time periods to study the growth and decline of population (Fig. 5.12). In some cases where surface distributions of artifacts are not heavily disturbed (and can be shown to be a good representation of what lies beneath the surface), these findings may mark the end of the data-gathering stage of research. In most cases, however, such survey results are preliminary, for they guide the archaeologist in choosing where to excavate to explore promising areas and test specific hypotheses.

EXCAVATION

The principal means by which the archaeologist gathers data about the past is **excavation,** used both to discover and to retrieve data from beneath the ground. As we have seen, survey is often an essential prelude to excavation. Collections of artifacts and ecofacts from the surface often provide clues about what lies beneath the ground and help the archaeologist plan excavations (see Fig. 5.12). Remote sensors such as magnetometers or ground-penetrating radar equipment may also detect buried features. But the only way to verify the presence and characteristics of subsurface data is through excavation.

Data from excavation are especially important for the archaeologist because subsurface remains are usually the best preserved and the least disturbed. In contrast, surface artifacts and ecofacts are seldom in primary context and are usually poorly preserved. Surface features such as ancient walls or roads, though they may still be in primary context, are often less well preserved than similar features buried, and therefore protected, below the surface. In addition, excavation often reveals associations of artifacts, ecofacts, and features in primary contexts. As we have seen, these kinds of data are the most useful to the archaeologist for inferring ancient function and behavior.

The two basic goals of excavation are (1) to reveal the three-dimensional patterning or structure in the deposition of artifacts, ecofacts, and features, and (2) to assess the functional and temporal significance of this patterning. For example, stone tools, pottery vessels, and animal bones may be found adjacent to house remains or other areas in which they were used. Determination of this three-dimensional patterning depends on documenting provenience and associations of the individual artifacts, ecofacts, and features with respect to one another and to their surrounding matrix. At the same time, evaluation of provenience and association allows the archaeologist to assess context. Attention to these relationships clearly differentiates the archaeologist from the looter.

By knowing which elements were found together (from provenience and association) and by inferring how they got there (from association and context), the archaeologist can reconstruct ancient behavior. As a result, proper excavation records are as crucial to interpretation as proper methods of excavation. Of course, reconstructing behavior also depends on the ability to determine the

FIGURE 5.13

Excavations at Cerén, El Salvador, exposed the remains of an adobe house and adjacent cornfield buried by a local volcanic eruption that collapsed and carbonized the roof beams and thatch. Later eruptions are represented by the upper deposits of ash.

functions of individual artifacts, ecofacts, and features; this analysis, as we will discuss in Chapter 6, is based on their provenience and association plus their form and other attributes.

The three-dimensional structure of an archaeological deposit is especially important. There is a fundamental distinction between the single vertical dimension that shows depth and the two horizontal ones that determine lateral extent. Ideally, the horizontal dimensions represent the associated remains of a single point in time. As already mentioned, the community of Cerén, El Salvador, was buried by a sudden volcanic eruption (ca. A.D. 600). Its buildings and their contents, household artifacts and food remains, along with adjacent agricultural fields, were preserved as if in suspended animation (Fig. 5.13). While only a few sites are frozen in time like Cerén or Pompeii, at most sites artifacts and features on the same horizontal surface represent use or discard that is approximately contemporaneous. New surfaces cover the old, and repetition of this process creates a vertical dimension (Fig. 5.14) so that the vertical dimension in an archaeological deposit represents accumulation through time.

Two contemporary houses at same ground level

One house is abandoned, collapses, and
is used as a rubbish dump.

Resulting mound is leveled and a new house is built
on its summit, which is now contemporary (although
at a higher level) with still-occupied house at right.

FIGURE 5.14

This is one means by which accumulation of occupational debris results in
vertical buildup.

Stratigraphy

Archaeologists have borrowed several key terms from geology to describe the
successive deposits of cultural materials found at many sites. **Stratification** in
archaeology refers to the observed layering of matrices and features. These layers or **strata** may be sloping or roughly horizontal, thick or thin. In some cases
they are well defined by contrasts in color, texture, composition, or other characteristics. Just as often, however, boundaries may be difficult or even impossible to
see; one stratum may simply grade into another. But in all cases stratified deposits reflect the geological **law of superposition:** the sequence of strata from bottom to top reflects the order of deposition from earliest to latest. The individual
strata of an archaeological deposit may represent the superimposed remains of
different occupations at the site; they may result from the sequential disposal of

material, such as accumulated layers of trash in a midden; or they may reflect deposits made naturally, as when floods cover an area with layers of alluvium. Whatever the source of deposition, the lowest levels were those *deposited* the earliest.

The law of superposition refers to the sequence of deposition, not to the age of the materials in the strata. Although in most cases the age of materials does follow their depositional sequence, there are exceptions. For example, strata may be formed of redeposited material, as when water erosion removes soil from a location upstream and redeposits it in a new location downstream. If this soil contains cultural material, chronologically later artifacts could be removed, redeposited, and then covered by chronologically earlier artifacts (Fig. 5.15). Thus, the redeposited matrix contains later artifacts in its lower strata and earlier artifacts in its upper strata. Note, however, that even in this case of reversed stratification, the law of superposition holds: the lower layers were *deposited* first, followed by the upper layers. The same reversal effect can result from human activity, as when stratified deposits are mined and reused for construction fill. Another reason superposition of artifacts or ecofacts may not directly reflect age involves intrusive strata. Pits or burrows dug by humans or by animals may insert later materials into lower levels.

The interpretation of stratification is called **stratigraphy.** That is, stratigraphy refers to the archaeological evaluation of the temporal and functional meaning of the observed strata. In stratigraphic analysis the archaeologist combines the law of superposition with a consideration of context. Because intact archaeological features are invariably in primary context, problems of temporal determination usually arise with portable data—artifacts and ecofacts. The archaeologist must judge whether the artifacts and ecofacts found in each stratum are the undisturbed result of human activity (primary context) or have been rearranged or redeposited by human agents or natural events (secondary context).

In some cases this judgment is aided by **conjoining studies** (or "refitting" studies), in which fragments of broken bone, stone, or other material can be fitted back together. For example, at Site FxJj50 in the Koobi Fora area on the east shore of Lake Turkana in Kenya, conjoining studies linked enough scattered stone flakes to suggest that they represented remains of tool manufacture and use within a 170-square-meter site area. Bone pieces were also conjoined with the same interpretation, and the weathering on the bone suggested that it had lain exposed to the elements for little more than a year at most, before burial by flood-laid soils. Together, these inferences established the 1.5-million-year-old site as a single complex feature and strengthened the behavioral interpretations for the distribution of these materials.

If, through means such as conjoining studies, archaeologists can demonstrate primary context with reasonable assurance—that is, if there is no evidence of redeposition or disturbance—then the temporal sequence of the archaeological materials within a deposit may be assumed to follow that of the strata. In this way a stratigraphic sequence is established.

ORIGINAL MIDDEN DEPOSIT

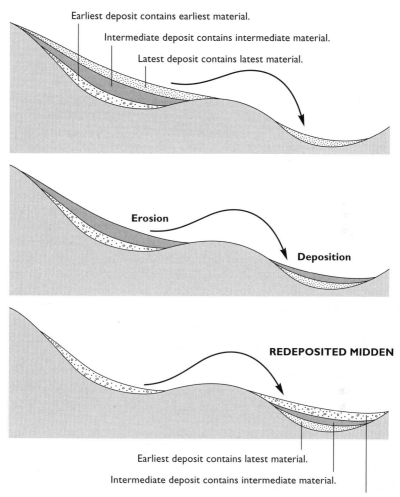

Earliest deposit contains earliest material.

Intermediate deposit contains intermediate material.

Latest deposit contains latest material.

Erosion

Deposition

REDEPOSITED MIDDEN

Earliest deposit contains latest material.

Intermediate deposit contains intermediate material.

Latest deposit contains earliest material.

FIGURE 5.15

This diagram depicts inverted layering. The uppermost (latest) material in the original deposit erodes first and is redeposited as the lowermost layer downstream.

Let us consider an example of stratigraphy. In northern Colorado bison hunters some 11,000 years ago camped in the area now called the Lindenmeier site. The hunting groups left stone tools, toolmaking debris, hearths, and the bones of prey animals. Although each group probably spent only a brief time at Lindenmeier, repeated use of the campsite over time led to a gradual accumulation of occupation debris. During this time the level of the ground surface was raised by natural processes: small depressions were flooded from a nearby stream, and plants grew in the wet areas, died, and decayed to form soil filling the old depressions. The new, raised surfaces created by such filling-in were used as hunting camps, and older cultural debris was buried and sealed in place when it was flooded. In this way the combined effects of geological buildup and repeated reoccupation produced a stratified deposit in which the natural matrix accumulation included (and preserved) evidence of human occupation. At Lindenmeier the law of superposition is relatively unaffected by disturbing factors; the basic stratigraphy is simply vertical accumulation through time, and the relative age of the artifacts correlates well with stratigraphic position.

The functional dimension of stratigraphy involves distinguishing natural activity from cultural activity. The archaeologist attempts to determine which layers in the stratified deposit result from human activity and which are naturally laid soils. For some deposits evidence of past human activity is obvious, as in burials, house foundations, and middens. In the absence of clear indicators, however, determining if a given stratum was produced by human agents may be more difficult. Clues to past human occupation include the presence in the soil of unusually high concentrations of diagnostic residues, such as phosphates, or of pollen from domesticated plants.

Stratigraphic evaluation, then, incorporates both temporal and functional aspects. Combining the law of superposition with assessments of context, the archaeologist interprets the depositional history of the excavated matrix. Functional interpretation begins with a distinction between those parts of the sequence that are natural strata and those that are cultural features. On the basis of these evaluations, the archaeologist establishes a stratigraphic sequence for each excavation and then, by comparing stratigraphy between excavations, a composite stratigraphic sequence for the entire site. This stratigraphic sequence forms the temporal framework for all further interpretation.

One of the best ways of recording and synthesizing stratigraphic information to create a stratigraphic sequence is by use of a schematic diagram known as a Harris Matrix (Fig. 5.16). A Harris Matrix can synthesize all stratigraphic information from a given site by using several standardized conventions to depict observable stratigraphic relationships, such as superimposition, and projected relationships between separate but equivalent deposits.

Stratigraphy emphasizes sequence and accumulation over time and follows from the vertical dimension of archaeological deposits. Distribution in the two lateral dimensions—that is, the spread of features and artifacts through a given horizontal layer—associates these data with one another within a single period or time span. Because horizontally associated materials within a stratum are ideally the remains of behavior from a single period of time, these lateral distributions provide data to reconstruct the range of activities carried on simultaneously. Taken together, stratigraphy and association—the vertical and the horizontal—define the three-dimensional physical structure that excavation attempts to reveal.

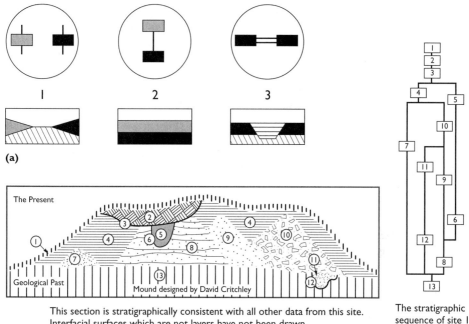

(a)

(b)

This section is stratigraphically consistent with all other data from this site.
Interfacial surfaces which are not layers have not been drawn.

The stratigraphic
sequence of site I

(c)

FIGURE 5.16

(a) A Harris Matrix depicts stratigraphic relationships as taking one of three
forms: (1) no direct connection between the elements, (2) one superimposed on the other, or (3) apparently distinct units interpreted as previously
parts of a single whole. Stratigraphic components of a mound are depicted
(b) in a schematic cross-section view and (c) in a Harris Matrix summarizing abstractly the stratigraphic relationships among the components.

Excavation Methods

An archaeological excavation is usually a complicated, time-consuming process. The aim of an excavation program is the acquisition of as much three-
dimensional data relevant to its research objectives as possible, given available
resources. The success of any particular program depends on a variety of factors,
the most important of which is the overall organization or strategy of the excavations. This strategy guides the archaeologist in choosing the location, extent,
timing, and kinds of excavation to meet the research goals with maximum efficiency. Obviously, each situation is unique, but the range of choices is limited. To
make the best decisions, the researcher must be thoroughly familiar with all the
alternatives and the ends each is best suited to accomplish.

FIGURE 5.17

Penetrating excavations: this view of an earthen structure at Las Tunas, Guatemala, was revealed by a trench; a second, smaller trench has now penetrated this structure and its two stairways.

The two basic kinds of excavations mirror the three-dimensional physical structure of most sites.

1. **Penetrating excavations** are primarily deep probes of subsurface deposits. Their main thrust is vertical, and their principal objective is to reveal, in cross section, the depth, sequencing, and composition of archaeological remains. They cut through sequential or adjacent deposits. This category includes test pits, trenches, and tunnels (Fig. 5.17).

2. **Clearing excavations** aim primarily at the horizontal investigation of deposits. Their main thrust is outward or across, and their principal objective is to reveal the horizontal extent of an archaeological deposit and the arrangement of objects within the deposit. Clearing excavations emphasize tracing continuities of single surfaces or deposits of varying extent (Fig. 5.18).

Archaeologists frequently use a combination of these types of excavations to meet the diverse goals of their research.

Many strategies are possible for excavating an archaeological site. More than one archaeologist has compared excavation to solving a three-dimensional jigsaw puzzle. Of course, excavation attempts not to put the pieces together, but to take them apart. The archaeologist reassembles the pieces later, on paper or by

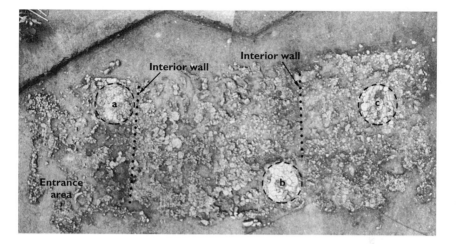

FIGURE 5.18

Clearing excavations: this labeled photograph shows House 14 at Divostin, Yugoslavia. This was the largest dwelling (18 meters long) found and cleared at this Neolithic site. Three hearths (a, b, c) and nearly a hundred pottery vessels were found on the fired mud-and-chaff floor.

computer. This need to reassemble the pieces explains the importance of using care in taking them apart (excavating) and in observing and recording precisely how they originally fit together. We will briefly consider the techniques for conducting and recording excavations—techniques that, when properly executed, enable the archaeologist later to reconstruct and interpret the original three-dimensional site.

Excavation Tools and Techniques

The tools used for archaeological excavation vary with each situation, balancing the needs for removing quantities of matrix with those for precision and control. For removal of large amounts of overburden (matrix overlying a buried site), mechanical equipment such as backhoes or front-end loaders can be used. Pick-and-shovel crews can efficiently remove matrix in secondary contexts, and they offer more precision and control than machines. For most excavation needs archaeologists use a sharpened mason's pointing trowel as a multipurpose tool, well suited for tasks such as following and clearing floors or walls. To expose small or poorly preserved remains in primary context, dental picks, fine brushes, and air blowers may be used, along with large amounts of patience.

The full inventory of archaeological tools is quite extensive and would include surveying and drafting instruments, notebooks, cameras, and laptop computers. A variety of containers are also necessary for the recovery and

TABLE 5.1
TABLE 5.1

Example of an Excavator's "Dig Kit"

1 mason's trowel	Assorted ballpoint pens
Assorted dental picks	Assorted drawing pencils
Assorted small brushes	String tags (provenience labels)
1 digital camera	1 marking pen (waterproof)
1 pocket compass	Assorted artifact bags (cloth & plastic)
1 small palette knife	Assorted ecofact bags (plastic)
1 Swiss army knife	1 field notebook
1 folding rule (English & metric)	1 clipboard
1 tape measure (English & metric)	Graph paper
Nylon line	1 canvas "dig kit" bag
2 line levels	1 laptop computer
1 plumb bob	
1 plastic ruler	

transport of artifacts, ecofacts, and other materials recovered by excavation. Table 5.1 lists items that may be found in a standard archaeologist's "dig kit" used by many research projects.

Excavation proceeds by removal of one stratum at a time, but not all deposits contain visible strata. In such cases, a block of matrix can be divided into arbitrary levels, usually 5, 10, or 20 cm in thickness, and excavated one at a time (especially thick stratified layers can also be subdivided this way). This increases control of provenience for any materials encountered during excavation and preserves at least an approximation of the temporal sequence reflected by the depth of the deposit.

Some contexts, such as floor surfaces, may preserve fine deposits of activity residues. **Micromorphology** is the microscopic study of these deposits in thin sections cut from excavated matrices, such as floors. In this way evidence for ancient uses of rooms, buildings, or other features is revealed based on the identification of residues from past activities. For example, excavated buildings in the royal Acropolis at Copán, Honduras, contained floor residues of pollen from several specific types of flowering plants. This, combined with soot deposits on building walls and the remains of incense burners found within the same rooms, provided evidence that specific buildings were used for religious rituals involving offerings of flowers and incense.

Provenience Control

A variety of methods are used to ensure accurate control of vertical and horizontal provenience during excavation. Horizontal location is determined with reference to a site grid. Within each excavation the location of artifacts and features

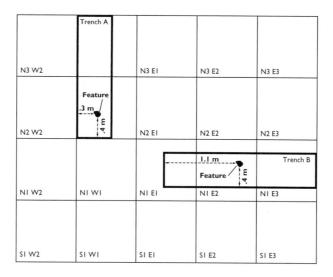

FIGURE 5.19

A site grid may be used to designate the horizontal provenience of excavated features in two ways. In Trench A measurements are made north and east of the N2 W1 stake, to record the provenience as "(N2).4m/(W1).3m." In Trench B horizontal provenience is measured from the limits of the trench, as "1.1 m east of the trench's west wall, .4 m north of the trench's south wall." The latter is convertible to a site grid designation as long as the location of the trench walls in relation to the grid is known.

can be related to the grid by reference to grid coordinates or to edges of the excavation (Fig. 5.19). Vertical location is determined with respect to a known elevation; this may be done with surveyors' instruments or by direct measurement. Either optical or electronic instruments may be used to measure relative elevation from a known elevation datum. Alternatively, elevation above or below a point nearby may be measured with a line level, steel tape, and plumb bob (Fig. 5.20). Elevation is given in relation to sea level.

Provenience control for artifacts and ecofacts is often complicated by their small size and abundance. When artifacts are relatively sparse, or when they are encountered in primary contexts, the location of each item is plotted precisely. Otherwise, provenience can be recorded by reference to a specified area within an excavation, such as a single stratum. The most common means of recovering artifacts and ecofacts under such circumstances are by screening, or trapping small finds by passing matrix through a wire mesh (Fig. 5.21); and by flotation, or catching small organic materials by immersing matrix in water. After recovery, artifacts are often bagged and ecofacts are put in suitable containers. Then both are taken to the field laboratory for processing. From this point on, of course, they must carry a label relating them to their provenience.

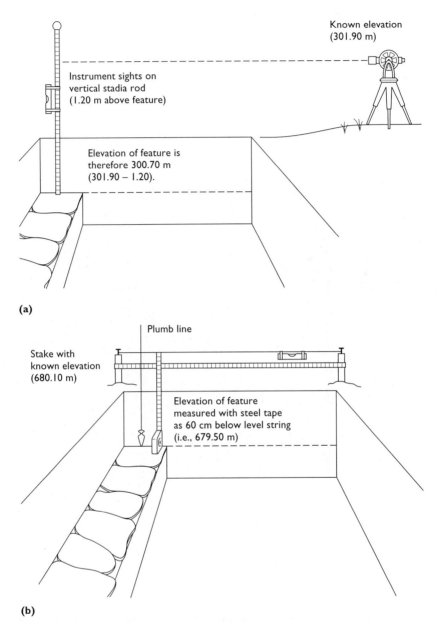

Known elevation
(301.90 m)

Instrument sights on
vertical stadia rod
(1.20 m above feature)

Elevation of feature is
therefore 300.70 m
(301.90 − 1.20).

(a)

Plumb line

Stake with
known elevation
(680.10 m)

Elevation of feature
measured with steel tape
as 60 cm below level string
(i.e., 679.50 m)

(b)

FIGURE 5.20

There are two ways of determining vertical provenience: (a) using an optical
or electronic instrument of known elevation; (b) measuring an elevation along
a plumb line that intersects a level string of known elevation.

FIGURE 5.21

Screening, as at Baker Cave, Texas, is a means of recovering small artifacts and ecofacts that might otherwise be missed during excavation.

Recording Archaeological Data

Apart from artifacts, ecofacts, and other samples physically removed from their provenience, all data retrieved by archaeologists are in the form of records. Because the portion of a site that is excavated is thereby destroyed, the way archaeological research is recorded is of crucial importance. The only record of the original matrices, proveniences, associations, and contexts

(a)

(b)

(c)

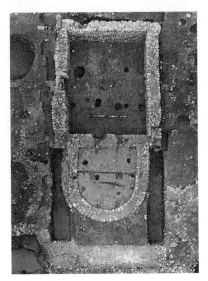

(d)

FIGURE 5.22

These photos trace successive stages in the excavation of the Church of
St. Mary, Winchester, England. Foundations visible in (a) date from ca.
A.D. 1150; those exposed in (d) represent an earlier building dated at
ca. A.D. 1000.

of the data is preserved in the field notes, scaled drawings, digital images, and standardized forms produced by the investigator.

These four kinds of data records are used for all types of data collection, but they are generally more detailed when used to record archaeological excavations. In such cases the most common and important are digital photos and scaled drawings (which are rendered either by hand on paper or electronically by computer drafting programs). Scaled drawings include sections, which depict the vertical or stratified relationships as exposed by excavation, and plans, which depict the horizontal relationships of features and other material remains. Sites and features are thoroughly photographed before, during, and after excavation. Initial photos document the appearance of sites and features before excavation disturbs them. Once excavation is under way, a continuous series of photographs is taken to chronicle everything as it is revealed (Fig. 5.22).

DATA PROCESSING

As archaeological data are collected and recorded in the field, recovered materials and records are organized and processed. The processing of these raw forms of data ensures their preservation, security, and availability for study. Although this step seems self-evident, it is essential to any further work. Imagine trying to do research in a library in which books and other publications are simply piled on the floor as they arrive instead of being cataloged. This suggests the importance of orderly processing of archaeological data for continued use. Several computer database programs are available that can be used to record all forms of archaeological data as they are processed.

For artifacts and ecofacts, processing consists of cleaning, conserving, labeling by provenience, and sorting into basic categories to prepare them for later analysis. Such processing is usually done during the course of fieldwork. In this way the archaeologist can evaluate the data as they are recovered and can continue to formulate and modify working hypotheses for testing while the research progresses. For example, if the archaeologist recognizes that evidence being recovered indicates occupation that is not consistent with a current hypothesis, further excavation can be carried out to test this finding. Should this expanded work validate the initial indications, the original hypothesis may be altered or replaced by a new proposition.

Artifacts usually undergo the most steps in processing and are often classified in some way in the field as well. Ecofacts are generally more delicate and are usually turned over to a specialist for identification. Obviously, features are not processed beyond being recorded as they are revealed. Of course, constituents of some features, such as offerings in a burial, are portable and can be taken to a laboratory to be processed. Recorded data, such as notebooks and drawings, also pass through the processing stage in the field laboratory (Fig. 5.23).

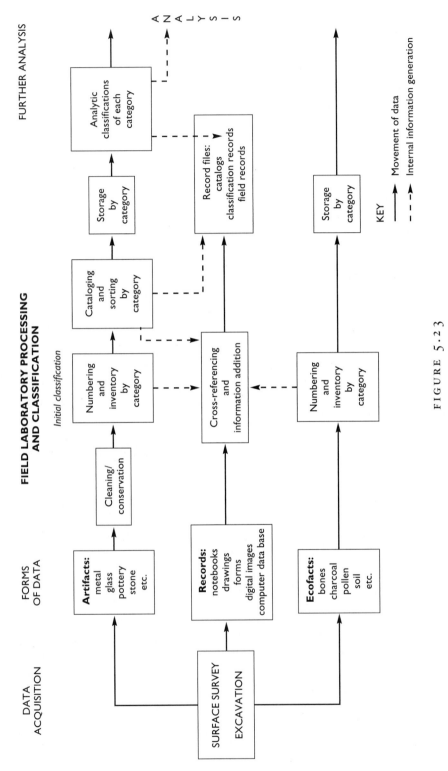

FIGURE 5.23

This flowchart illustrates the data-processing and data-analysis stages normally undertaken in a field laboratory.

CLASSIFICATION

In all branches of science, classification provides the working basis for further study. As mentioned in Chapter 2, much of the work of early archaeologists was devoted to the description and classification of their collections. Although classification is no longer the archaeologist's major concern, it remains a first step toward reconstructing the past. As such, initial classifications done during fieldwork may be vital to checking research progress and reorienting ongoing investigations.

Classification refers to the process of arranging or ordering objects into groups on the basis of the sharing of particular characteristics called **attributes.** An attribute is any observable trait that can be defined and isolated. Three basic categories of attributes apply to archaeological data (Fig. 5.24):

1. **Stylistic attributes** usually involve the most obvious descriptive characteristics of an artifact believed to reflect choices of its maker: its color, texture, decoration, alterations, and other traits.

2. **Form attributes** include the overall three-dimensional shape of the artifact and aspects of that shape. These include measurable dimensions (or metric attributes) such as length, width, thickness, and weight.

3. **Technological attributes** include the characteristics of the raw materials used to make artifacts (called constituent attributes) and any other traits that reflect the manufacturing process.

The kind of attribute selected will determine the kind of archaeological classification that results. Archaeologists select attributes based on the questions they ask about the data, starting with choices between technological types, form types, and stylistic types. Examples of **technological types** include Southwest Asian metal artifacts in which different copper alloys can be distinguished by their constituents, such as brass (copper and zinc) or bronze (copper and tin or copper and arsenic). In defining **form types,** component shape attributes—for example, the inward or outward curve of a vessel's walls—are especially important in classifying fragmentary artifacts such as pottery sherds; metric attributes such as vessel height are usually more applicable to intact specimens. An example of form types is the common classification of handheld grinding stones by their cross-sectional shape (round, ovoid, rectangular, and so on). **Stylistic types** are generally based on color, surface finish, and decorative attributes. Pottery classifications usually derive from such attributes, including types based on the presence or absence of painted decoration and, if decorated, the number of colors and style of painting.

These kinds of classifications are based on directly observable traits. Artifacts can also be classified using inferred characteristics, which are attributes measurable only by tests such as spectrographic or chemical analysis. Classifications

STYLISTIC ATTRIBUTES

FORM ATTRIBUTES

TECHNOLOGICAL ATTRIBUTES

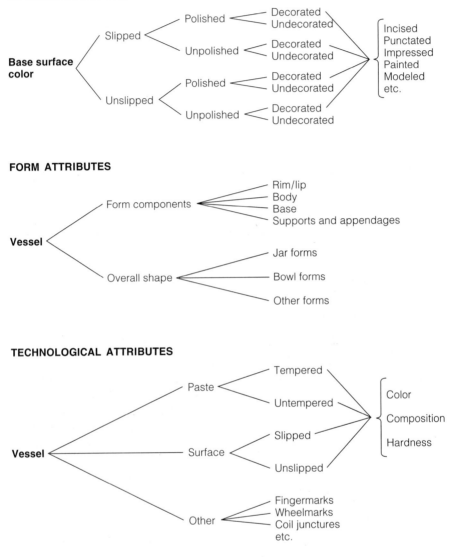

FIGURE 5.24

In the classification of pottery, these kinds of attributes are used to define stylistic, form, and technological types.

based on these kinds of criteria are seldom carried out in the field, however, because they usually require specialized laboratory facilities and technicians.

All classifications serve a variety of purposes. First and most fundamentally, classifications create order from apparent chaos by dividing a mass of undifferentiated data into groups (classes). Classification thus enables the scientist to organize vast arrays of data into manageable units. We have already done this by distinguishing artifacts from ecofacts and features for their respective collection and processing requirements. Artifacts are often further subdivided into gross categories such as chipped stone, pottery, or metalwork. These classes may then be subjected to more detailed classification, breaking them down into kinds of chipped-stone artifacts, kinds of pottery, and kinds of metalwork.

Second, classification allows the researcher to summarize the characteristics of many individual objects by listing only their shared attributes. Most archaeological classifications result in definition of **types.** Types represent clusters of attributes that occur together repeatedly in the same artifacts. For example, the potsherds and whole vessels in a given pottery type will share attributes such as color and hardness of the fired clay; other attributes, such as evidence of ancient vessel repair or of ritual vessel breakage, may not be defining traits of the type. Thus, reference to types enables the archaeologist to describe large numbers of artifacts more economically, ignoring for the moment other attributes that may be used to differentiate among members of a single type.

Third, classifications define variability. The explanation of such variability often leads to further understanding of the past. For example, recognition of different pottery styles can suggest distinctions in social status within an ancient society.

Finally, by ordering and describing types, classification enables the scientist to suggest a series of relationships among classes. These relationships generate hypotheses that stimulate further questions and research. For instance, the most obvious kind of question that emerges from a classification concerns its source: how did the order originate, and what is its significance? In classifications of artifacts, the described order and relationships among categories or types represent aspects of the artifacts' raw materials, techniques of manufacture, use (function), and decorative style.

Classifications are used to support a variety of conclusions about past behavior. Some form classifications can be correlated with function to make inferences about ancient activities. Technology classifications often provide the basis for reconstructing manufacturing processes. Stylistic classifications have long been used to define chronological changes to date artifacts (discussed in Chapter 7), or to define spatial distinctions that may reflect different cultural, ethnic, and social groups. Used with caution, such studies can be helpful. For example, a number of archaeologists have defined pottery stylistic classifications and proposed that these can be correlated with prehistoric Native American tribal or other social groups. Yet ethnoarchaeological studies of living societies (discussed in Chapter 8) have shown that the relationship between artifact styles and social distinctions (such as ethnicity) is more complicated and subtle than often assumed. For example, an ethnoarchaeological study in the Lake Baringo region of Kenya concluded that while the spatial patterning of some artifacts corresponded to tribal affiliations, others did not.

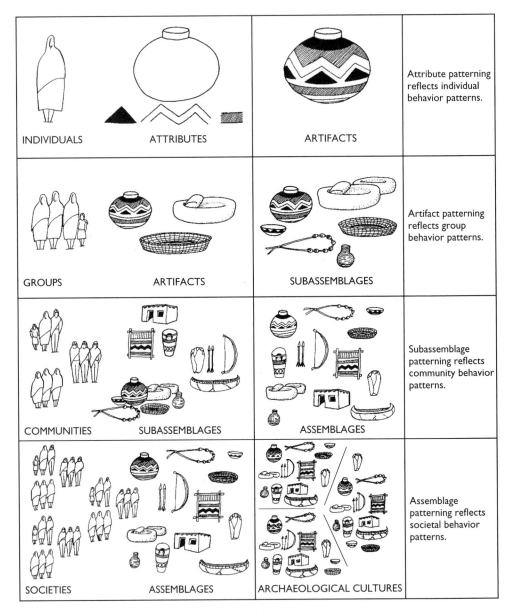

FIGURE 5.25

This behavioral reconstruction is based on hierarchical classification, independent of archaeological context.

The point to remember is that classification is a convenient working tool, organizing artifacts or other archaeological data into manageable and meaningful groups and facilitating further analysis. There is no single right classification. The attributes the investigator chooses to look at depend on the research issues he or she wants to explore. For example, a researcher interested in food storage patterns in different parts of a community or in different time periods would look at shapes and sizes of storage vessels (form types) rather than at the designs used to decorate them (stylistic types).

One approach attempts to reconstruct the past by correlating hierarchical classifications with various levels of behavior. A widely cited example of such behavioral reconstruction was outlined by James Deetz (Fig. 5.25). According to this scheme, the individuals who created artifact types adhered to culturally defined standards. Patterned sets of artifacts used by occupational groups (defined by form and functional attributes), such as the various tools used by farmers or hunters, are called **subassemblages.** Patterned sets of subassemblages, representing the sum of social activities, define the **assemblage** of an ancient community. At the highest level patterned sets of asssemblages are used to define **archaeological cultures** (the sum total of material remains assumed to represent the culture of a past society).

This kind of behavioral reconstruction, often based on style and form types, relies on the validity of the assumption that archaeological classifications reflect the structure of ancient cultural patterns. The best test of the utility of this kind of hierarchical classification rests with the context and associations of the data on which it is based.

SUMMARY

Archaeological fieldwork involves the collection and processing of data. Fieldwork may begin with surveys to discover and locate sites. Surface survey is the oldest and most common way to identify sites, but it is often slow and not useful for detecting deeply buried sites. Aerial survey provides rapid coverage of wide areas and is efficient for identifying sites that have at least some surface indications. Subsurface detection methods, using mechanical probes or electronic instruments, are slow but may be the only way to find buried sites.

Once sites are identified and located, surface survey is used to gain representative data without resorting to excavation. Sometimes this may be the only way data are acquired; more often, however, surface survey is a prelude to excavation, aiding in selecting areas to excavate and producing hypotheses to be tested by excavation. Ground survey is the most common method, acquiring data by mapping sites and by collecting surface artifacts and ecofacts. Subsurface sensors, like those used to discover sites, may be used as part of surface survey as well. Together, ground survey and subsurface detection methods are used to produce maps showing the distributions and densities of features, artifacts, and ecofacts at sites and within regions.

Excavation is used to investigate the three-dimensional structure of buried archaeological data and to determine the functional and temporal significance of these data. These three dimensions reflect the processes of site formation: activities that took place at any one point in time are represented by the horizontal dimensions, while sequential activities are represented by the vertical dimension. Archaeologists, therefore, investigate stratigraphy—the interpretation of the sequence of deposition—to determine which data reflect simultaneous (and functionally related) activities and which reflect the sequence of activities over time. There are two basic kinds of excavations: (1) penetrating excavations, which cut through deposits to reveal the depth, sequence, and composition of sites, and (2) clearing excavations, which expose the horizontal extent and arrangement of remains within a single stratum.

Provenience control is crucial to the collection of archaeological data: to reconstruct later how a site was formed, the location of all recovered materials must be accurately recorded. All data from excavations or surface collections are given distinctive labels and plotted with reference to horizontal location and vertical elevation. Data gathering is a destructive process, so records—field notes, standardized forms, scaled drawings, and photographs (the first three are often rendered in paper and computerized formats)—are essential to all later analysis and interpretation.

Both data and records are usually processed in a field laboratory to ensure that they are preserved, secured, and available for further study and analysis. After this, portable data, such as artifacts and some ecofacts, are classified by attributes (stylistic, form, and technological) that the archaeologist selects to address particular research questions. Classification is a convenient means of ordering, summarizing, relating, and understanding a mass of data, and each classification used to match specific research situations is only one of many possible organizing schemes. All, however, are useful to the archaeologist in providing a starting point for further analysis and interpretation.

FOR FURTHER READING

ARCHAEOLOGICAL SURVEY

Allen, Green, and Zubrow 1990; Billman and Feinman 1999; Chase et al. 2011; Collins and Molyneaux 2003; Cowgill 1974; Davis 1975; Ebert 1984; Fish and Kowalewski 1990; Lasaponara and Masini 2011; MacNeish et al. 1972; Sabloff and Ashmore 2001; Schliemann (1881) 1968; Weiner 2010

EXCAVATION

Blau and Ubelaker 2009; Bunn et al. 1980; Carmichael, Lafferty, and Molyneaux 2003; Harris 1989; Hodder 1999, 2000; Matthews et al. 1997; Matthews and Hastorf 2000; Rapp and Hill 1998; Roskams 2001; Stein and Ferrand 2001; Wheeler 1954

DATA PROCESSING

Appelbaum 2011; Hodder 1999, 2000; Matero 2000; Sullivan and Childs 2003; Weiner 2010

CLASSIFICATION

Deetz 1967; Ford 1954; Hill 1970; Hill and Evans 1972; Hodder 1982a; Longacre and Skibo 1994; Ramenofsky and Steffen 1998; Spaulding 1953; Spector 1993; Whallon and Brown 1982

ADDITIONAL SOURCES

J. M. Coles 1984; Cowgill 1974; Davis 1975; Flannery 1976; Hamilton and Woodward 1984; Kipfer 2007; Levin 1986; MacNeish et al. 1972; Villa 1982; Willey 1953

6

Analyzing the Past

Archaeologists use various studies to analyze artifacts, ecofacts, and features. Because each of these broad categories covers a wide variety of archaeological remains, in this chapter we will consider only those most commonly encountered by archaeologists. This study includes consideration of the characteristics that differentiate one kind of data from others to show the ways each can contribute to an understanding of past behavior. Bear in mind that the information gleaned from these remains is influenced by their physical characteristics, their state of preservation, and the specific questions being asked.

ARTIFACTS

Artifacts are classified into **industries,** which are defined according to both materials used and manufacturing techniques. Our discussion will highlight lithic and ceramic industries because stone and fired clay are the most commonly encountered archaeological materials.

Lithic Artifacts

Stone tools were undoubtedly among the earliest implements used by human societies; in fact, their use predates the emergence of modern *Homo sapiens* by more than a million years. The first stone tools used by the ancestors of modern humans were probably unmodified rocks or cobbles used only once for tasks such as hammering or pounding. But **lithic technology** has its roots in the first attempts to modify and shape stone to make tools.

There are two basic kinds of lithic technology: (1) the chipped-stone industry, which involves fracturing or flaking stone, and (2) the ground-stone industry, which is based on pecking and grinding or polishing stone. Because chipped stone is the oldest preserved form of culture and technology, archaeologists have used it to name the earliest period of cultural development, the Paleolithic (Old Stone) period. In this traditional scheme the later development of a stone technology involving grinding signals the advent of the second developmental age, the Neolithic (New Stone) Age. Ground-stone tools did not, of course, replace chipped stone; rather, the two technologies coexisted for thousands of years in both the Old and New Worlds. Of the two, chipped stone is more commonly encountered.

Chipped-stone technology takes advantage of the characteristics of several hard, nonresilient, and homogeneous minerals, including flint or chert, obsidian (a natural volcanic glass), basalt, and quartz. When struck, these materials fracture in a uniform manner, not following any natural cleavage planes in the rock. Instead, shock waves from the blow spread through the struck stone or **core** in a cone-shaped pattern, detaching a fragment called a **flake** (Fig. 6.1). Chipped-stone tools are produced either by removing flakes to give a sharp edge to the core (core tools) or by utilizing one or more of the detached flakes (flake or blade tools).

Chipped-stone tools can be made by a variety of techniques; we will briefly summarize the more important of these. Some techniques have been inferred from traces left on the tools themselves, others from ethnographic observations of peoples still manufacturing stone tools, and still others through archaeologists' experiments in duplicating the ancient forms. Some of these techniques are as old as the origins of stone tools; others represent later refinements during the long development of lithic technology.

The shape and size of the flake detached from a core depend on the physical characteristics of the stone itself, on the angle and force of the blow being struck, and on the physical characteristics of the tool being used to detach the flake. Short, rather thick flakes are produced by **direct percussion,** which is achieved by either striking the core with a hammer stone or another tool (Fig. 6.2a) or striking the core against a fixed stone called an anvil. The earliest recognizable stone tools, manufactured during the earliest part of the Paleolithic period more than 2 million years ago, were produced by these methods.

Although not a common technique, **indirect percussion** uses a punch made of bone or wood placed between the core and the hammer stone to direct and soften the resultant blow, producing longer and thinner flakes. Another refinement, called **pressure flaking,** uses steady pressure on the punch to detach flakes (Fig. 6.2b). The usual result of either indirect percussion or pressure flaking is a series of long, thin, parallel-sided flakes called **blades** (see Fig. 6.1). True blades produced from prepared cylindrical cores are typical of the later Paleolithic in the Old World and of much of the pre-Columbian era in the New World.

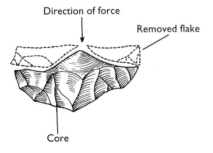

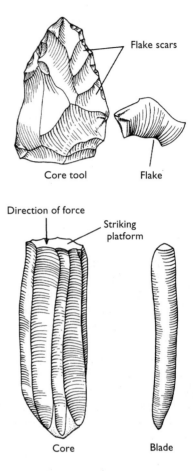

FIGURE 6.1

The terminology used in describing lithic core, flake, and blade tools reflects the manufacturing technology.

Once a flake or blade tool has been detached, it may be ready for use as a cutting or scraping tool, or it can be further modified. Edges that required strength and durability rather than sharpness, such as those on scrapers, were **retouched** by finely controlled pressure flaking to remove small, steep flakes (see Fig. 6.2b). Skillful pressure flaking can sometimes completely alter the shape of a flake, as in production of barbed or notched projectile points and miniature forms (microliths).

During the Paleolithic, new techniques and forms gradually emerged that increased both the efficiency of tool production and the available inventory of tool forms. By the end of the Paleolithic, however, a new lithic technology was also being developed—the shaping of harder, more durable stone by pecking and grinding against abrasives such as sandstone. These tools, which took the form of axes and adzes, had much longer lasting edges than their chipped counterparts and were thus more efficient for such tasks as cutting trees and splitting lumber.

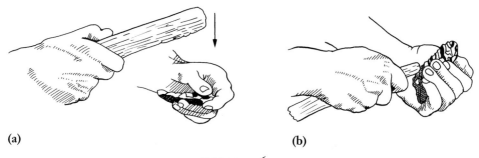

(a)   **(b)**

FIGURE 6.2

Manufacturing techniques for chipped-stone tools include: (a) direct percussion using an antler and (b) pressure flaking using an antler or similar tool.

Ground-stone techniques were also used to shape large basins, known as **querns** or **metates,** used for grinding grain and other tasks.

Lithic analysis has traditionally involved classification based on form, often using direct or implied functional labels such as scrapers and handaxes. Although still used, form classifications have been refined to specify more precisely the sets of criteria that distinguish form types.

To a large extent lithic typologies based on overall form have given way to more sophisticated attribute analyses based on either manufacturing technology (technological types) or actual use (functional types). Stone tools are particularly well suited to such analyses and classifications because stoneworking and use are subtractive actions: each step in shaping and use permanently removes more of the stone. Clues to most steps in ancient manufacturing and use are preserved and can be detected in flake scars, striking platforms, and other identifiable attributes (see Fig. 6.1). By analyzing the full range of lithic material, both artifacts and **debitage** (workshop debris), the archaeologist can often reconstruct most or all of the steps in tool manufacture (Fig. 6.3).

To test and refine reconstructions of ancient tool manufacture, pioneering lithic specialists such as François Bordes and Don Crabtree experimentally duplicated ancient chipped-stone technology. Through these experiments, and through their training of other archaeologists in the techniques used to manufacture stone tools, lithic specialists have increased the precision with which ancient manufacturing practices can be analyzed, as well as proposing alternative methods that may have been used in the past. Several studies have shown that what were once considered waste flakes were, in fact, cutting tools.

Microscopic or chemical examinations of stone are sometimes useful for establishing the source of the raw material. By comparing quarry samples with artifact samples microscopically, analysts can sometimes identify distinctive quarry signatures—particular patterns of constituent minerals that come from one source alone. For example, Herbert Thomas used such evidence in 1923 to

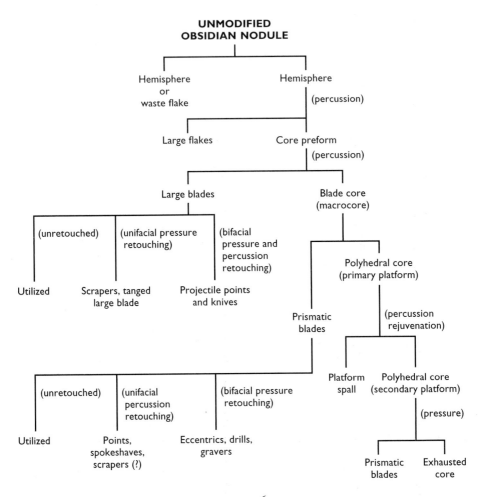

FIGURE 6.3

This technological classification represents manufacturing steps used in production of chipped-stone artifacts at Chalchuapa, El Salvador.

argue that the bluestones of Stonehenge had been brought from the Prescelly Mountains of Wales, some 240 miles away, by a feasible transport route. More recently, O. Williams-Thorpe and R. S. Thorpe have reexamined a broader range of similar source evidence, concluding that the distinctive bluestones were actually available locally to ancient builders, transported by glaciers to within perhaps 5 miles of where Stonehenge was built. Diagnostic trace elements within lithic materials such as obsidian can be identified and measured by neutron activation (measuring the material's response to brief and harmless bombardment by neutrons) or similar analyses. The use of these techniques for detection of raw material sources has allowed reconstruction of ancient exchange networks in many parts of the world.

Determining how stone tools were used requires other approaches. At one time inferred function was often a primary criterion for lithic classifications. One common distinction was between supposedly utilitarian objects (those with domestic or household uses) and ceremonial objects (those with ritual or non-domestic uses). This categorization might work for artifacts from secure contexts, such as tools from household living floors versus those from burials. But the distinction was often misused by automatically associating elaborate forms with ceremonial use and those of simpler shapes with utilitarian use. Artifacts from secure ceremonial contexts may once have served multiple functions, including utilitarian ones, prior to their final deposition in a burial or cache. Today, lithic analysts usually identify stone-tool function through detailed attribute study. They examine specific aspects of form, such as angle of the cutting edge, and attributes of wear resulting from use—microscopic fractures, pitting, or erosion of the edge—to establish the range of tasks an artifact once performed.

These analyses of form and wear use analogy—comparing the attributes of archaeological materials with those of modern examples whose function is known—to determine probable ancient function. For example, ancient spear points are identified by the similarity of archaeological forms to modern versions. In other cases analogs are provided by imitative experiments in which archaeologists make stone tools and use them to chop, scrape, slice, whittle, or saw various materials such as meat, bone, or wood. After an experimental tool is used, its edges are examined microscopically to detect the pattern of wear resulting from each kind of use. Wear signatures can be identified and used to infer the functions of archaeological specimens that have similar wear patterns.

Residues left on working edges may provide direct clues to ancient function. Thomas Loy has found that edges of stone tools may preserve traces of blood that allow identification of the kinds of animals killed by these weapons, even after thousands of years. Another well-known example of residue detection is the identification of silica, which provides evidence of the harvesting of grains or other grassy plants in sites occupied during the early stages of agricultural development.

Ground-stone tools can also preserve clues to manufacture and use. Examination of residues may reveal what was ground on the implement in question. For example, a quern or mortar could have been used to grind food or pigments; only analysis to detect possible residues or wear will tell.

Ceramic Artifacts

The term **ceramics** covers all industries in which artifacts are modeled or molded from clay and then made durable by firing. In addition to pottery, this category includes ceramic figurines, musical instruments, and spindle whorls (used for spinning thread or yarn). Although clay figurines—such as the Venus figurines from Dolni Vestonice in the Czech Republic, which date from the European Upper Paleolithic—appear to be the earliest known form of ceramic technology, pottery is undoubtedly the most abundant and widespread kind of ceramics.

Pottery is a distinct ceramic industry because of its unique manufacturing techniques and specialized functional attributes. Archaeological evidence throughout the world indicates that pottery originated with humanity's first attempts at settled life. In Southwest Asia, East Asia, and South America, pottery developed as part of a more complex, expanding technology that was fostered by the relative stability of settled village life. Pottery was and still is used to transport, cook, and store a wide range of foods, liquids, and other supplies. But as societies became increasingly complex, pottery also assumed other, specialized functions, including such ritual uses as burial urns and incense burners.

Compared with the age of the chipped-stone industry, pottery's 12,000-year history seems short. But the widespread occurrence of pottery vessels, combined with their extreme durability and capacity for great variety in form and decoration, makes pottery one of the most frequently analyzed and useful artifacts available to archaeologists. The importance of the common potsherd in archaeological research can hardly be overstressed; one unabridged dictionary even defines *potsherd* as "a broken pottery fragment, esp. one of archaeological value."

Pottery technology ranges from simple household hand-production to specialized mass-production methods. First, however, the potter must acquire and prepare the proper clay. The moist clay must be thoroughly kneaded (or wedged) to drive out air bubbles and create a uniform, plastic mass. (*Plasticity* refers to the capacity to be molded and shaped.) As part of the clay processing, nonplastic substances such as sand or ground shell that retain their shape and size may be added—as temper—to reduce shrinkage and thus lessen breakage during drying or firing.

Hand-forming pottery involves modeling a vessel either from a clay core or by adding coils or segments and welding the junctures with a thin solution of clay and water (Fig. 6.4). It is the oldest kind of pottery technology and is usually associated with small-scale production. Mold-forming is commonly used to mass-produce pottery and small clay artifacts such as figurines and spindle whorls. Wheel-forming, a relatively recent invention that appeared in Southwest Asia sometime before 3000 B.C., is the most common means of mass-producing pottery vessels throughout the world. The potter's wheel is used to form the vessel by manipulating a rapidly rotating clay core centered on a vertically mounted wheel, powered by the potter's hands or feet or by other power sources.

Once the vessel is formed, it is usually smoothed to create a uniform surface, often using a coating of a thin clay solution or **slip.** Slips or paints may be used to decorate the vessel in a variety of patterns and colors. Specialized slips that vitrify during high-temperature firing are called **glazes.** A vessel may be further modified or decorated by modeling, either adding clay (welding appliqués) or subtracting clay (incising, carving, cutting, and so on). When dry, the vessel may be polished by rubbing with a smooth, hard object, such as a beach pebble, to compact the surface and give it a shine.

(a)

(b)

(c)

(d)

FIGURE 6.4

Steps in pottery manufacture include (a) hand-forming vessels (Chinautla, Guatemala), (b) burnishing with a smooth stone (Zambia), (c) adding coils to form the rim (Nigeria), and (d) firing pottery in an open kiln (Chinautla).

Firing transforms clay from its natural plastic state to a permanent nonplastic one. During the firing process clay may pass through as many as three stages:

1. Dehydration or loss of water, occurring at temperatures up to about 600°C.

2. Oxidation of carbon and iron compounds in the clay, occurring at temperatures up to about 900°C.

3. **Vitrification**—a complex process in which glass and other new minerals are formed in the clay, occurring at temperatures above about 1000°C. Vitrification fuses the clay so that the vessel walls become waterproof. The earliest glazed pottery appears to have been produced in China by 1500 B.C.

Pottery analysis uses a variety of approaches, depending on the objectives of the research. Any of the three broad approaches discussed earlier—studies based on stylistic attributes, form attributes, and technological attributes—are frequently used with pottery.

Stylistic analyses of pottery have usually received greatest emphasis. Pottery lends itself to a variety of stylistic and decorative treatments—painting, appliqué, incising, and so on—that have no effect on the vessel's usefulness as a container. Because of this underlying freedom of choice in pottery decorations, it is often assumed that stylistic patterns represent culturally guided choices rather than technological or functional limitations. Stylistic classification remains one of the most important methods of analyzing ancient pottery, using decorative attributes to trace ancient social and cultural links in time and space.

The analysis of vessel form may be combined with stylistic classifications to assist in the definition of types. Because they can take a wide variety of shapes, differences in form among pottery vessels may represent the potter's choices rather than technological limits (Fig. 6.5). Of course, vessel form is also a clue to function. The use of general shape-function analogs is common in archaeological studies. For instance, ancient jars with necks were often used for storing and dispensing liquids, as they are today in most areas of the world without running water; the restrictive neck helps to control spills and thus to reduce waste.

Vessel function may also be determined by detecting residues from use, whether those remnants are visible or discovered through microscopic or chemical analyses. Cups for drinking chocolate, for example, have been identified from residues in pottery cylinders in Mesoamerica and in Chaco Canyon, New Mexico. Archaeologist Patricia Crown teamed with analyst W. Jeffrey Hurst at Hershey company labs (yes, as in Hershey chocolates!) to examine organic residues on the pottery cylinders. They identified traces of cacao, inferring as well that cacao drinking suggested ties with Mesoamerica, where such practices developed. Cooking vessels, too, may have identifiable interior residues. In such cases the archaeologist can not only infer vessel function but also reconstruct ancient cooking practices and food preferences. Other residues, such as incense resins, cereal pollen, or unfired clay, can also help in identifying the function of incense burners, grain storage jars, or potter's equipment.

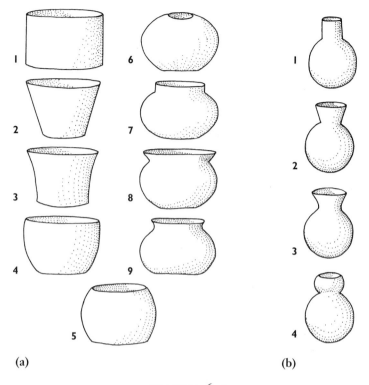

FIGURE 6.5

This example of pottery form classification shows: (a) nine defined bowl categories and (b) four defined jar categories.

The provenience of pottery may also allow the investigator to determine past uses. Vessels associated with burials are usually regarded as ritual paraphernalia used in funerary rites. Funerary vessels, however, often show traces of prior use, indicating that they served different purposes before being assigned their final, ritual function. Identifying all the multiple uses of recycled pottery vessels is often not possible, but these complicating factors should be kept in mind in interpreting vessel function.

Analysis of ancient pottery may reveal clues about manufacturing behavior, but in contrast to a subtractive technology such as stone-tool manufacture, pottery involves a plastic, additive technology. Manipulation of the clay in the later stages of manufacture often obliterates the diagnostic markings and features left by earlier stages. To overcome this difficulty, archaeologists use analogy with documented instances of pottery production today. Clues may be recognized by observing actual production and matching these with similar features on ancient pottery.

Metal Artifacts

Metallurgy is the complex technology used to extract metal from ores to produce metal artifacts. The earliest examples of this technology are found in Southwest Asia, where between 8000 and 9500 years ago people began to shape copper into simple tools and ornaments. Independent traditions of metalworking appeared in the New World, beginning with the making of copper ornaments in the upper Great Lakes region and the central coast of Peru, both by 3000 B.C. These traditions were based on working pure copper nuggets without extracting metal from ores. Somewhat later a more sophisticated metallurgy developed in the Andes of South America and in Mesoamerica. Over time, metallurgy has developed and spread throughout the world, almost completely replacing lithic technology. Today, of course, sophisticated metal technology has become an essential part of our own civilization.

Metal technology originated in the prehistoric exploitation of three hard metals—copper, tin, and iron—and, to a lesser degree, of two rare or precious metals—silver and gold. Because the development of metallurgical technology followed a fairly regular sequence, gradually replacing the two established lithic industries in the Old World, 19th-century archaeologists classified the apparent progress of Old World civilization with labels referring to successive ages of metal. Thus, the first metal to be used gave its name to the Copper Age, or Chalcolithic. The combination of copper and tin that was produced in later times gave its name to the Bronze Age, which was followed in turn by the Iron Age.

Since the 19th century, archaeologists have learned a great deal more about the origin and development of prehistoric metallurgy. As a result, the course of technological innovation can now be traced not only in Southwest Asia but also in Southeast Asia, China, Africa, and the New World.

The sequence of metallurgical development is still best known for Southwest Asia, however. The first uses of metal in that area, some time before 7000 B.C., involved **cold hammering** of copper. Copper is malleable enough to be shaped by hammering, but the progressive pounding cracks and weakens the metal. **Annealing**—heating and slow cooling—heals the cracks and stresses produced by hammering, thus providing renewed strength to the metal tool. By 4000 B.C., however, copper technology had changed. The change involved melting and casting the metal in molds into a variety of shapes, from axe heads to spear points, swords, and ornaments. At the same time, intense heat was used to **smelt** copper from ores, thereby greatly expanding the range of sources for the raw material.

Another significant advance involved deliberate production of metal **alloys.** Most scholars believe that experimental attempts to remove impurities from copper led to the realization that some of these impurities were beneficial. Most notably, inclusion of small quantities of tin or arsenic in copper forms a new metal combination, or alloy, called bronze. Bronze has several advantages over copper. Its melting point is lower, and it also cools into a harder metal capable of retaining a sharper, stronger edge. Further hammering, after cooling, hardens it further. Bronze was being produced in Southwest Asia by about 3000 B.C. (Fig. 6.6); Southeast Asia has yielded some bronze artifacts that date to about

FIGURE 6.6

These bronze vessels, from the first millennium B.C., were found in a tomb chamber at Gordion, Turkey.

the same era. Bronze metallurgy spread swiftly. Some of the most sophisticated products of bronze casting were created in China during the Shang Dynasty, which extended from about 1500 to 1027 B.C.

Ironworking was the next major development in metallurgical technology. Meteoritic iron was known and used during the Bronze Age, but in the later part of the second millennium B.C., ironworking displaced bronze casting as the principal means of metal tool production. Because iron melts at a higher temperature than bronze, ironworking is also more complicated than bronze casting. The principal iron output of early Southwest Asian furnaces was a spongy mass called a bloom, which was then reheated in a forge and hammered by a blacksmith to shape the tool, increase the metal's strength, and drive out impurities. Even so, forged iron is relatively soft. Use of a charcoal fire for the forge, however, introduces carbon and strengthens the iron, producing carburized iron—or steel—a much harder and more durable metal. By the end of the second millennium B.C., Southwest Asian blacksmiths were making steeled iron tools, and the age of iron metallurgy was under way.

The analysis of metal artifacts has varied with the geographical area and reflects differing research priorities. Because metal—especially molten metal—is a malleable material, like pottery, it is well suited to stylistic analyses and classifications. One example is the classification of bronze fibulae, or safety-pin brooches, from La Tène sites of Iron Age Europe (Fig. 6.7). Other studies have focused on the form of metal artifacts and on functional attributions based on form variation, similar to studies done for stone and ceramic artifacts.

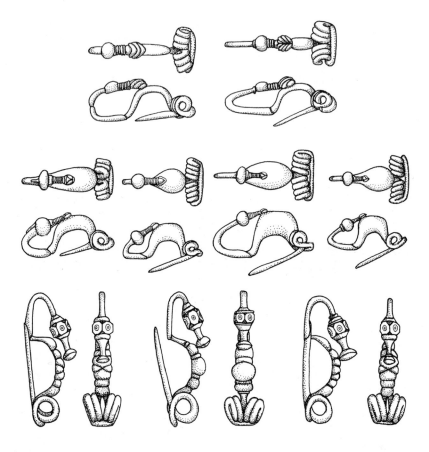

FIGURE 6.7

One classification scheme identifies three stylistic types of bronze fibulae (safety pins) from an Iron Age grave at Münsingen, Switzerland.

The general focus in metal artifact analysis, however, is reconstruction of ancient technology. Classifications divide the metal industry into subindustries according to the metal being worked. More technical analyses are then performed, including constituent analysis and microscopic examination of the metal structure. These studies help the archaeologist understand the range of technology involved in the procurement of raw materials, the production process, and refinement of the final product. Constituent analysis not only can identify the metals and nonmetallic materials present but also may allow specification of the metal sources. Examination of the microstructure of an artifact may yield clues about the precise techniques used in its production—hammering, annealing, and so on.

A complicating factor in these analyses is that metallurgy, like pottery, is an additive and correcting process in which mistakes can to some extent be covered and smoothed away by subsequent treatment. Unlike pottery, however, in which firing permanently alters the raw material, metal artifacts can also be melted down and the raw material reclaimed and reused. Such recycling may, for example, account for a relative lack of bronze artifacts early in the Iron Age: to save valuable alloying materials, many whole implements may have been refashioned into a succession of new tools, with only the final version left to the archaeological record.

Organic Artifacts

The class **organic artifacts** includes a variety of objects made from organic materials such as wood, plant fibers, bone, antler, ivory, and shell. Although such items are known to be important—and even dominant in the material culture of some modern societies, such as the Inuit (Eskimo)—they are especially susceptible to decay processes and thus are encountered by archaeologists only under special conditions. Many kinds of organic materials have been used to produce artifacts, each of which involves a specialized technology. We will restrict discussion here to the most frequently encountered artifact categories: bone and related materials (such as antler and ivory), wood, and shell.

Despite some controversy over the precise origins of bone technology, there is no doubt that by the Upper Paleolithic, people were making artifacts from a variety of animal parts. In both the Old and New Worlds, bone was split and carved with stone tools to form spear points, fishhooks, and other tools. Antler, usually from deer, was split or carved to make projectile points, especially barbed points for spears or harpoons. In the Arctic the prehistoric tradition of carving ivory to make harpoons and other artifacts has survived to this day (Fig. 6.8).

The technology involved in the production of bone, antler, and ivory tools is subtractive, like stoneworking. The simplest such tools were those that involved no form modification—for example, an animal bone used as a club. The same bone could also be broken to produce a sharp or jagged edge. The earliest finds suggest that such working was first confined to chipping and cracking, but by the Upper Paleolithic the production of bone, antler, and ivory tools showed great variety, skill, and sophistication; some forms even had engraved decoration.

Because wood is even more perishable than bone, antler, and ivory, the origins of woodworking remain obscure. Isolated finds, particularly from waterlogged sites, attest to woodworking by the Early Paleolithic in Africa and the Middle Paleolithic in Europe. Being a subtractive industry, this technology is preserved in the finished implements themselves, but due to the rarity of their discovery, methods of manufacturing (cutting, sawing, or carving) are more often inferred indirectly, from stone or metal woodworking tools.

Shell artifacts have been found the world over, even substituting for stone tools where stone is scarce. Other shell artifact forms include cups, spoons, fishhooks, and a variety of ornaments. Shellworking is another subtractive industry; one of the most remarkable ancient means of modifying

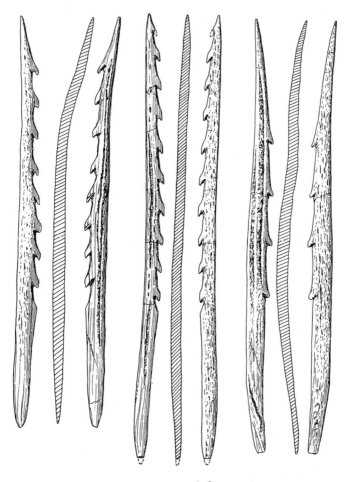

FIGURE 6.8

Bone harpoon heads from Alaska illustrate one kind of artifact fashioned
from organic materials.

shell surfaces was a delicate etching by application of a cactus-derived acid,
used among the Hohokam in the American Southwest (Fig. 6.9).

Analysis of organic artifacts yields information on the range of biotic
resources exploited by an ancient society and may give clues to communication
links with other areas, as when shell artifacts at an inland site are found to be
marine (saltwater) species. We will consider the ecofactual aspects of organic
artifacts in more detail later on.

Most classifications of organic artifacts are based on criteria of form. Sometimes
these form taxonomies have stylistic overtones, but more often they involve functional inferences, and the types may be labeled with direct or implied functional

FIGURE 6.9

In this example of a Hohokam decorated shell from Arizona (ca. A.D. 800–1200), the design was etched with acid from a saguaro cactus.

names. For example, the well-known artifact assemblages of the European Upper Paleolithic include a great variety of barbed bone projectile points, almost always referred to as harpoons. Such designations provide convenient, easy-to-remember names, but they do not establish the actual function of these artifacts.

ECOFACTS

Because they are natural objects, ecofacts yield only indirect information about technology, but they are no less important than artifacts as clues to understanding past human societies. For example, at the Olsen-Chubbuck site in southeastern Colorado, a series of bison skeletons was found associated with some stone tools, all strewn along the base of a ravine (Fig. 6.10). The site represents the remains of human hunting behavior some 8500 years ago. The location and arrangement of both ecofacts and artifacts have been used to infer a good deal about hunting strategy (how and from what direction the animals were driven over the ravine edge, including which way the wind may have been blowing), butchering techniques (how the carcasses were dismembered, which bones were stripped of meat on the spot, and which were carried off to the presumed campsite), and yield (how much meat and byproducts would have been available from the kill).

Ecofacts can also tell us about noneconomic activities such as ritual. In Peru's Upper Mantaro River Valley, Christine Hastorf and Sissel Johannessen analyzed woody plant remains from prehistoric sites spanning a thousand years' time, from about A.D. 500 to beyond A.D. 1500. They found that in the final century, the time of Inca expansion into the area, one local tree type came to dominate the woody remains. For the Inca this particular tree was linked symbolically to ancestry, especially to

FIGURE 6.10

Remains of bison killed and butchered by hunters some 8500 years ago
were excavated at the Olsen-Chubbuck site, Colorado.

mummified ancestors and the strength of the ancestral line. According to historical
accounts human figures carved from its wood were burned in ritual sacrifice to the
divine ancestor of the Inca dynasty. Drawing on documentary evidence as well as
the plant remains themselves, Hastorf and Johannessen suggest that the trees were
deliberately cultivated, an act likely fostered by the Inca during their conquest and
consolidation of the Upper Mantaro Valley.

Most frequently, however, ecofacts are used to reconstruct the environment
in which past societies lived and the range of resources they exploited. In fact,
as we discuss further in Chapter 10, plant and animal remains from archaeological context, as well as soils and sediments, can tell us about environmental
change in the past in ways that are important for understanding climate and
other changes today. Grahame Clark and his coworkers analyzed pollen samples
from Star Carr, a 10,000-year-old site in northern England, and inferred that the
surrounding area was largely covered by forest of birch and pine; the presence
of pollen from plants that thrive in open areas points to localized clearings, one

of which became the site of Star Carr. By examining both the plant remains and the abundantly recovered antlers of red deer, roe deer, and elk, the investigators could establish the times of year the site had been occupied. This was done by comparing the distribution of antlers broken from the animals' skulls with those that had simply been collected after being shed naturally and then correlating the results with the known seasonal cycles of deer antler growth and shedding. The work at Star Carr was a landmark, showing the wealth of interpretation that could be gained from ecofactual data.

As with artifacts, the first step in analysis of ecofacts is classification. Clearly, however, the classification of ecofacts must use different criteria than those used for artifacts, borrowing schemes from botany, zoology, and geology. Analyses of ecofacts are often done by interdisciplinary specialists who combine archaeological expertise with expertise in these fields. Thus, plant materials from archaeological sites are often analyzed by archaeobotanists, and animal remains are often analyzed by zooarchaeologists. The study of archaeological soils and sediments is the work of geoarchaeologists. Ecofacts may be classified in many specific ways, according to properties that might relate them to past human societies. For example, some plants and animals are available for harvesting only at limited times of the year; these, as the Star Carr case indicates, may be used to determine seasonality of exploitation. Animals can also be studied in terms of the amounts of meat they would yield and therefore the size of the human population they could support. Soils can be classified as to their relative potential fertility under given kinds of agricultural exploitation.

Floral Ecofacts

Floral remains in archaeological contexts fall into two basic categories: (1) microspecimens and (2) macrospecimens. Microspecimens include pollen and **phytoliths,** the more durable silica bodies formed in plants. Macrospecimens include seeds, leaves, casts or impressions, and so forth. Both categories require technical identification. As part of this process, many plants (and animals) are identified as wild or domesticated. The domestication of plants and animals in the Old and New Worlds was a significant cultural development, giving people more direct control over the quantity and quality of their food supply. Accordingly, a good deal of study has been done concerning when, where, and how this process was carried out. Critical to such study, of course, is the ability to identify wild and domesticated forms. Because domestication is a gradual result of repeated selection for desired traits—as when larger or quicker-growing strains are deliberately replanted and nurtured—there is no single "original" domesticated maize cob or wheat kernel. Rather, one can discern trends in form from fully wild to fully domesticated (Fig. 6.11).

Another dimension in the study of floral ecofacts is the context in which they are found. Some plants may be found in economic contexts, such as charred wood in kitchen hearths; in other cases contexts suggest ritual use. On the other hand, the only sure indication that a plant was a food resource is contextual—from its occurrence

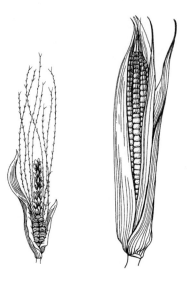

FIGURE 6.11

As drawings of early maize
(left) and a later domesticated
maize variety (right) show, over
time selection favored more
and longer rows of kernels.

in the digestive tracts of mummies or bog corpses, or in human **coprolites** (preserved feces). Food remains and residues may also be found adhering to the interiors of food storage vessels or to preparation surfaces such as grinding stones.

Faunal Ecofacts

Animal remains in archaeological contexts take a number of forms, from intact specimens to partial ones, such as bones or coprolites. Bones and teeth, the most commonly recovered forms, have received the most attention.

A basic question of faunal studies involves the kinds of animals being exploited. Zooarchaeologists attempt not only to identify the species distinctions but to establish the proportions of adult versus juvenile and, for some adult animals, male versus female. Tallies of this kind have been used as evidence for the very beginning of animal domestication, before bone changes due to selective breeding can be detected. In this case the presence of large numbers of young-animal remains may indicate direct access to and control of a herd or selective culling before breeding age to remove certain characteristics. In other cases the presence of immature animals may point to use of the site in the season when the young animals would have been available. In contrast, changes in bone mass of sheep and goats of the third millennium B.C. in Israel suggest that older females were more numerous in later occupation levels: from this shift in herd composition, the same analysts inferred a rising emphasis on milk production.

Archaeologists can also examine the parts of animals present at a site. At Star Carr the occurrence of stag frontlets and detached antlers gave evidence not only of the season during which the site was occupied but also of the range of antler raw materials that were used by the site's occupants. At Olsen-Chubbuck study of the presence or absence of various skeletal elements led to inferences about butchering techniques by indicating which parts of the animals were taken back to the residence area for more leisurely consumption.

Special characteristics of particular animals may lead to specific interpretations. Some small animals, such as snails, are very sensitive to climate and thus can serve as indicators of local climatic change or stability. An increase in white-tailed deer could, for example, signal an increase in cleared areas or a decrease in local forest cover. Presence of large mammals as prey often suggests organized group hunting practices, and hunting herd animals requires different tactics from those for hunting solitary animals. Ideological interpretations may also be made from faunal evidence.

Contextual associations can be related to various kinds of human-animal relations. For example, the occurrence of mummified cats in ancient Egypt and of jaguar remains in elite Maya burials reflects the high symbolic status enjoyed by those animals in the two societies. Bones found in middens, on the other hand, are usually interpreted as remains of food animals or scavengers.

As part of the consideration of context, the archaeologist must be careful to distinguish, as far as possible, which animals are related to human presence and exploitation and which are not. For example, burrowing animals such as gophers or opossums found in graves may have gotten there on their own, independent of the ancient burial. Other animals may simply take advantage of the shelter provided by occupation areas, such as bats roosting in abandoned Maya temples. As an example of how critical such a determination can be, consider the debate over Makapansgat, an early site in South Africa. Raymond Dart used the pattern of occurrence of the nonhuman bones—how they were broken, what elements were present, and how they were deposited—to argue that these bones include tools, as well as ecofacts, used by early human ancestors 2 million years ago. Other scholars, however, argue that the bones are neither artifacts nor ecofacts, but are the result of animal activity and breakage, like those found in the dens of modern carnivores.

Human Remains

From a scientific viewpoint, human remains represent an extremely important category of nonartifactual data and are the domain of a branch of anthropology—biological or physical archaeology. Yet for many people, human remains represent far more than scientific data; they are the sacred remains of the ancestors of living people. Thus, more than anything else encountered and studied by archaeologists, human remains raise significant and difficult ethical issues. This is most apparent when living descendants of the dead express their concerns about the excavation and analysis of skeletal remains. Archaeologists have an obligation to respect the concerns and wishes of living descendants of past peoples, and this is especially important when it comes to the ethical treatment of human remains. The term **bioarchaeology** refers to the joint biological and cultural study of human remains and mortuary sites to investigate how people in a society lived, including all the dimensions cited in this paragraph.

In Chapter 10 we consider at length archaeologists' professional responsibilities in the treatment of human remains. Here we review some of the ways human remains from archaeological contexts further our understanding of past peoples and societies. Scientific studies of human remains can yield a wealth of unique information about our human ancestors, including past life expectancy, health and disease, diet and nutritional status, genetic relationships and migrations, individual life histories and traumas, and even social standing, cultural practices, and customs. Much of this information has practical benefits for people today, such as increased understanding of the origins of disease and the effects of diet and nutrition on human populations.

Forms of human remains include intact or well-preserved examples, such as mummies; fragmentary bones and teeth; and coprolites. Bones and teeth are most often preserved, so they will receive the most attention.

Analysis of human remains begins with identification of the particular elements (bones, teeth) present and of the number of individuals represented. Because people are often buried in individual graves, this may not be a difficult task, but mass graves or reused ones present special problems. Once the elements are identified, however, an assessment is made of each individual's sex and age at death. Some skeletal elements are more reliable or easier to interpret in these assessments. For example, sex can be most readily judged from the pelvis. Age can be assessed by a variety of means, including eruption sequence and degree of wear on teeth, fusion between bones of the skull, and fusion of the ends (epiphyses) to the shafts (diaphyses) of limb bones.

Once age and sex identifications are made, a number of other studies may be done. Paleodemographic analysis seeks to understand the structure of the ancient population under investigation, including determination of sex ratio and life expectancy (Fig. 6.12).

Aspects of ancient diets can be reconstructed from skeletal samples. One technique is stable carbon isotope analysis of human bone collagen. Because plants metabolize carbon dioxide according to different ratios of two carbon isotopes, ^{13}C and ^{12}C, measurement of the ratios can indicate which plant groups were used in the ancient diet. Such important foods as maize, sorghum, sugarcane, and millet, for example, belong to one major group, called C_4 plants, while spinach, manioc, barley, sugar beets, and peas belong to another, the C_3 group. Among the results of these studies is independent corroboration of the conclusion that maize, a C_4 plant, was domesticated in Mexico and Peru and later became a staple crop in North America. Stable carbon isotope analysis of human skeletal material from Tehuacán, Mexico, by Paul Farnsworth and his colleagues revealed that C_4 plants (including maize) composed 90 percent of the diet by 4500 B.C. and remained at this level for the remainder of the pre-Columbian era. This contrasts with far lower estimates of plant use in the Tehuacán diet based on preserved macrospecimens (seeds and other plant remains). The discrepancy seems due to a sampling bias, because the pollen samples came from only one type of habitation site (dry caves). The stable isotopic analysis of the

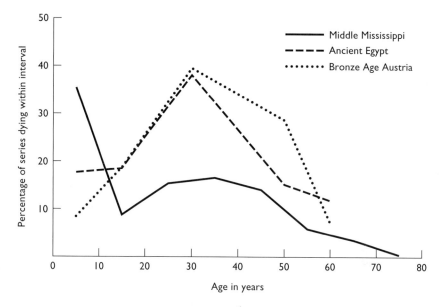

FIGURE 6.12

As the comparative mortality profiles from selected ancient populations show, Middle Mississippians of the southeastern United States after A.D. 1000 were two to three times as likely to die before 10 years of age than were ancient Egyptians or Austrians of the Bronze Age several thousand years earlier. Once past childhood, however, members of all three groups reached a peak death rate between ages 25 and 35.

human skeletal sample more likely represents the complete dietary inventory of the Tehuacán population.

Other isotopes present in human skeletal remains also provide clues for dietary reconstructions. Stable nitrogen isotope analysis reveals distinctions between reliance on marine versus land-based food resources. Strontium isotope analysis can detect distinctions between meat and plant diets, and whether an individual has moved to a new place, different from his or her homeland.

Combining analyses can give a detailed picture of the lives of the deceased. At Cahokia, Illinois, for example, 272 individuals were buried in the small Mound 72 (see Fig. 5.10a, lower center); one of the deceased might even have been the first leader of Cahokia society, at about A.D. 1050. We discuss more about Cahokia and its founding in Chapter 8. Of importance here about the decedents in Mound 72, Stanley Ambrose and his colleagues found that individuals buried separately, with prestigious grave goods and those buried in mass graves with no grave goods differed in health and diet, based on stable carbon and nitrogen isotope evidence. Mound 72 was already an important ritual focus in the first century of Cahokia's existence, and the isotopic analyses point to rising inequality in people's access to high-quality food—what the authors call the "nutritional dimension of social complexity."

Biological anthropologists also study ancient DNA (deoxyribonucleic acid), the molecular material that controls genetic heritage. Although the amount of DNA preserved in ancient remains is often small, and the risk of contamination from modern DNA high, great strides have been made, yielding important insights about such questions as ancestry and migrations of ancient humans. For example, although in initial analysis, DNA from Ötzi the Iceman (see Chapter 1) was contaminated in handling, subsequent work confirmed that he was most likely of northern European, not Mediterranean, ancestry. Broader studies have contributed importantly to more far-reaching issues, such as how people colonized different parts of the world, especially Polynesia and the Americas.

Human remains also yield information on the health and nutrition of the population. Not all diseases or injuries affect the skeleton, but many do, and these can be detected by specialists such as paleopathologists. Obvious examples are bone fractures and tooth caries; other maladies, including arthritis, yaws, and periodontal disease, leave tangible marks as well. Prolonged stress from carrying heavy loads or similar hard work likewise leaves traces, such as enlarged muscle attachments on bone. These diagnostic traces make ancient human remains important to the study of the physical quality of life in ancient times and the origins and development of diseases such as tuberculosis.

Of course, if mummified bodies are available for study, analysis can be much more detailed, akin to a regular autopsy. Mummies from arid climates like Egypt and Peru have yielded varied evidence of parasites, injury, and other sources of ill health in antiquity. Ötzi was examined by X-ray, CAT scan, and other means, revealing healed fractures of several ribs, some hardening of blood vessels (probably due to high cholesterol), and arthritis.

Human bones also offer clues to ancient social standing. William Haviland has attributed differences in male stature at the Maya site of Tikal, Guatemala, to social class and accompanying wealth differences. The taller males, found in richer tomb burials, were probably also richer in life and thus able to secure better food supplies than could their shorter counterparts, buried in less well-made and less well-furnished interments.

Some cultural practices also leave their mark on skeletal remains. One example is cranial modification, practiced in pre-Columbian times in North, Central, and South America. According to this custom, infants' heads are shaped or bound until they take the desired form (Fig. 6.13); the past Chinese practice of binding girls' feet to make them smaller is comparable.

Soils and Sediments

The soils and sediments recovered by excavation represent one of the most important categories of ecofacts available for study. These materials represent more than just the matrix in which cultural remains may be embedded. The

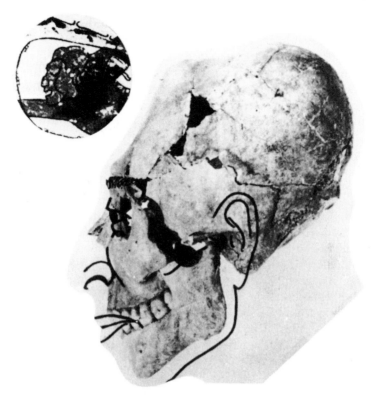

FIGURE 6.13

This photograph of an artificially modified skull from the Classic Maya site of Altar de Sacrificios, Guatemala, also contains a superimposed reconstruction of the individual's profile in life. The inset shows an individual with a similarly shaped skull painted on a pottery vessel from the same site.

analyses of archaeologically recovered soils and sediments by trained geoarchaeologists provide essential information about the past.

The analysis of soils and sediments by geoarchaeologists has four main objectives: (1) to establish the stratigraphy of a site (see Chapter 5), (2) to date the site (discussed in Chapter 7), (3) to understand natural site formation processes, and (4) to reconstruct the ancient landscape in which the site's inhabitants lived. We will look at several examples to illustrate the importance of site formation processes and the reconstruction of ancient landscapes.

The processes of site formation usually derive from a combination of human activities and natural geological processes. It is basic to stratigraphic evaluation to distinguish between natural and cultural origins for all deposits encountered. But in some cases the soils have a particularly dramatic story to tell. For example, Alan Kolata has found water-laid soils capping the occupation levels at 750-year-old sites on the south shore of Lake Titicaca, in Bolivia. He suggests the soils likely account for a sudden decline in this part of the ancient Tiwanaku state: flooding and a rise in the lake level may have waterlogged and thereby ruined what had been a productive agricultural landscape.

Even more dramatic is the fate of the island of Thera (now called Santorini) in the Aegean, where an earthquake destroyed the town of Acrotiri in the 17th century B.C. In Chapter 4 we discussed the explosion of the volcano on that island and how this event completely disrupted local human occupation. However, excavations at Acrotiri have established that a considerable time elapsed between the earthquake and the volcanic explosion, because a thin humus layer (the result of natural, gradual soil formation processes) was found between the remains of the fallen, abandoned buildings and the volcanic deposits. Indeed, two distinguishable eruptions apparently took place—a small one followed by the catastrophic one. The smaller eruption apparently worked as a warning, allowing most of the residents of Thera to leave: the finds at Thera are relatively lacking in human remains compared to Pompeii, where many residents had no time to flee before the eruption of Vesuvius in A.D. 79.

Soil characteristics were observed by ancient inhabitants as well as modern investigators. Soil surveys in many areas of the world have indicated that occupation by agriculturalists correlates well with the distribution of well-drained and fertile areas. Fertility potentials must be tested, however, and not simply assumed. For example, volcanic ash is generally a fertile parent material for agricultural soils. But the ash fall from the eruption of Ilopango volcano in El Salvador around A.D. 200, traced by Payson Sheets and his associates, blanketed the area with an infertile layer that would have decreased local agricultural production capacities for as long as several centuries.

Reconstructing the original landscape of a site is fundamental to understanding the past. Because landscapes are dynamic, the ancient settings of most archaeological sites were often quite different from those encountered today. For example, the small Maya site of Quiriguá is located on an active floodplain of the Motagua River in eastern Guatemala. Quiriguá was occupied from about A.D. 400 to 900. Today the Motagua channel is several hundred meters south of the site and appears unrelated to the form or location of the civic center. In archaeological investigations in the 1970s, however, the site was argued to have been a trading center controlling commerce in jade, obsidian, and other products, transported by canoe on the Motagua River. How could Quiriguá control river trade if it was so far from the river channel? The answer was provided by geoarchaeological study of buried soils and sediments. Commercial ditchdigging in areas adjacent to the site exposed sands and gravels consistent with an extinct river channel, and buried ground surfaces revealed a natural levee on which Quiriguá's buildings had been erected. Together, the location of channel sediments and the shape and location of the buried levee revealed an ancient Motagua River directly adjacent to Quiriguá. Not only had Quiriguá been constructed exactly along the river, but a silted-in basin in the heart of the site identified a possible docking area for the canoe travelers.

FEATURES

Features, like artifacts, owe their form to human intervention, so it is not surprising that analysis of features is similar to that for artifacts. Formal, stylistic, and technological analyses are all appropriate approaches to the study of features. As when dealing with artifacts, the archaeologist attempting to understand the significance of a particular feature makes use of provenience, association, and context. Two characteristics of features are particularly important in analysis: location and arrangement. Intact features directly reflect the original makers' and users' intentional placement, while the locations of artifacts are used to infer (by determination of context) whether a use-related placement has been preserved. Features are most valuable in understanding the distribution and organization of human activities, for they represent the facilities—the space and often some stationary equipment—with which these activities were carried out. Sometimes, of course, features are not intact and, as with artifacts, some interpretations can only be inferred. For example, when a multistory house collapses, features from the upper floors, such as hearths or grain-grinding bins (Fig. 6.14), may still be inferred from their disarrayed component parts, but the original form, placement, and arrangement of the feature can only be estimated.

We will discuss features in two categories that have behavioral implications: constructed features and cumulative features.

Constructed Features

Constructed features were built to provide space for some activity or set of activities. Examples range from simple windbreaks to elaborate houses (Fig. 6.15) and temples, from burials and tombs to roadways and fortification walls, and from artificial reservoirs and stone-lined hearths to agricultural terraces and irrigation canals. The important criterion is that there is some human construction that formally channels the ongoing use of space.

Classification and analysis of constructed features may involve examining attributes of form, style, technology, location, or some combination of these. Technological analysis includes consideration of the materials used in the construction and the ways these materials were put together. When complex architecture is involved, as with such imposing features as the Egyptian pyramids, intricate analysis is required. The technological analysis of such features usually yields data not only about the physical act of construction, such as the use of particular materials and the sequence of their incorporation in the growing structure, but also about related social aspects of the construction process. For instance, in the prehistoric Moche Valley in Peru, adobe bricks from large structures were marked with distinctive labels. Michael Moseley has concluded that each mark represents a separate group of brick producers (a little more than a hundred of these marks were identified). Each work force responsible for supplying a certain number of bricks could thus have verified that its proper contribution had indeed been made.

(a)

FIGURE 6.14

Features may often be
identified even after disturbance: (a) an intact
mealing bin, where
stones were set for
grinding grain, in a pre-
historic pueblo from the
southwestern United
States; (b) a feature presumed to be a collapsed
mealing bin, the distur-
bance seemingly result-
ing from destruction of
the building's roof or
upper story.

(b)

FIGURE 6.15

House 1 at Skara Brae, in the Orkney Islands of Scotland, provides a good illustration of features. Not only is the house itself a complex feature, but its furnishings are features, too, from the bed platforms in the upper left to the stone hearth at center and cupboard in the upper right.

Well-preserved structures can yield complex data about construction methods and materials. For example, among the oldest known roadways are wooden tracks built to cross wetlands, which have then helped preserve these features. The oldest known example, the Sweet Track in the Somerset Levels of southwest England, dates to about 4000 B.C. (Fig. 6.16). Its excavation has led to a wealth of information about technology, environment, and other aspects of life in the Neolithic, including a variety of preserved wooden implements dropped by people walking across the track and then preserved in the bog below.

Even seemingly simple constructed features can have great significance. For example, bedrock mortars of the western Sierra Nevada of California are roughly circular depressions, of various sizes, ground into granite outcrops or huge boulders. They and associated cobbles served as mortars and pestles, used to pulverize seeds and other plant materials. These features are known to have been used by women of the Mono and related Native American groups to prepare acorn flour and other food. Thomas L. Jackson's combined archaeological and ethnographic study shows that bedrock mortars are keys to understanding Mono society and economy. Archaeologists had previously argued that the variation in mortar depths was due to differential wear: the longer a mortar was used,

(a)   (b)

FIGURE 6.16

An artist's reconstruction (a) of the Sweet Track, in England, in use can be
compared with a photograph (b) of its archaeological traces as revealed
by excavation.

the deeper it got. Jackson questioned this conclusion, citing accounts of Mono
women who describe their mortars as being of three deliberately distinct depths,
each for a different phase in acorn processing. The location, spacing, and associations of the mortars also reflect deliberate decisions to accommodate annual
movements across the landscape to collect and process food. Because the mortars were made and owned by Mono women, the site distribution leads to a new
appreciation for the central role of women's activities and decision making in
structuring Mono life.

Internal arrangement, elaboration, and orientation of features are often
important attributes. A good example of this is the range of features now being
studied as astronomical observatories. In the 1960s Gerald Hawkins analyzed
the astronomical alignments found in the component parts of Stonehenge, interpreting the range of observations that could have been made from this Bronze
Age station. Although many of Hawkins's findings are now disputed, his work
led scholars to examine other monuments to see if their arrangements suggest

similar use. The kinds of features under investigation range from the Big Horn Medicine Wheel in northern Wyoming to entire community plans that may incorporate astronomical layouts.

Location of constructed features can also be informative for particular research questions. For example, location of burials in special mortuary structures or elite areas, such as the North Acropolis of Tikal, Guatemala, or the Great Pyramids of Egypt, may indicate special social status and privilege. Study of locations of these or other particular kinds of features may suggest factors involved in siting or placement decisions, such as preference for elevated ground or proximity to water sources in locations of houses. With the increased use of quantitative methods and with the adoption of analytical techniques from fields such as geography, archaeologists are beginning to study the attributes of different locations more thoroughly and to specify more rigorously whether the choices of location that we observe are due, in fact, to human preferences and decisions or to chance.

Cumulative Features

Cumulative features are those formed by accretion rather than by a preplanned or designed construction of an activity area or facility. Examples include middens, quarries (the result of subtraction of the exploited resource, sometimes accompanied by an accumulation of extracting tools), and workshop areas. We have already seen, in Chapter 5, how conjoining studies helped define a cumulative workshop feature at Koobi Fora.

Conjoining studies also aided interpretation of the features defined by some 16,000 lithic artifacts at Meer II, a 9000-year-old campsite in northern Belgium, dispersed vertically through nearly 50 centimeters of deposit. Enough of the lithics could be refitted, however, to see that this site was a single complex feature—and still essentially intact. Evidence on manufacturing sequences among the conjoinable pieces was used to show spatial relations between making and using the stone tools. When data were added concerning general debris density, hearth location, and wear patterns on the tools, a detailed map of overall activities could be created, defining a domestic area in the southwest, where hide processing and bone and antler working took place around a hearth. From wear patterns Daniel Cahan and Lawrence Keeley could even show that the bulk of the rough work was done by a right-handed person, with a left-hander working alongside for perhaps a shorter time.

Although stylistic analysis is rarely appropriate here, cumulative features can be analyzed according to attributes of form, location, and sometimes technology. Form attributes include size and content. Because we are dealing with accumulated entities, size can indicate either the duration or the intensity of use. For example, a midden will be larger if it is used for a long time or with great frequency in a short period of time. It is not always possible to distinguish the relative importance of these two factors in cumulative features. But, when available, long-term stratified middens are particularly valuable to the archaeologist because they yield evidence concerning the temporal span of occupation at a site.

Analysis of the location of cumulative features may give information on the distribution of ancient activities. For example, distribution of quarries relative to habitation sites might indicate how far people were willing to travel to obtain stone raw materials, and the location of workshop areas reveals the distribution of manufacturing activities within or among settlements.

Because they are unplanned accretions of artifacts and other materials, cumulative features have different technological attributes from constructed features. That is, even though cumulative features were not built, they may still yield technological information. For example, quarries may preserve extraction scars as well as abandoned mining tools; these may indicate various techniques used to mine raw materials. A study of the debris from stone-chipping stations may help in reconstructing the chipping technology, and artifacts from a midden—molds or bowl sherds containing unfired clay or pigments—may indicate the nearby presence of a pottery production area and aid in determining the technology involved in its use.

SUMMARY

Analysis of the three categories of archaeological data—artifacts, ecofacts, and features—is influenced by their physical characteristics, their state of preservation, and the specific questions being asked of the data.

Artifacts are divided into industries based on shared raw materials and manufacturing techniques. The industries most commonly encountered by archaeologists are those of stone (lithic) and fired clay (ceramic). Lithic industries involve subtractive production processes that often preserve evidence of the steps taken during manufacture. This makes technological analysis, especially with chipped-stone tools, a rewarding avenue of investigation. Functional analysis of lithic artifacts is also useful in reconstructing past activities when based on detectable wear and residues.

Ceramic industries, such as pottery, are made by additive processes that often destroy evidence of manufacturing steps, so that technological analysis is more difficult. But clay is a plastic and easily manipulated substance that can be shaped and decorated in a variety of ways, thus lending itself to stylistic classifications that define variations in both time and space. Pottery vessel shapes and the identification of residues are used to infer function as a means to reconstruct past activities.

Metal artifacts also possess characteristics that allow technological, stylistic, and functional analyses. Artifacts made from organic materials are usually classified by form as a basis for functional inferences. Constituent analyses of most kinds of artifacts can identify raw material sources and allow the reconstruction of past trade and distribution networks.

The various categories of ecofacts—plant, animal, human, and inorganic remains—can be analyzed to yield culturally meaningful information. Floral remains include both microspecimens (pollen and phytoliths) and macrospecimens (seeds, plant fragments, and impressions). Faunal remains include mummies, skeletal remains, and coprolites. Once identified as to species, both floral and faunal samples can yield information on ancient environments and subsistence activities, as well as medical and ritual behavior. Human remains provide direct evidence about ancient populations, including nutritional and health status, vital to understanding not only the past but also the present (as in the origins and evolution of human disease). Their study also raises significant ethical issues, expressed by a commitment to respect the concerns of living descendants of past peoples. The analysis of soils and sediments can yield clues to the presence or absence of past human activity, insight into the way sites were formed, and information about ancient land use and environments.

Features preserve in their form and location a record of the spatial distribution of past human activities. Some features are deliberately constructed to house activities; others represent cumulative activities (additive or subtractive) that modify the environment. Constructed features usually represent attempts to channel use of space. Their analysis allows reconstruction of past technologies, while their attributes of form and location yield inferences about ancient behavior and culture. In addition, variations in building or decorative style provide important markers of age or cultural identity. Cumulative features result from gradual accumulation of artifacts and ecofacts, as in workshops or middens, or progressive removal of materials, as in mines or quarries. Both provide important clues to ancient technology and other forms of behavior.

FOR FURTHER READING

ARTIFACTS
Andresen et al. 1981; Clark (1954) 1971; Crown and Hurst 2009; Drooker 2001; Gero 1991; Hastorf 2001; Hosler 1994; Keeley 1980; Knapp, Pigott, and Herbert 1998; Lambert 1997; Oakley 1956; Rice 1987, 1996a, 1996b, 1999; Sabloff 1975; Schick and Toth 2001; Schmidt 1997; Torrence 1989

ECOFACTS
Binford 1981; Hastorf and Johannessen 1991; Katzenberg and Harrison 1997; Klein and Cruz-Uribe 1984; Lambert 1997; Olsen 1964; Pearsall 1989; Reitz and Shackley 2012; Smith 2001; Stein and Farrand 2001; Weiner 2010; Wheat 1972; Williams-Thorpe and Thorpe 1992; Windes and McKenna 2001; Zeder 1999; Zeder, Buikstra, and van der Leeuw 2010

HUMAN REMAINS

Ambrose, Buikstra, and Krueger 2003; Bahn 2003; Blau and Ubelaker 2009; Boutin, Baadsgard, and Buikstra 2011; Boyd 1996; Buikstra 1981; Buikstra and Beck 2006; Geller 2008; Rakita, Buikstra, Beck, and Williams 2005; Verano and Ubelaker 1992; White 1990; Wing and Brown 1980; Zeder, Buikstra, and van der Leeuw 2010

FEATURES

Aveni 2000; Coles 1984, 1989; Coles and Coles 1986; David and Thomas 2008; Hawkins 1965; Hyslop 1984; Jackson 1991; Knapp, Pigott, and Herbert 1998; Steadman 1996; Stein and Farrand 2001; Van Noten, Cahan, and Keeley 1980

ADDITIONAL SOURCES

Cahan, Keeley, and Van Noten 1979; Crabtree 1972; DeNiro 1987; Farnsworth et al. 1985; Haviland 1967; Jovanovic 1980; Kolata 1987; Loy 1983; Moseley 1975; Potts and Shipman 1981; Toth 1987; van der Merwe and Avery 1982; Wertime and Wertime 1982

7

Dating the Past

To RECONSTRUCT THE PAST, we must define the time dimension. That is, we need to determine which remains are from the same period and which are from different periods. Only then can we examine behavior systems at specific points in time and trace how these systems change over time.

In this chapter, we discuss a few of the most important methods used by archaeologists to determine age and chronological sequence. It is important that each method has some limits or built-in inaccuracies. Thus, a chronology based on several different methods and many dated samples is more reliable than a sequence based on a single method or only a few dated samples.

Throughout much of its history, archaeology has emphasized methods for establishing the age and proper sequence for past remains. As a result, archaeologists now have a variety of ways to determine the age of this evidence. Recent advances in chemistry and nuclear physics have greatly expanded the inventory of available dating techniques, freeing archaeologists from much of the traditional work of determining the age of their evidence. Because of the radiocarbon revolution in the 1950s and a host of newer age-determination methods, the archaeologist today can focus research on behavior-oriented studies rather than chronological issues.

Before we discuss specific techniques, however, we should consider a few basic definitions. First, **direct dating** uses analysis of the artifact, ecofact, or feature itself to arrive at its age. **Indirect dating** uses analysis of material associated with the artifact, ecofact, or feature being studied to evaluate its age. For example, organic remains found in a tomb might be dated directly by the radiocarbon method (discussed later in this chapter); other artifacts found in the same tomb and the tomb

TABLE 7.1

Major Archaeological Dating Techniques

RELATIVE METHODS	ABSOLUTE METHODS
Seriation	Obsidian hydration
Sequence comparison	Dendrochronology
Stratigraphy	Radiometric (radiocarbon,
Geochronology	potassium-argon, etc.)
Bone chemistry	Archaeomagnetic

itself could then be dated indirectly by assigning them the same age as the organic material with which they were associated. Of course, the reliability of indirect dating depends on the security of the context—in this case, the evidence that the organics and the other materials were deposited at the same time.

The second distinction is that between relative and absolute (also called chronometric) dating techniques (Table 7.1). **Relative dating** refers simply to evaluating the age of one item relative to other items—for example, determining that artifact A is older than artifact B. In relative dating, actual ages are not assigned to data. **Absolute dating** refers to placing the age of a sample on an absolute time scale, usually a calendrical system (for example, determining that artifact A was used ca. 400–300 B.C.). Although absolute methods assign an age in years, they are seldom precise. Instead, as our example indicates, most absolute methods assign an age expressed as a range in years and often include a statement of the degree of statistical probability that the true age of the sample falls within that range (expressed by a "±" symbol).

The most precise dating is possible with artifacts or features inscribed with calendrical notations, even if these refer to a calendar different from the one in use today. For instance, most coins minted during the Roman Empire refer to a specific year in the reign of a particular emperor. And in the Americas, most monuments carved by the Maya of the Classic Period (ca. A.D. 250–900) are inscribed with dates in their calendrical system. In both of these cases, the ancient calendrical system can be correlated to our own, so that the Roman and Maya notations can be assigned a date in our system—in some cases, down to the month and day. This dating can, in turn, be used for indirect absolute dates for materials associated with such calendrical inscriptions.

A series of relative or absolute dates arranged in order of their age defines chronological sequences. These sequences provide time frameworks used to organize all subsequent data. Establishing these sequences is crucial since they enable archaeologists to reconstruct the order of ancient events. In many areas of the world, these sequences are well defined, so newly discovered data can be placed in the existing scheme. In other areas, however, basic chronologies have yet to be established.

1900 1910 1920 1930 1940 1950 1960 1970 1980 1990 2000

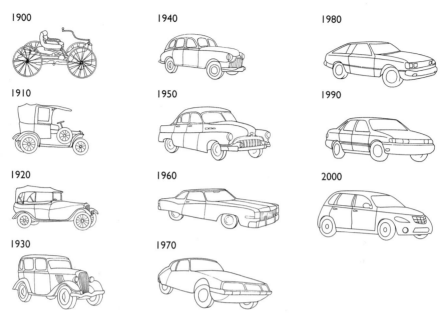

FIGURE 7.1

Gradual changes in design are clearly evidenced in familiar aspects of our own culture, such as automobiles.

SERIATION

Patterns of human behavior change continually, and as behavior changes, so do the material products associated with that behavior. We have all observed how changes in design and style alter familiar objects in our society. Many of us can identify the trends of change well enough to place any particular item in its approximate time period. For instance, when shown automobiles of varying ages, many of us can arrange them in rough chronological sequence (Fig. 7.1); similar sequential changes are noticeable in clothing styles, art, music, and so on.

The artifacts and features of past societies also exhibit changes over time, and by observing and studying their attributes, archaeologists can discover the trends. By identifying the attributes that change most rapidly, the archaeologist can construct a sequence that will most accurately reflect the passage of time. Surface decorative or stylistic attributes usually shift most rapidly and tend to be the best chronological indicators because they are least affected by functional or technological requirements. For example, a water storage jar must be deep enough to hold water and should have a restricted mouth to lessen evaporation and reduce spills, but it can be any color or design. Artifacts made from such plastic materials as clay or metal are usually good sources for deriving temporal sequences because they can be decorated in a variety of ways.

ARBITRARY SEQUENCE DATES

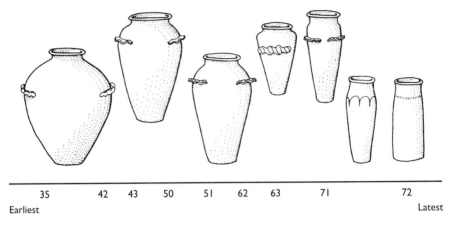

| 35 | 42 | 43 | 50 | 51 | 62 | 63 | 71 | 72 |

Earliest   Latest

FIGURE 7.2

One of the earliest applications of stylistic seriation was Petrie's chronological ordering of tombs at Diospolis Parva, Egypt, based on changes in associated pottery vessels.

Seriation is a relative dating method derived from these cultural regularities. It refers to a variety of techniques that seek to order artifacts in a series so that adjacent members in the series are more similar than members farther apart in the series. Seriation has two basic applications: (1) stylistic seriation and (2) frequency seriation.

Stylistic Seriation

Stylistic seriation is a technique for ordering artifacts and attributes according to similarity in style. The variation may reflect either temporal change or spatial distance; the archaeologist must determine which factor (or both) was involved in each situation. Generally, the more limited the source area of the artifacts in question, the more likely the seriation reflects the passage of time.

One of the first studies to use stylistic seriation was the Diospolis Parva sequence outlined by Sir Flinders Petrie at the close of the 19th century. Petrie was faced with a series of pottery jars from predynastic Egyptian tombs that were not linked stratigraphically (dating by stratigraphy is discussed later in the chapter). He ordered the pottery by shape and ranked their similarities by using a series of numbers (Fig. 7.2). The numbers, of course, did not refer to age in years, but indicated instead the relative age of each jar within the seriation. This technique allowed Petrie to organize the pottery chronologically and, by association, to order the sequence of tombs as well.

Petrie's study also shows that the archaeologist cannot assume that the trend of change always implies progress as our own culture defines that term. In the Diospolis Parva sequence, for example, vessel handles began as functional attributes and ended as decorative lines mimicking handles. Thus, for a sequence to be valid, the archaeologist must ensure that it is free from presumptions of progress, increasing complexity, or other ethnocentric biases. Of course, one must also have some idea which end of the resulting seriation is the earlier and which the later. In most cases, links with other dating methods (usually absolute) will provide this information.

Frequency Seriation

Frequency seriation orders the sequence of sites or deposits by studying the relative frequencies of their artifact types. This is based on the assumption that the frequency of each artifact type follows a predictable career, from the time of its origin to an expanding popularity and finally to total disuse. The length of time and the degree of popularity (frequency) vary with each type, but when presented diagrammatically most examples form one or more lenslike patterns known as **battleship-shaped curves.** The validity of this pattern has been verified by plotting the frequencies of artifact types from long-term stratified deposits and by testing historically documented examples. The best-known historical test, by James Deetz and Edwin N. Dethlefsen, involved dated tombstones from 18th- and early-19th-century New England. This study demonstrated that the popularity of various decorative motifs on headstones did indeed show battleship-shaped distribution curves over time (Fig. 7.3).

SEQUENCE COMPARISON

If seriation cannot be used for the artifacts being studied, the archaeologist has another recourse. If other well-documented artifact sequences exist in the geographical area being investigated, the artifact classes in question may be compared to those already defined from nearby sites and placed into a corresponding temporal order. This is **sequence comparison** (also known as cross-dating), which presumes the existence of past cultural connections, such as trade, so that the resemblances are not accidental. But even if such connections can be documented, there is no guarantee that two similar types are exactly the same age. The work of Deetz and Dethlefsen, for example, showed that even among neighboring colonial communities, the time ranges for particular tombstone motifs were rather variable. Because of these difficulties, the comparative method is usually the weakest means for inferring a local chronological sequence; it is generally used only when other means are impossible.

Sequence comparison is very useful, however, for building broad chronologies for a region. By matching sequences already established for individual sites or regions, archaeologists produce the time-space grids important to the reconstruction of culture history (see Chapter 3), allowing the identification of trends in cultural change and stability across broad expanses of space and time.

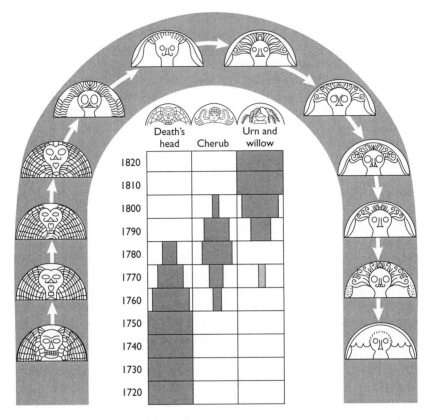

FIGURE 7.3

A study of dated New England tombstones shows the changes in popularity of particular styles depicted by width of the bar graphs ("battleship-shaped curves"), and it supports assumptions used in both stylistic seriation and frequency seriation. The outer ring shows the gradual change in one motif, the death's head.

STRATIGRAPHY

The age of archaeological materials can sometimes be assessed by their association with geological deposits or formations. Often these assessments are relative, as in cases based on superposition, where materials in lower strata were deposited earlier than those in higher strata. As discussed in Chapter 5, **stratigraphy** refers to the archaeological interpretation of the significance of stratification. Archaeological stratigraphy may represent a combination of both behavioral and natural transformation processes (as in a midden composed of alternating strata of cultural materials in primary context and redeposited alluvium). As long as the context—and, therefore, the temporal order—of a stratified deposit is clear, the archaeologist can use stratigraphy to determine the relative age of the deposition of artifacts and other materials in the deposit.

GEOCHRONOLOGY

Many methods have been developed for determining the age of geological formations. Because the earth existed for billions of years before humans appeared, however, only a few techniques of **geochronology** apply to the relatively recent span of archaeological deposits. Often these assessments are relative, based on stratigraphy. But when geologists have determined the absolute age of geological formations using radiometric or other techniques (discussed shortly), the archaeologist can, in turn, assign an indirect date to artifacts found in these matrices.

The effects of long-term geological processes, such as glacial advance and retreat or fluctuations in land and sea levels, can sometimes be quite useful in dating archaeological remains. Again, if the chronology of the geological events is known, associated archaeological materials can be fit into that scheme. For example, the successive post-Pleistocene shorelines at Cape Krusenstern, Alaska, provided J. Louis Giddings with a means of ordering sites chronologically. As the beach expanded seaward over time, people continued to locate their camps near its high-water limit. In this progression, the younger beaches—and, by association, the more recent sites—are those located closer to the current beachfront. More than 100 old beach lines are discernible at Cape Krusenstern, representing some 5000 years of accumulation (Fig. 7.4). Through this relative sequence— which some have called **horizontal stratigraphy**—Giddings arranged the sites in temporal order. By applying other dating techniques, he then converted the relative dating to an absolute scheme.

OBSIDIAN HYDRATION

In 1960, Irving Friedman and Robert L. Smith announced a new age-determination technique called **obsidian hydration,** based on the cumulative adsorption of water by volcanic glass. Over time, the adsorbed water forms a hydration layer on the exposed surfaces of obsidian (Fig. 7.5). The thickness of this layer is measured in microns (1 micron = 0.001 mm) and is detectable microscopically. Since the hydration layer penetrates deeper into the surface over time, the thickness of this layer can be used to determine how long the surface has been exposed. In other words, the age of manufacture or use—either of which could fracture the obsidian, exposing a new surface for hydration—can

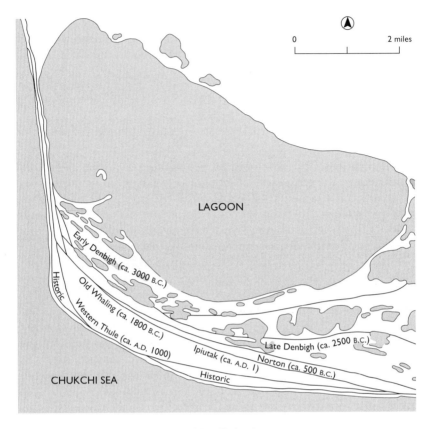

LAGOON

CHUKCHI SEA

Early Denbigh (ca. 3000 B.C.)

Historic

Old Whaling (ca. 1800 B.C.)

Western Thule (ca. A.D. 1000)

Ipiutak (ca. A.D. 1)

Historic

Late Denbigh (ca. 2500 B.C.)

Norton (ca. 500 B.C.)

0   2 miles

FIGURE 7.4

This map of Cape Krusenstern, Alaska, emphasizes some of the series of ancient beach ridges that have been related to particular periods of occupation during the last 5000 years.

be calculated if the rate of hydration is known. Once this rate is established, the thickness of the hydration layer from any obsidian sample can be compared to a chronological conversion table to provide the sample's age.

Since the method was originally applied, issues have emerged that create problems for determining reliable dates. First, the hydration rate varies with the composition of the obsidian, which differs from one source deposit to another. Second, the hydration rate also changes in response to temperature variations of the matrix in which the obsidian was deposited. Because of these variations, obsidian hydration dating has proved less reliable as an absolute method and more useful as a relative method—dating obsidian samples within a single site or region in relation to one another. But as long as its limitations are known, obsidian hydration can still be a simple and inexpensive means for directly dating obsidian artifacts.

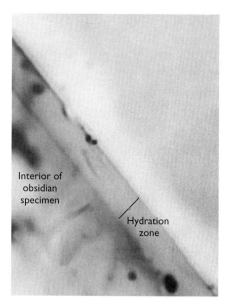

Interior of
obsidian
specimen

Hydration
zone

FIGURE 7.5

In this magnified view, a 3μ
(3-micron)-wide hydration
zone appears as a wide band
at the edge of the obsidian.

FLORAL AND FAUNAL METHODS

There are several methods based on floral and faunal remains that can provide either direct or indirect dates for archaeologists. We will discuss two of the most familiar techniques.

Dendrochronology

Dendrochronology, or tree-ring dating, is the best-known method of directly determining absolute age for wood. This approach is based on counting the annual growth rings in the cross-sections of cut trees. As early as 1848, E. G. Squier and E. H. Davis (see Chapter 2) determined the minimum age of mounds in the Mississippi River Valley from the age of the oldest trees growing on them. Assuming that trees would not be allowed to grow on earthen constructions while they were in use, they reasoned that if the oldest tree growing on these mounds were 300 years old, the site itself would have to be at least three centuries old.

The modern method of dendrochronology involves a refinement of tree-ring counts. It uses the cross-linkage of tree-ring growth patterns among a series of trees to extend a sequence of growth cycles into the past, far beyond the lifetime of a single tree (Fig. 7.6). Because of this, as we will see, dendrochronology has become the critical means to calibrate radiocarbon dates. The compilation of a long-term sequence of tree-ring growth patterns was first established by astronomer A. E. Douglass, working in the southwestern United States in the early 20th century. Douglass's original research was aimed at relating

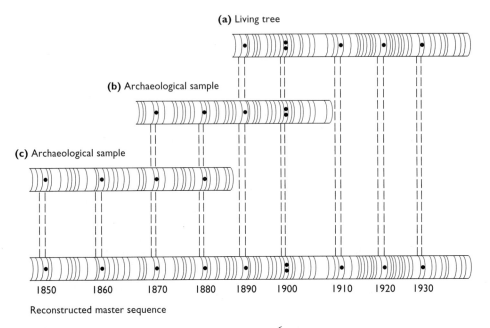

(a) Living tree

(b) Archaeological sample

(c) Archaeological sample

| 1850 | 1860 | 1870 | 1880 | 1890 | 1900 | 1910 | 1920 | 1930 |

Reconstructed master sequence

FIGURE 7.6

A master dendrochronological sequence is built by linking successively older specimens, often beginning with living trees (a) that overlap with archaeological samples (b, c), based on matching patterns of thick and thin rings. Provided the sequence is long enough, specimens of unknown age can be dated by comparison with the master sequence. The rings are marked with dots at 10-year intervals for ease of reading.

past climatic cycles—as reflected in patterns of wider and narrower tree-ring growth—to sunspot cycles. Although variations in tree-ring growth do provide valuable clues to past climatic cycles, the added benefit in establishing an absolute chronological sequence for archaeology was soon realized. By counting back from a known starting point and matching patterns of rings from trees with overlapping lifetimes, the tree-ring sequence could be projected back for thousands of years. Then a given tree segment from an archaeological context could be dated by matching its ring pattern to the known sequence. The longest tree-ring sequences are those of oak trees in Germany (some 9500 years) and bristlecone pines in southeastern California (more than 10,000 years and discussed further later on).

Although potentially useful anywhere that trees were used by prehistoric peoples, dendrochronology has been applied in only a few parts of the world, notably in the southwestern United States, Alaska, northern Mexico, Germany,

Norway, Great Britain, the eastern Mediterranean, and Switzerland. The method is limited by its dependence on four conditions that cannot be met everywhere:

1. The species must produce well-defined annual rings and be sensitive to minute variations in climatic cycles. Many species of trees cannot be used because they produce roughly uniform rings regardless of climate changes.
2. The ring-growth variation must depend primarily upon one environmental factor, such as temperature or soil humidity.
3. The prehistoric population must have made extensive use of timbers, especially in construction.
4. Cultural and environmental conditions must allow for good preservation of timbers in archaeological contexts.

Dendrochronology determines the date a tree was cut down by placing its last or outermost growth ring within a local sequence. If the outermost ring is missing from the sample, the exact cutting date cannot be assessed. Even with a cutting date, the validity of a dendrochronological date depends on correct evaluation of the archaeological context and association of the timber. Specimens that form parts of construction features—and thus are in primary context—are more reliable. Even so, Bryant Bannister has listed four types of errors in interpreting tree-ring dates:

1. The wood may have been reused, and so its cutting date would be older than the construction in which it was used.
2. The use of the feature—such as a house—may have extended well beyond its construction date, so that the timber's cutting date would be much older than the final use or abandonment of the house.
3. The replacement of old, weakened timbers by newer, stronger ones may have resulted in the wood being younger than the original construction.
4. Wooden artifacts or ecofacts found within a feature—such as furniture or charcoal in a house—may be *either younger or older* than the building's construction date.

To help offset these problems, the archaeologist tries to recover multiple samples for dendrochronological analysis. The dates from the various specimens can then be used to check one another. Good agreement among several samples from the same feature makes accurate dating far more likely.

Bone Chemistry

Bone chemistry techniques enable the archaeologist to see if bones found in the same matrix were indeed deposited together. Bone buried in the same deposit will lose organic components, principally nitrogen, and gain inorganic components, such as fluorine and uranium, at steady rates. Since the rates of nitrogen

TABLE 7.2

Fluorine, Nitrogen, and Uranium Content
of Piltdown and Related Bones

REMAINS	PERCENTAGE OF FLUORINE	PERCENTAGE OF NITROGEN	URANIUM PARTS PER MILLION
Fresh bone	0.03	4.0	0
Piltdown fossil elephant molar	2.7	—	610
Piltdown cranium	0.1	1.4	1
Piltdown jaw	0.03	3.9	0

SOURCE: *After Oakley 1970, Table B, p. 41.*

loss and fluorine gain differ because of varying local environmental conditions (temperature and humidity), the rates vary from one deposit to another. Thus, these rates can be used to determine only relative dates—that is, to show that one bone is older than another from the same deposit. They cannot be used to establish absolute dates.

The classic applications of these relative dating techniques involved human skeletal remains of disputed antiquity, the most dramatic of which was the exposure of the great Piltdown hoax. The Piltdown finds, unearthed between 1911 and 1915, revealed an apelike mandible (jawbone) apparently paired with a modern-looking human cranium. The two were anatomically mismatched overall, but the apparent geological association, combined with the uniformly discolored appearance of age in all the bones and some humanlike traits in the otherwise apelike jaw, convinced all but a few disbelievers that Piltdown Man represented a significant new discovery that altered conceptions about the course of human evolution. The skeptics held out, however, and finally prevailed. In 1950, Kenneth Oakley tested the bones for fluorine content and later for nitrogen; he found that the mandible was much younger than the cranium (Table 7.2). Uranium tests reinforced these findings. On further examination, the apparently human traits of the mandible and its discoloration were shown to be due to deliberate alteration of a modern ape jaw.

RADIOMETRIC METHODS

Several age-determination techniques exploit the principle of radioactive decay, the transformation of unstable radioactive isotopes into stable elements. These are all termed **radiometric** methods. Although they can sometimes be used to date archaeological materials directly, they more frequently provide indirect age determinations. Because the radiometric technique most commonly used by

TABLE 7.3

Half-Lives and Utility Ranges of Selected Radioactive Isotopes

ISOTOPES	HALF-LIFE (IN YEARS)	LIMITS OF USEFULNESS FOR ARCHAEOLOGICAL DATING
$^{14}C \rightarrow {}^{14}N$ (radiocarbon) (Cambridge half-life)	5730 ± 40	Particle counts: up to 40,000–50,000 years AMS: up to 100,000 years
$^{234}U \rightarrow {}^{230}Th$ and ^{231}Pa (uranium-series)	ca. 75,200	50,000–500,000 years
$^{40}K \rightarrow {}^{40}Ar$ (potassium–argon)	1.3 billion ± 40 million (.04 × 10⁹)	100,000 years and older
$^{238}U \rightarrow {}^{206}Pb$ (fission-track)	ca. 4.5 billion	Generally 100,000 years and older

archaeologists is radiocarbon dating, the discussion here emphasizes this particular technique. Most other radiometric techniques are applicable to extremely long time spans (Table 7.3), beyond the time range of human existence, and are used mainly by geologists to determine the age of geological formations.

The physical properties of radioactive decay can be used for dating purposes if three facts are known: (1) the original amount of the radioactive isotope present at the onset of decay, (2) the amount now present, and (3) the rate of radioactive decay. In most cases, the first factor is computed indirectly. The amount of the radioactive isotope now present is counted directly. Since the decay of any unstable isotope is a random process, it does not produce a steady rate of decay; it is possible, however, to calculate the statistical probability that a certain proportion of the isotope will decay within a given time (Fig. 7.7). This rate is usually expressed as the **half-life** of the isotope—the period required for one half of the unstable atoms to decay and form a stable daughter isotope. The half-life of any radioactive isotope represents not a fixed rate, but rather a statistical average with a specified range of error.

Radiocarbon

Radiocarbon dating is the most important radiometric technique for archaeologists. Radiocarbon (^{14}C) is produced in our upper atmosphere by constant cosmic ray bombardment. As carbon dioxide ($^{14}CO_2$), it is distributed throughout the atmosphere, with most of it absorbed in the earth's oceans (Fig. 7.8). Only about 1 percent is absorbed into living creatures; it enters plants through photosynthesis and animals when they eat plants. Thus, all living things constantly

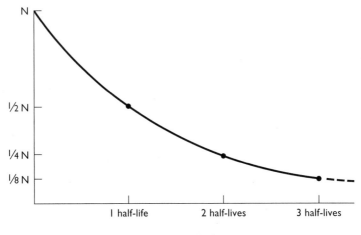

FIGURE 7.7

The decay rate of a radioactive isotope is expressed by its half-life, or the period after which half the radioactive isotopes will have decayed into stabler forms. After two half-lives, only one quarter of the original amount of radioactive isotopes will remain, and by the end of the third half-life, only one eighth ($\frac{1}{2} \times \frac{1}{2} \times \frac{1}{2}$) will remain radioactive.

take in both ordinary carbon (^{12}C) and radioactive carbon (^{14}C) throughout their lifetimes. The proportion of ^{14}C to ^{12}C in an organism remains constant until its death. At that point, no further ^{14}C is taken in, and the amount present begins to decrease through radioactive decay. The rate of this decay process is measured by the half-life of ^{14}C (about 5700 years; see Fig. 7.7 and Table 7.3). The measurement of the amount of ^{14}C still present (and emitting radiation) allows the dating of the sample by calculating the length of time elapsed since the death of the plant or animal providing the sample.

Any archaeological specimen of organic origin is a candidate for direct radiocarbon dating. Charcoal from burned materials, such as is found in ancient hearths or fire pits, is most commonly used, but unburned organic materials such as bone collagen, wood, seeds, shells, and leather—and even the carbon in worked iron—can also be dated. Most of these latter materials require larger sample amounts, however, because they contain a smaller proportion of carbon.

In the original method developed in the late 1940s by Willard F. Libby, the amount of ^{14}C is detected by Geiger counters, used to measure the rate of decay emissions from a sample, usually for a period of 24 hours or more. A method based on accelerator mass spectrometry (AMS) technology enables the physicist to more efficiently measure the amount of ^{14}C in an archaeological sample. The AMS method counts the ^{14}C isotopes after they have been separated from all other isotopes and molecules in the sample. This allows dates from much smaller

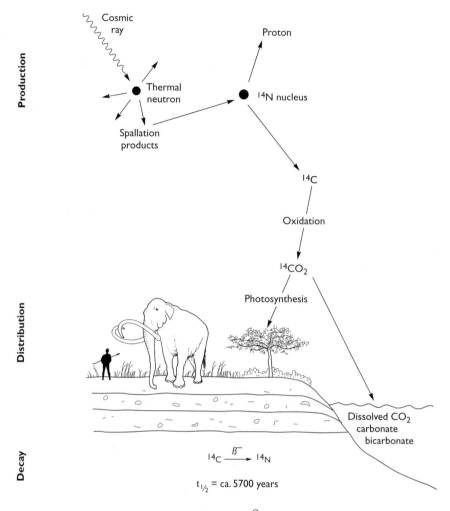

FIGURE 7.8

This diagram illustrates the production, distribution, and decay of ^{14}C.

samples and can be done in far less time (several minutes per sample, compared to several days or even weeks for the particle counting method). In some cases, the AMS method can extend the range of radiocarbon dates further into the past (see Table 7.3) and increase the precision of radiocarbon dates.

Radiocarbon age determination has revolutionized archaeological dating. It provided the first means of relating dates and sequences on a worldwide basis, because, unlike other methods available at the time, it did not rely on local conditions. The great wave of enthusiasm led, however, to uncritical acceptance of and overconfidence in the precision of radiocarbon dates. Although it is still the most popular method and among the most useful of all dating techniques available to the archaeologist, it does have a number of limitations.

The limitations begin with the archaeologist. Any radiocarbon date is only as meaningful as the evaluation of the archaeological context from which it derives. Organic samples from disturbed or secondary contexts can furnish dates, but these often have no bearing on the ages of associated materials. To use radiocarbon to date associated materials indirectly, the archaeologist must establish that all were deposited together.

The second limitation derives from the small amount of ^{14}C available for detection. The third is the built-in statistical uncertainty inherent in all radiometric techniques, since both the decay rate *and* the half-life are averages. Thus, a radiocarbon age expressed as 3220 ± 50 years **B.P.** (before present) does *not* mean that the analyzed sample died 3220 years ago; rather, it means that there is a 67 percent probability that the original organism died sometime in the 100-year span between 3170 and 3270 years before A.D. 1950 (the arbitrary zero date used in all radiocarbon analyses). The probability that a reported range includes the right date can be improved to 97 percent by doubling the range of error—in this case to 200 years, or 100 years on either side of the central date.

A fourth limitation to the radiocarbon technique is the fluctuation of past levels of ^{14}C on earth, detected by measurements of radiocarbon dates for wood samples with ages determined by dendrochronology. Radiocarbon age determinations before 1500 B.C. furnish dates that are increasingly out of line (Fig. 7.9). At 1500 B.C., radiocarbon dates are about 150 years too recent; by 4000 B.C., they are about 700 years too young. The solution to this problem has emerged from dendrochronology. Extensive radiocarbon testing of known-age samples of wood has yielded a calibration formula, which allows a date calculated in radiocarbon years to be corrected to a more accurate time value. The correction tables are limited by our ability to secure known-age samples of wood; but use of the oldest living tree, the bristlecone pine found in southeastern California, has enabled scientists to extend the correction range further back in time.

Colin Renfrew termed the original radiocarbon dating method the "first radiocarbon revolution," because it gave archaeologists a uniform means to develop absolute chronologies anywhere in the world. The revisions and refinements to the original method produced the second radiocarbon revolution, especially the dendrochronological calibrations that revised many radiocarbon dates. A third radiocarbon revolution has resulted from advances in AMS dating and improvements in calibrating dates, so that the corrected time scale for ^{14}C dates has been extended at least another 3000 years into the past (to ca. 11,300 B.P.).

Before radiocarbon dating was available, archaeologists used dating techniques based on stylistic and form comparisons to interrelate European and Southwest Asian sequences. Whenever a question arose as to the source of an Old World invention or innovation—such as copper metallurgy or the construction of megalithic (monumental stone) tombs—it was assumed to have come from Southwest Asia to Europe. The first sets of radiocarbon dates seemed to

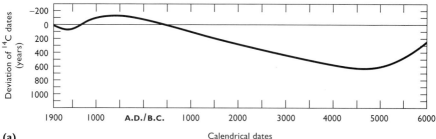

(a)

(b)

FIGURE 7.9

(a) The discrepancy between the ideal ^{14}C chronological scale (straight line) and a plotted series of samples, dated by radiocarbon analysis, whose ages were independently determined by dendrochronology is due to past fluctuations in the amount of ^{14}C on earth. (b) The bristlecone pine, found in the White Mountains of California, is the longest-living tree species known and is the key to increasing the accuracy of age determinations using the radiocarbon method.

support these assumptions. However, calibrated radiocarbon dates indicate that many archaeological remains, such as megalithic constructions, once thought to be the result of Southwest Asian influence actually occurred earlier in Europe!

Potassium-Argon

Potassium-argon dating is based on the radioactive decay of a rare isotope of potassium (^{40}K) to form argon (^{40}Ar) gas. The half-life of ^{40}K is 1.31 billion years, but the method can be used to date materials as recent as 100,000 years old. The technique is used principally to determine ages for geological formations that contain potassium. The basic principles of radiometric age determination, already described for the radiocarbon method, are used with rock samples to measure the ratio of ^{40}K to ^{40}Ar.

The K-Ar technique has been particularly helpful in dating geological formations associated with the remains of fossil hominids (human ancestors) and Lower Paleolithic tools. When Mary and Louis Leakey found the remains of *Zinjanthropus*, an early hominid (now included in the genus *Australopithecus*), they were able to assign the bones an age of about 1.75 million years on the basis of K-Ar dating of the volcanic strata in which the remains were found.

Argon-Argon

Argon-argon dating is a refinement of the K-Ar method that allows several age determinations to be made from each sample, thus increasing the reliability of the date and producing more accurate results from smaller samples. Dates are determined by measurements of argon isotope ratios in mineral samples without requiring separate measurements of potassium content as in K-Ar dates. Ar-Ar dating has corrected many of the original K-Ar dates from East Africa. For example, Ar-Ar dating has revised the age of *Zinjanthropus* back to 1.98 million years. Early hominid finds in the Lake Turkana/Omo Valley area on the border between Kenya and Ethiopia, once dated to over 2 million years by K-Ar dating, have been revised to 1.88 million years by Ar-Ar. The Ar-Ar method also has been used to show that some of the earliest-known hominid fossils found in Ethiopia date between 3.4 and 4.4 million years.

Uranium-Series

Uranium-series dating is based on the half-lives of a few uranium isotopes that are short enough to be useful to archaeology (see Table 7.3). U-series dating based on ^{230}Th, an isotope of ^{234}U, can date the formation of calcite deposits in caves, springs, and lakes. When such deposits are associated with archaeological remains, U-series methods can provide indirect absolute dates by measuring the ratio of ^{230}Th to ^{234}U. Calcite formations in a series of European Paleolithic cave sites have been dated by U-series methods to furnish absolute dates for associated Paleolithic bones and tools.

Fission-Track

Fission-track dating is similar to other radiometric methods, except that instead of being based on the counts of daughter isotope particles, it is based on the number of fission tracks preserved in a mineral sample. Fission tracks are the scars left by fission particles produced by the decay of trace elements like ^{238}U as they pass through a mineral. The age of a given mineral deposit can be determined by counting the number of fission tracks it contains. A number of fission-track dates have been consistent with Ar-Ar dates for geological deposits used to date early hominid finds from Ethiopia, thus increasing confidence in both methods.

ARCHAEOMAGNETISM

Dating by **archaeomagnetism** relies upon the fact that the earth's magnetic field varies over time, shifting in the horizontal plane (expressed as *declination* angle) as well as vertically (expressed by the *dip* angle). The course of these shifts over the past few centuries has been determined from compass readings preserved in historical records. This changing magnetic course can be extended back in time by the analysis of mineral compounds, such as clay, that contain iron particles that align to magnetic north when clay is heated above its *curie* point, the temperature at which the particles lose their magnetic orientation. When the minerals cool again, the new magnetic alignment of the iron particles is frozen in the clay body. Thus, if a sample of baked clay is not disturbed, it will preserve the angles of dip and declination from the time when it was heated. By using known-age samples of fired clay, such as hearths dated by radiocarbon associations, archaeologists have traced the location of the magnetic pole into the past. When enough cross-dated archaeomagnetic samples have been analyzed, the variations in dip and declination can be matched to a time scale, thus allowing newly discovered fired-clay samples to be dated directly, using the archaeomagnetic data alone (Fig. 7.10).

LIMITED AND EXPERIMENTAL METHODS

There are numerous dating methods beyond those we have discussed, and new techniques are being developed all the time. Most of these are less frequently used or more limited in their application than are the ones considered here. Nonetheless, some of these additional methods are well established and accurate, such as calendrical dating (using deciphered ancient calendars) and varve analysis (using strata deposited annually in lakes by retreating glaciers).

Several others have great potential to directly date archaeological materials but remain experimental and under development to improve their accuracy and usefulness. Such methods include electron spin resonance (ESR), used to date

(a)   **(b)**

FIGURE 7.10

Age determinations can be made based on archaeomagnetism. (a) Careful collection and recording in the field are essential. One sample has been removed and preserved in the small square container to the left (above the leveling device); another is about to be removed. (b) The specialist measures and analyzes magnetic alignments in the laboratory later by replicating the original orientation of the sample.

teeth and shell; thermoluminescence (TL), for burned flint and pottery, as well as to identify clay sources; optically stimulated luminescence (OSL), for stones in buildings; and aspartic acid racemization, used to date bone.

ESR has been used to date samples of Neanderthal tooth enamel from several cave sites in Israel. Some of these dates have been consistent with TL dates from burned flint found at the same sites although others have been too scattered and divergent to be useful. But ESR still holds great promise as a direct absolute method for dating teeth. Because of lack of consistent accurate results, TL dates are used to authenticate pottery suspected of being recently manufactured fakes, since the method can readily distinguish recently fired pottery from authentic ancient samples. Aspartic acid racemization can be used for relative dates of bone from the same site. It is sometimes useful for gaining absolute dates from eggshells and land snail shells.

SUMMARY

Control over the dimension of time is crucial; reconstruction of the past depends on the archaeologist's ability to distinguish contemporaneous and sequential events. Various techniques are used to determine the age of recovered data, either directly (by dating the artifact, ecofact, or feature itself) or indirectly (by association with other remains that can be dated). Absolute dating refers to age in calendrical years or years before present (B.P.). Relative dating refers to age in relation to another date (older, younger, or the same age).

Archaeologists have long used relative dating techniques based on provenience, such as stratigraphy, or based on the characteristics of recovered remains, such as stylistic or frequency seriation. Geological associations may also provide dates for archaeological evidence, as in use of geochronological sequences. Obsidian hydration yields direct dates for obsidian artifacts based on hydration rates. Floral and faunal remains can be dated by several means, including absolute age from tree-ring sequences (dendrochronology) and relative age from the detection of chemical changes in bones. Radiometric methods provide absolute dates based on the radioactive decay of unstable isotopes; the most useful method, radiocarbon dating, relies on an isotope of carbon (^{14}C) present in all living tissue. Potassium-argon and argon-argon dating determine the age of some geological deposits and can provide indirect dates for associated archaeological remains. Other indirect radiometric methods include uranium-series dating, used to date calcite deposits associated with archaeological materials, and fission-track dating, used to date minerals found with archaeological remains. Traces of ancient magnetism, preserved in features such as hearths, can be dated by correlation to magnetic sequences (archaeomagnetism) of known age.

Some methods, such as calendrical correlations and varve dating, have limited but very precise dating applications, as both relative and absolute methods. Others continue to be developed as absolute methods, such as electron spin resonance for dating teeth and shells, and thermoluminescence for dating burned flint and pottery. A relative dating method, aspartic acid racemization, can be used to directly date bone.

New and improved methods continue to be developed. But all archaeological dating techniques have some limiting factors. While the various methods of age determination can lead to accurate control of the time dimension for archaeological data, archaeologists must be aware of each method's limits and, whenever possible, compensate for inaccuracies by applying two or more methods as cross-checks to produce an internally consistent chronological sequence.

FOR FURTHER READING

SERIATION
  Blinman 2000; Deetz and Dethlefsen 1967; Petrie 1901

STRATIGRAPHY
  Harris 1989; Rapp and Hill 1998; Stein 2000

GEOCHRONOLOGY
  Giddings 1967; Rapp and Hill 1998

OBSIDIAN HYDRATION
  Beck and Jones 2000; Friedman and Trembour 1983; Friedman et al. 1997; Michels 1973

FLORAL AND FAUNAL METHODS
Baillie 1995; Nash 2000a; Oakley 1970; Towner 2000

RADIOMETRIC METHODS
Hedges and Gowlett 1986; Michael 1985; Renfrew 1971, 1973; Taylor 2000; Taylor and Aitken 1997; Weiner 2010

ARCHAEOMAGNETISM
Eighmy 2000; Sternberg 1997; Wolfman 1984

ADDITIONAL SOURCES
Aitken 1990; Bannister 1970; Biscott and Rosenbauer 1981; Feathers 2000; Nash 2000b; Orme 1982; Ramenofsky and Steffen 1998; Sharer 2006; Taylor and Aitken 1997; Zeuner 1958

8

Reconstructing the Past

Now THAT WE HAVE described how archaeologists control the time dimension of their data, we can consider the ways data are used to reconstruct the past. Here we move from analysis, or gaining information by breaking down the data into their component parts and analyzing their relationships, to interpretation, or putting these elements back together to form a meaningful reconstruction that addresses the research goals.

There is no definite line between analysis and interpretation. As we noted in discussing research design in Chapter 4, the collection and analysis of archaeological data often overlap in time, and the archaeologist is always looking for new ways to answer the questions formulated as the research progresses. Even in examining the tiniest bit of evidence—such as a decorative motif on a painted sherd—the archaeologist works with an eye to how this might bear on the larger questions the investigation is attempting to answer. In this chapter, we consider how archaeologists use analogy and analyze data to reconstruct the activities of past people.

ANALOGY

A basic paradox underlies archaeology: the archaeological record exists in the present, while the archaeologist is interested in the past—specifically, in the past conditions and human activities that created that record. Since events in the prehistoric past cannot be observed directly, the archaeologist reconstructs those events using **analogy**—a form of reasoning whereby the identity of unknown things or relations is inferred from those that are known. Everyone uses this kind of reasoning, and while analogy is fundamental to science generally, its application in archaeology merits a more detailed consideration. Reasoning by analogy is founded on the premise that if two classes of phenomena are alike in one respect, they may be alike in other respects as well. In archaeology, analogy is used to infer the identity of and relationships among archaeological data by comparing them with similar phenomena documented in human societies that are living or recorded historically.

Uses of Analogy

On the most basic level, analogy is what allows the archaeologist to identify artifacts, features, ecofacts, and sites as the remains of past human behavior. After all, the archaeologist does not observe the ancient human activity that produced chipped-stone implements. However, ethnographers and other observers have recorded hunters and gatherers in several parts of the world continuing to make and use similar tools into this century. Because of the similarity in form between the artifacts and the ethnographically observed examples, analogy has identified many of the ancient tools and, by extension, has allowed reconstruction of manufacturing techniques and use behaviors associated with them (Fig. 8.1).

Analogy underlies all prehistoric archaeological reconstruction, but historical archaeology can often rely on documentary sources to identify archaeological remains. In cases that can be directly linked to later records, this historical information is sometimes projected back in time to assist archaeological reconstructions. But in clear-cut prehistoric situations, with no direct links to historical information, the archaeologist must rely on inferences using analogy.

In many cases, the archaeologist's use of analogy draws simply and unconsciously from everyday experience; in this way, masonry foundations that support modern houses suggest that similar archaeological features are remains of a dwelling. Often the archaeologist will encounter a feature or an artifact that is not familiar to his or her experience; in such cases, identification by analogy becomes most clearly a conscious, rational process.

A good example of detailed analogical reasoning is Lewis Binford's study of a certain type of feature encountered in sites of the middle and lower Mississippi River Valley and adjacent areas after A.D. 1000. These features are small pits dug into the ground, averaging about 30 centimeters or less in length and width and slightly more than that in depth. Found around houses and domestic storage areas, but never near public buildings, the pit features contain charred and carbonized twigs, bark, and corncobs. Clearly, the charred contents had been burned in place, in an oxygen-starved atmosphere that must have produced a lot of smoke, so these features were called "smudge pits." Although their specific function was unknown, a variety of suggestions were made, ranging from offerings of corncobs to ovens to fires built to drive away mosquitoes.

In seeking a firmer way to interpret these smudge pits, Binford combed the ethnographic literature describing the Native American groups in the area. These

FIGURE 8.1

Iranian women stand by a grain bin built by the woman spinning wool, at right.

accounts included descriptions of hide-smoking procedures in which untanned deerskins were tied over small pits. Smoldering, smoky fires were then set in the pits and allowed to burn until the hides were dried and toughened, ready to be sewn into clothing. Binford pointed out that the details in the ethnographic accounts on the form and contents of the hide-smoking pits corresponded well with equivalent attributes of the archaeological smudge pits. Because there was a high degree of correspondence in form between ethnographic and archaeological examples, because the geographical areas involved were the same, and because a good case could be made for the continuity of practices in that area from the archaeological past (after A.D. 1000) to the time of ethnographic observations (1700–1950), Binford argued—by analogy—that the archaeological smudge pits represented facilities for smoking animal skins.

More precisely, Binford offered this interpretation based on analogy as a hypothesis to be tested. If this identification were correct, other aspects of hide smoking described in ethnographies should also be found associated with the archaeological smudge pits. For example, since the ethnographic accounts describe tanning activities as occurring between, rather than during, peak hunting seasons, the smudge pits should be found in sites used in the spring and summer rather than in hunting sites. The more such correspondences found between the ethnographic and the archaeological data and the more specific attributes identified as being associated with a particular kind of feature, the stronger the case becomes for the analogical interpretation.

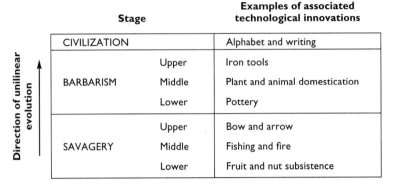

FIGURE 8.2

Lewis Henry Morgan's unilinear stages were used to equate past and present societies on a scale of evolutionary progress.

Abuse of Analogy

Before examining in more detail the different kinds of analogy and the ways they should be used, we should first understand some of the errors that have resulted from their improper use.

In the 19th century, when the theory of unilinear cultural evolution dominated anthropology (see Chapter 2), living societies were often equated directly with stages of the proposed evolutionary sequence (Fig. 8.2). These stages were defined largely by technological attributes (Stone Age, Iron Age, and so on), and each stage was presumed to have its own corresponding developmental level of social system, political organization, and religious beliefs. By means of these combined technological, social, and ideological attributes, living societies were ranked with respect to their progress along the evolutionary scale.

Obviously, this kind of analogy is suspect: it is dominated by only one criterion—technology—and ignores other variables such as time and space. In linking the Australian Aborigines with the peoples of the European Paleolithic, for instance, 19th-century anthropologists applied an analogy that ignored a temporal separation of more than 10,000 years and a spatial separation of over 10,000 miles. Since the 19th century, anthropologists have compiled a great deal of information about all the varieties of human societies, including those using hunting and gathering as a means of subsistence. These studies show that while some regularities of social structure and cultural organization can be recognized, a single trait such as hunting cannot be used to predict the forms the rest of the culture will take. Yet this is essentially what the 19th-century unilinear evolutionists attempted to do.

The use of technological or other limited criteria to make wide-ranging analogies like those of the 19th-century unilinear cultural evolutionists is not reliable. Unfortunately, careless equations between living cultures and those of the past may be found in some more recent archaeological publications. Further, the general analogy between the hunters of the European Paleolithic and certain contemporary peoples still occurs—especially in popular accounts reporting discovery of supposedly lost tribes that are usually described romantically, somewhat condescendingly, and certainly erroneously as "peoples from the Stone Age."

The obvious abuses of analogy in reconstructing the past have led to reactions, both by cultural anthropologists and by archaeologists, against the use of this method of reasoning. Much of the criticism of analogy has been concerned specifically with the uncritical use of ethnographic studies as analogs for archaeological interpretation. However, as we will see, the use of analogy in archaeology involves a wider range of analog sources, including historical accounts and modern experimental techniques.

Specific and General Analogy

It is important to distinguish between specific and general analogy. **Specific analogy** refers to particular comparisons within a single cultural tradition, while **general analogy** refers to broad comparisons that can be documented across many cultural traditions.

Specific analogy has rich potential for detailed interpretation of archaeological remains, but to use it, the archaeologist must defend its appropriateness on three grounds (all of which had been controlled in Binford's interpretation of the smudge pits):

1. *Cultural continuity.* Specific analogies begin with continuity within a single cultural tradition. In the southwestern United States, for instance, there is considerable evidence that the contemporary Native American societies documented in ethnographic and historical accounts are the direct descendants, both culturally and biologically, of local prehistoric occupants (Fig. 8.3). This cultural link allows the archaeologist to propose reasonable analogies for past cultures of the American Southwest.

2. *Comparability in environment.* Even where cultural continuity exists, environmental changes can alter links between past and present. Thus, an analog drawn from a society living in an environment different from that of the ancient society will be less reliable than one based on a society living in the same or a similar environment.

3. *Similarity of cultural form.* Analogs must be based on observable similarities, which will usually be determined by the degree to which traditional behavior is maintained by the analog society. For example, in Southeast Asia, conservative highland tribal groups provide more likely analogs for local prehistoric reconstructions than do their urbanized neighbors in Bangkok.

(a)

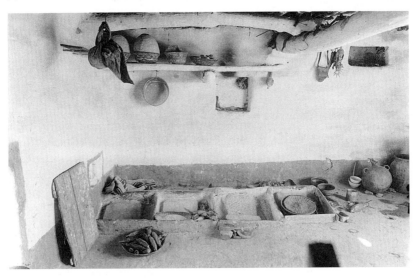

(b)

FIGURE 8.3

Cultural continuity, in the southwestern United States, for example, is an important criterion for using ethnographic studies as specific analogs for understanding ancient societies. These photographs were taken around the turn of the 20th century and show (a) an overall view of Oraibi Pueblo, Arizona, and (b) a room with equipment for preparing meals. Compare (b) with the mealing bin in Figure 6.14.

General analogies can be applied in situations in which specific analogies are unavailable. Because of the lack of cultural continuity, the problems involved in using living societies of hunters and gatherers as detailed analogs for Paleolithic groups have already been cited. Rather than throwing up their hands in dismay, however, archaeologists have developed better general analogies, each usually involving a narrow range of activities. Much of this has been accomplished through **actualistic studies,** in which behavior can be tied to diagnostic material remains, regardless of the cultural setting. These studies range from observing modern trash-disposal patterns to examining how one group of hunters differs from another in consuming its prey. In all cases, the key is rigorous specification both of the material traces of the past behavior and of the range of conditions under which certain kinds of behavior would be expected—and therefore might turn up in archaeological contexts.

Sources of Analogs

Analogs used in archaeological interpretation come from diverse sources: historical accounts and documents that describe societies in the past, ethnographic studies that describe present-day societies, and actualistic studies that attempt to duplicate conditions that existed in the past.

Historical sources include the full range of past records, studies written by professional historians, and descriptions made by casual observers such as travelers, merchants, soldiers, or missionaries. In the New World, much of our understanding of the pre-Columbian cultures of Mesoamerica and the Andes rests upon documents from the Spanish conquest of the 16th century (Fig. 8.4).

Ethnographic studies of living human societies are probably the most common source of archaeological analogs. Written by professional anthropologists, ethnographies are generally more focused and useful to the archaeologist than are other sources. However, professional ethnography is only about a century old, and most such work has been conducted among people influenced to some degree by European customs for far longer than that. Moreover, not all ethnographers conduct research relating behavior to material remains—that is, in ways that facilitate archaeological analogy. As we have said earlier, actualistic studies are undertaken by archaeologists to resolve precisely this dilemma, through either ethnoarchaeology or experimental archaeology.

Ethnoarchaeology refers to ethnographic research done by archaeologists so that the kinds of information needed to understand the past as well as the present are recorded. Of particular importance are the correlations between activities and durable remains, which help researchers understand the ways materials enter the archaeological record and the kinds of behavior they reflect. For example, studies of the manufacture of stone tools and pottery reveal the kinds of traces these activities leave behind, such as hammer stones, debitage, or misfired pottery. In another example, mapping modern house contents, with the owner's permission, and watching house construction can give scientists clues

FIGURE 8.4

This 16th-century map of the Aztec capital of Tenochtitlán, Mexico, is illus-
trative of Spanish records used to complement the archaeological record
of pre-Columbian societies. Although, in this case, spatial relationships are
shown differently from those of modern maps, the document provides valuable information, such as means of access (causeways and canoes) to the city
and the layout of its central plaza.

FIGURE 8.5

Studies of contemporary human
behavior provide analogies for
interpreting archaeological data.

about how to interpret ancient house remains (Fig. 8.5). A recent trend in ethnoarchaeological studies has directed attention toward material diagnostics of
behavior more likely to be otherwise invisible in the archaeological record, such
as ideology or ethnicity.

Experimental archaeology is another aspect of actualistic studies done by
archaeologists. Although experiments have a long history in archaeology, only
recently have they gained recognition as a fundamental source for past reconstructions. Early examples often involved using actual archaeological materials
or replicas, such as cutting tools and musical instruments, in an attempt to discover their ancient functions. Similar experiments continue, but in many cases
experimental archaeology has been reoriented to provide analogs for a broader
range of behavior—acquisition, manufacture, use, and disposal—associated with
archaeological materials.

Experimental work with stone artifacts is particularly well known. Don
Crabtree and François Bordes were leaders in reconstructing techniques used
to manufacture ancient stone tools by experimental stone chipping designed to
duplicate the archaeologically recovered forms. S. A. Semenov and Lawrence
Keeley pioneered in studying the wear patterns produced on stone tools by various kinds of use (slicing, chopping, and so on) so that the functions of artifacts
can be identified by analogy.

The most elaborate experimental studies involve reconstruction and maintenance of households and communities under past conditions. Archaeologists dealing with historically documented periods are in a better position to do experiments of this kind. Plymouth Plantation in Massachusetts and Colonial Pennsylvania Plantation in eastern Pennsylvania are examples of reconstituted colonial American communities. In these experimental projects, crops are raised; food is stored, processed, and cooked; buildings are constructed; and tools are manufactured and used—all according to colonial customs. The experience provided by these cases is comparable to ethnoarchaeology, for the archaeologist has the opportunity to observe, participate in, and record the behavior associated with the material remains.

An important category of experimental archaeology involves study of what happens to archaeological materials upon disposal. Such experiments consider the taphonomic and other transformational processes discussed in Chapter 4. Although these processes do not always involve human behavior, they are relevant to the interpretation of human behavior. For example, Glynn Isaac and his colleagues sought to outline details that would help in distinguishing whether stone-tool scatters in riverbank locations are intact sites (use-related primary context) or merely reflect the cumulative effects of artifacts being washed downstream from their original deposition points (natural secondary context). To accomplish this, they systematically scattered groups of artifacts in the valley of a stream feeding into Lake Magadi, Kenya, returning annually to chart how artifact positions change in these experimental analogs.

IDENTIFYING ACTIVITIES

The spatial distributions and associations of archaeological data are often directly observable; plotting finds on plans and maps, for example, is an essential part of data collection. But until the artifacts, ecofacts, and features are described, analyzed, and sorted in terms of time, archaeologists do not know which parts of these spatial distributions are remains of related activities. Past behavior cannot be reconstructed until the archaeologist knows whether bits of evidence go together in time or are from different periods. If they are from the same time span, they can give information about behavior and human interaction; if they are not, they allow the archaeologist to look at continuity and change in behavior over time.

In the following discussion, we use the threefold division of culture commonly used by archaeologists in reconstructing ancient behavior:

1. **Technology** is the means by which human societies interact most directly with the natural environment. It consists of the set of techniques and the body of information that provide ways to procure raw materials and convert them into useful items, such as tools, food, and shelter. Because technology

relates so closely to the natural environment, our discussion will include the ways archaeologists reconstruct ancient environments.

2. **Social systems** assign roles and define relationships among people: kinship organization, political structure, exchange networks, and the like are all facets of the way people organize themselves and their social interactions. We consider settlement patterns and evidence of exchange systems as examples of means for reconstructing ancient social systems.

3. **Ideology** encompasses the belief and value systems of a society—its attempts to explain its world. Religious beliefs and practices come most readily to mind as illustrating ideological systems, but art styles, writing, and other records also provide information about how human groups have codified their concepts about their world and existence.

The divisions among these three categories of human activity are not rigid. For example, exchange systems serve to move tools and raw materials, thus acting as part of the technological system, but they also reflect (and affect) social relations. These categories simply represent broad distinctions among cultural behavior that relate people to their environment, to one another, and to ideas.

Technology

In Chapter 6, we discussed the technologies involved in the production and use of various kinds of artifacts. This information, focusing on the analysis of artifacts, enables the archaeologist to answer specific questions about how stone tools or pottery vessels were made and used. At this point, we need to expand our focus to determine what means were available to a given group to relate or adapt to their environment. To do this, archaeologists must ask another question: what evidence indicates the presence of a given technology? An archaeologist usually forms a series of working hypotheses about the technologies employed by the ancient people being studied and tests these against the recovered evidence to answer the research questions.

Projectile points, for instance, are usually taken as evidence of hunting; discovery of these points in association with the bones of slaughtered animals, as in the Olsen-Chubbuck, Lindenmeier, or Folsom kill sites mentioned previously, clearly reveals aspects of the subsistence technologies for these prehistoric societies. Other hunting technologies, however, leave few artifacts. Trapping equipment, for example, is seldom preserved; use of this kind of technology is reconstructed from recovering particular kinds of animal remains and applying analogy with modern trapping techniques used by inhabitants in the same area to capture the same game animals.

Remains of workshops provide extremely valuable technological evidence. Workshops are activity-specific clusters of artifacts, sometimes including specially constructed features such as kilns, that preserve a variety of details about manufacturing processes. There are as many kinds of workshop features as there are different manufacturing technologies. The elaborateness of the workshop facility often depends on the scale of the activity. For example, flint-knapping might be the work of nonspecialized individual hunters using a few simple tools at varied locations over time; archaeologists would encounter remains of separate casual chipping stations in the area examined. Activities that require specialized individuals and facilities, however, such as iron metallurgy with its need for skilled labor and intense, controlled heat, are more likely to have readily identifiable areas set aside as workshops. In such a workshop, one would expect to find residues that reflect the manufacturing process, including raw materials, partially finished artifacts, mistakes (such as pottery vessels that cracked during firing), debris (such as stone debitage), and, of course, any special tools or features needed for production.

Technology mediates human interaction with the environment in many ways. People build shelters and make clothing to protect themselves from heat, cold, rain, wind, and snow. They also make baskets to help in plant collecting, fashion spears and arrows to kill food animals, dig irrigation ditches to provide water for crops, and build roads to ease travel (such as the Sweet Track roadway discussed in Chapter 6). The precise techniques and equipment used for a given task in a given time and place depend on past accumulation of technological knowledge. But they depend as well on the nature of the environment and the raw materials it supplies. The Inca of Peru, for example, built roads to unite their far-flung empire, including bridges to link segments of these roads. Where rivers and other gaps were narrow, builders used stone and timber; where gaps were wider than those materials could span, however, they used plant fibers to make suspension bridges of stout rope, bridges so strong the Spaniards could later cross them on horseback (Fig. 8.6).

As we saw in Chapter 3, environment does not determine culture, but it provides a flexible framework within which every culture operates. Similarly, culture does not determine environment, but cultural values and technological capacity may serve to define the extent to which available resources are harnessed. These principles are at the heart of one of the most enduring theoretical frameworks in anthropology, cultural ecology.

As introduced in Chapter 3, **cultural ecology** examines interaction of people with both the natural and the cultural environment recognizing that the relation between technology and environment is itself complex and interactive. For example, an innovation in technology may redefine the nature of the available environment: irrigation ditches can make gardens in the desert. The ecological questions asked by archaeologists center on which aspects of the range of environmental resources a prehistoric society used. To answer these questions, archaeologists must reconstruct not only the techniques and equipment used by a past society but also the nature of the environment that could be harnessed. In most research, the meeting ground for these approaches is the study of subsistence technology: what resources were available for food? which of these food resources were chosen and how were they obtained?

FIGURE 8.6

The Inca used fiber rope to build strong sturdy bridges across rivers that were often hundreds of feet below.

Archaeologists take two approaches to reconstruct ancient physical environments: (1) observation of the modern landscape, including topography and the range of biotic and mineral resources, and (2) collection of ecofacts. Such data give archaeologists evidence as to whether, and how, the available resources may have differed in ancient times. Pollen studies have proved to be especially useful indicators of ancient environments. Combining these kinds of approaches, archaeologists attempt, usually in consultation with other specialists, to reconstruct the nature of the environment in which the past society lived.

Examples of studies using both modern observation and the collection of ecofacts are easy to find. For instance, the Tehuacán Archaeological-Botanical Project defined its region for archaeological data collection to correspond to its resource area for modern environmental data collection. The overall goal of the project was to trace the development of agriculture in the New World. The Tehuacán Valley, in the Mexican state of Puebla, was chosen as the research location partly because it contained a number of dry caves that seemed to promise the climatic conditions under which maize and other domesticated plants would be preserved. At the same time, however, Richard MacNeish and his colleagues needed to determine the range of food resources available to the ancient residents of the Tehuacán Valley in order to outline the conditions under which they increasingly chose food production over food collection as their subsistence base. To get this information, the investigators surveyed the Tehuacán Valley and divided it into four microenvironmental zones, each with its own set of seasonally or perennially available resources. Combining this information with analysis of the ecofacts recovered from the region's archaeological sites, MacNeish and his coworkers were able to reconstruct the subsistence-related migrations of ancient human populations within the valley, postulating their movements in search of shifting food resources as the seasons passed. A few years later, MacNeish applied the same approach to the Ayacucho Basin of Peru, defining the correlations between seasonal shifts among subsistence technologies (Fig. 8.7).

Social Systems

All societies define themselves and distinguish among their members by assigning various roles and statuses. The most fundamental distinctions are those based on age and gender differences, but most human groups organize social interaction along a number of other lines as well. Kinship studies, a well-known part of anthropological research, have revealed the great variety of ways people have developed for naming relatives, reckoning descent, governing what family members one lives with, and so on. Principles of social organization extend beyond consideration of family organization, however, to include other social orders, such as how power is channeled (political organization) and who controls production and distribution of wealth and other resources (economic organization).

Much of the evidence of social structure recorded by ethnographers is intangible. Social, political, and economic categories and kinship patterns often leave little or no trace in the archaeological record. In recent years, however, archaeologists have tried to recognize how aspects of material remains might be clues to past social organization. In this section, we discuss two different approaches to reconstructing past social relationships and social structure: (1) settlement archaeology and (2) exchange systems.

Settlement archaeology is the study of the spatial distribution of ancient human activities and occupations, ranging from the differential location of activities within a one-room dwelling to the arrangement of sites across a region (see Fig. 8.7). Because they are concerned with locational information, settlement studies use features and sites as their principal databases. Since the focus is on understanding the distribution of ancient activities, the archaeologist doing settlement studies needs locational information preserved by primary context, and

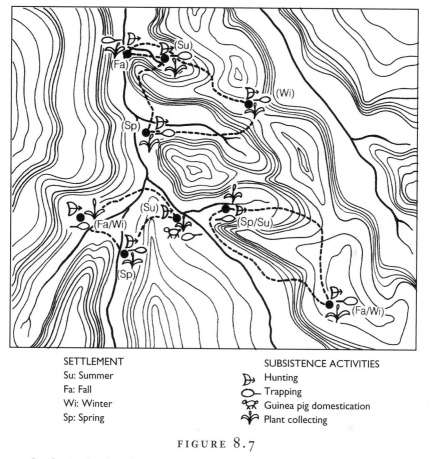

SETTLEMENT
Su: Summer
Fa: Fall
Wi: Winter
Sp: Spring

SUBSISTENCE ACTIVITIES
Hunting
Trapping
Guinea pig domestication
Plant collecting

FIGURE 8.7

Synthesis of archaeological data from the Ayacucho Basin of Peru has led
to postulation that ancient populations moved seasonally among sites to use
different subsistence resources.

features and sites retain such information intact. Artifacts and ecofacts are also
considered when they are in primary context, especially when their arrangement
reflects ancient activities (such as broken artifacts and debitage in a workshop).

Because they place sites and features in space, settlement studies have much
potential relevance for examining ancient uses of the environment. This potential has certainly been recognized by archaeologists doing settlement research.
In the Ayacucho Basin cited earlier, for example, MacNeish and his colleagues
not only examined ecofactual evidence of specific food use but also looked at
the distribution of occupational sites or base camps. The latter allowed them to
reconstruct the seasonal cycle of shifting residence and food procurement (see
Fig. 8.7). In this section, however, we focus on how settlement archaeology can
be used to reconstruct past social systems.

FIGURE 8.8

This artist's reconstruction highlights Çatalhöyük buildings (background) and some outdoor work areas (foreground).

The assumption underlying settlement archaeology is that spatial patterns in the distribution of archaeological remains result from and reflect spatial patterns of ancient human behavior. Archaeologists analyze spatial patterns on three broad levels: (1) activities within a single structure or on a single occupation surface, such as a cave floor; (2) arrangements of activities and features within a settlement or site; and (3) distribution of sites within a region. We consider examples on each of these levels.

At the smallest level of human settlement, archaeologists reconstruct the spatial organization of activities within a single structure—a dwelling or some other kind of building—or a comparably limited space. Such a study can consist of identifying areas in which various activities were carried out, as in distinguishing food preparation areas from storage areas. Identifying what went on in this kind of archaeological space is inferred by analogy, comparing the archaeological remains with material remains of documented activities. For example, excavated remains of hearths, fire-blackened jars, and grinding stones would indicate a cooking area, based on ethnographic observations of activities associated with similar features and artifacts.

Sometimes the findings from past research may be modified by new evidence (Fig. 8.8). At the Neolithic site of Çatalhöyük, Turkey, James Mellaart's excavations in the 1960s unearthed an astonishing complex of rooms, many of which were richly decorated with impressive plaster sculptures. The themes of the sculpture, together with associated figurines, were thought to indicate that the rooms were shrines for rituals dedicated to bulls and women. Female figurines and sculptures there came to be interpreted as representing a Great Goddess, a prehistoric deity linked to southern Europe in those early times.

In the 1990s, however, Ian Hodder and his colleagues reexamined the original finds at Çatalhöyük, including rooms, figurines, and sculptures, and greatly expanded the sample of rooms excavated within the overall settlement. As interpreted by Hodder, Lynn Meskell, and others, the identity of the figurines (as women, or men, or animals) is often ambiguous, and what had been interpreted as shrines were probably decorated houses. That is, the relatively elaborate decoration in Mellaart's sample of rooms fit within a much larger continuum of room treatment revealed in the new excavations, making it difficult to distinguish between domestic and ritual settings.

Even where rooms appear to be empty and unadorned, and their floors seem to have been swept clean, fine-scale techniques for retrieving plant, bone, and chemical residues can reveal how the space was used. **Micromorphology,** a microscopic technique described in Chapter 5, can sometimes yield unexpected insights about how individual rooms and buildings were used. At Neolithic Çatalhöyük, for example, Wendy Matthews and her colleagues encountered animal dung that had been trampled into microscopic layers, strongly suggesting that these were once stables for keeping animals, probably sheep and goats. Using both microscopic evidence and materials visible to the naked eye, then, archaeologists focus on this level of settlement analysis to understand how ancient societies divided up space into areas appropriate for particular activities.

At this microsettlement level, one of the most frequently studied kinds of features is the dwelling. A number of scholars have examined the potential determinants for house form. Bruce Trigger's list of such factors includes subsistence strategy (whether the society is sedentary or mobile), climate, available building materials, family structure, wealth, incorporation of special activities (such as craft production), ideology, security, and style. Although a number of these factors are related to environmental variables, several reflect the social system of the culture being studied. The arrangement of walls, doors, furnishings, and debris in a house provides clues about which areas were more public or private, how domestic tasks were organized, and which household members performed those tasks. Colin Richards's study of Neolithic stone houses in Scotland's Orkney Islands, for instance, focuses on how interior walls, doors, and immovable furnishings like those of Skara Brae (see Fig. 6.15) channeled movement, allowed for greater or lesser amounts of light within the house, and separated one work area from another. Even with simpler or more perishable structures, important differences in the use of space can be identified, and, at least in warm climates, many activities also took place outdoors.

In Peru's Upper Mantaro Valley, Christine Hastorf recognized changing distribution of plant remains on late pre-Hispanic patios and house floors after the Inca conquest in A.D. 1460. She suggests that maize remains increasingly marked women's making beer for social and political gatherings, thus representing intensified women's domestic production in support of men's expanding public activities. These examples hint at the range of studies taking place as "household archaeology." The latter is an expanding specialty within archaeology that recognizes how important households are as organizational units in society and how much can be learned about a society by looking at the diverse ways individual members of households lived their lives.

The next level of settlement analysis is the layout of the settlement itself. Here, the site is the unit of analysis, especially sites with evidence of residences (as opposed to kill sites, for example). At this level, archaeologists consider how smaller settlement and social units fit together to form larger ones, allowing them to examine aspects of prehistoric social systems from multiple perspectives.

Social stratification, for example, is frequently inferred partly on the basis of evidence from settlement analysis. At the Maya site of Tikal, Guatemala, archaeologists have found that houses are consistent in form throughout the site, but they range considerably in size, decoration, and the relative use of perishable versus stone construction materials. Larger, more substantial dwellings are assumed to have housed people who had more wealth or other means of controlling and acquiring goods and labor.

Aspects of social control can also be inferred from the regularity of settlement layouts. The site of Teotihuacan, Mexico, with its gridded streets and its orientation to cardinal directions is a striking example of imposed planning, which implies the presence of a powerful elite class able to command and direct the placement of structures and facilities over the landscape. Ancient Chinese political centers, too, were laid out according to a plan whose basis was partly religious but whose execution required effective social control.

Social and political distinctions, as well as levels of privacy or security, can be detected archaeologically. For instance, settlement remains at the urban site of Chan Chan, in the Moche Valley of Peru, can be divided into three categories: (1) small, poorly constructed residences, (2) intermediate-size residences, and (3) monumental structures. The three categories reflect differences both of complexity and of regularity in arrangement; the monumental structures, a set of ten enclosures (Fig. 8.9), are the most complex and regular of all. The ways the three categories of residences relate—or were allowed to relate—in space reflect several aspects of Chan Chan social organization. The small dwellings were segregated from the areas of intermediate-size residences, but the monumental compounds were the grandest and most exclusive of all. Although they encompassed great amounts of space, each had only one or two entrances, allowing its occupants to control strictly with whom they would interact. Each residence category can be equated with the social and status groups in this society. The ten compounds are interpreted as private royal residential complexes, the intermediate category as the residences of a distinct wealthy elite class, and the small category as dwellings of the poorest commoners.

At the broadest level of settlement analysis, archaeologists have traditionally considered the distribution of sites within a region. This can be approached

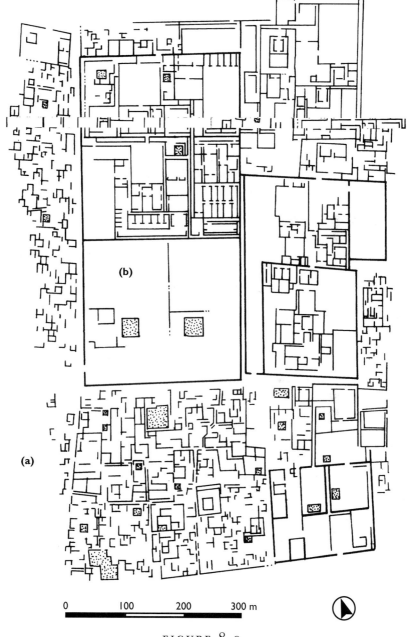

0   100   200   300 m

FIGURE 8.9

This portion of the map of Chan Chan, Peru, shows remains of (a) commoner residential areas contrasting with (b) one of the ten royal walled enclosures with restricted access from the outside.

in two ways, and GIS (Chapter 5) is a great help in organizing the data in both cases. The first is to reconstruct the function of each component in the settlement system and then to look at the various ways in which all the components may have been organized into an interacting social network. The same settlement pattern can reflect a number of different systems of social relationships (Fig. 8.10). MacNeish's Ayacucho subsistence cycle is one example of a particular view of settlement systems. Two different analyses of Paleolithic sites in Europe sharing a stone-tool assemblage known as Mousterian demonstrate how intangibles like social systems can yield divergent interpretations. Mousterian sites have been divided into multiple types based on their specific tool sets. François Bordes, a leader in delineating variation in Mousterian artifacts, argued that the different sites reflect occupations by contrasting social groups who used distinct styles of tool manufacture. Lewis and Sally Binford, however, used statistical analysis of the tool assemblages to contend that the variability represents, instead, different tasks being carried out from site to site. Their analysis led them to posit that some of the sites were residential base camps, while others represent hunting/butchering or other task-specific work camps. The contrast in the kinds of social interaction implied by the two interpretations is clear. In one view, the different Mousterian sites represent distinct human social groups doing similar things in different ways; in the other, a single overall group was simply dividing up activities according to appropriate locales. This underscores how all aspects of the settlement system must be examined in order to reconstruct the ancient social system.

The second way archaeologists have studied the distribution of sites is regional analysis, borrowed from economic geography. Many of the actual techniques refer more specifically to **locational analysis** and a particularly important example of these locational techniques called **central place theory.** Underlying this and similar techniques derived from economic geography is the assumption that efficiency and minimization of costs are among the most basic factors in spatial organization of human activities. For instance, an individual settlement will be located where a maximum number of resources can be exploited with the least effort; these resources will include not only aspects of the natural environment but also communication with neighboring groups. As the landscape fills with people, settlements will tend to space themselves evenly across it, and central places—settlements providing a wider variety of goods and services than their neighbors—will arise at regular intervals within the overall distribution. The most efficient pattern for the spacing of communities is a hexagonal lattice. This is all in theory, of course; in practice, landscape variables such as steep topography or the presence of uninhabitable areas break up the predicted pattern. Still, a reasonably close approximation of the hexagonal-lattice pattern has been observed in a number of both modern and ancient situations, including Romano-British towns (Fig. 8.11).

More recently, archaeologists working at this broadest spatial scale have focused on whole landscapes, emphasizing the relationships among all cultural and natural features on the land. A frequent goal is to identify the symbols attached to natural features in the landscape by evidence preserved in buildings,

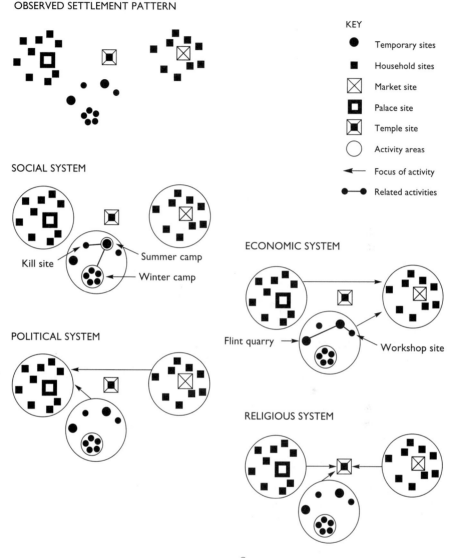

OBSERVED SETTLEMENT PATTERN

KEY

●   Temporary sites

■   Household sites

⊠   Market site

▢   Palace site

▣   Temple site

○   Activity areas

←   Focus of activity

●—●   Related activities

SOCIAL SYSTEM

Kill site

Summer camp

Winter camp

ECONOMIC SYSTEM

Flint quarry

Workshop site

POLITICAL SYSTEM

RELIGIOUS SYSTEM

FIGURE 8.10

A single settlement pattern may be the physical expression of a number of
systems of social relations, each of which can be studied at several scales.
For example, within the region, some households may live permanently
in one place while others move seasonally from one place to another.
Although the diverse people of the region may all be governed from a
single political capital, it need not be located in the same place as the economic hub or the ritual center.

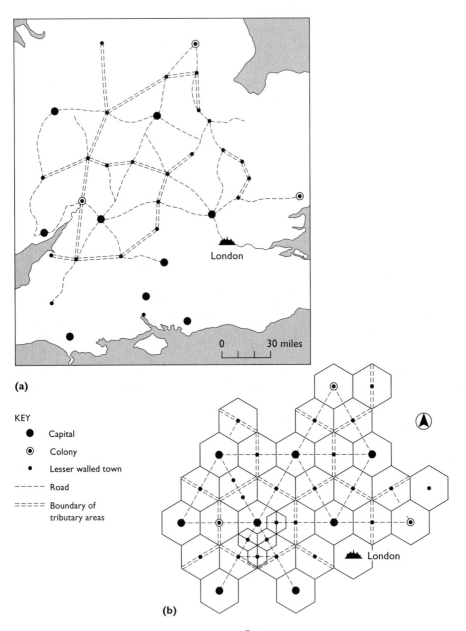

(a)

KEY

● Capital

◉ Colony

• Lesser walled town

----- Road

===== Boundary of
tributary areas

(b)

FIGURE 8.11

This Romano-British settlement from the 3rd century A.D. is (a) plotted on
a conventional map and (b) fitted to an *idealized* hexagonal lattice demon-
strating central place theory.

rock art, or other forms of marking the land. Archaeologists recognize frequent similarities between natural and built forms, as when temple pyramids resemble artificial mountains. Sometimes such interpretation benefits from historical texts and scenes in sculptures or wall paintings, as in Janet Richards's description of the ancient sacred landscape at Abydos, Egypt. But prehistoric landscapes can also yield important insights about ancient—and modern—attitudes toward the land and people's use of it. Barbara Bender and Christopher Chippindale have considered more than three millennia of occupation of the lands around Stonehenge, in England. Their studies include a record of confrontations between different interest groups seeking to control Stonehenge, its meaning, and its use, right up to the present day.

With the growth of indigenous archaeologies and collaborations with descendant communities, research on landscapes recognizes the deep history embodied in the land. In Chapter 1, we cited the collaborative work integrating archaeological traces and oral histories to expand understanding of social dynamics in the 1680 Pueblo Revolt, in what is now New Mexico. Elsewhere in the Southwest, collaboration among archaeologists and leaders of multiple Native American communities is significantly reshaping—and enriching—our grasp of the whole sweep of the human past and present in Arizona's San Pedro River Valley. Participants visit and discuss sites documented earlier by archaeologists, resituating the places in the narratives of indigenous history. As Ferguson and Colwell-Chanthaphonh acknowledge in titling their book about the project, the multivocal research demonstrates that people's "history is in the land."

Another way that archaeologists can understand a past society is by studying evidence of its exchange system. **Exchange systems** are established so that people can acquire goods and services not normally available to them locally. Trading ventures and institutions arise to carry out cooperative and peaceful exchanges between two or more parties. Of course, there are other means to acquire nonlocal goods and services. For example, foraging expeditions may be used to collect materials from distant sources, and raids or military conquest may plunder foreign lands for wealth and slaves.

The archaeologist may have difficulty in distinguishing trade goods from those acquired by other means, but the distinction is important for at least two reasons. First, the recognition of trade in the archaeological record leads to the reconstruction of past economic systems and thus contributes to a fuller understanding of the organization of entire ancient societies. Second, since cooperative exchange between individuals and between societies provides a primary means for the transmission of new ideas, recognition of trade helps lead the archaeologist to an understanding of cultural change.

Sometimes imports are recognized by the rarity of their appearance in contrast to other artifacts from the same site (Fig. 8.12). But identifying exotic items and their sources more specifically requires sophisticated technical analyses, such as X-ray fluorescence (XRF) or neutron activation analysis (NAA). Performed in specialized laboratories, such analyses can characterize the physical and chemical

(a)   (b)

FIGURE 8.12

Some nonlocal artifacts can be distinguished as imports because of their
style. These two seals are both about 4000 years old and are similar in style.
Each depicts a humped bull with a brief inscription above its back. Seal
(a) comes from the Indus site of Mohenjo-daro, in Pakistan, where this style
of seal is common and where stylistically related artifacts are also found.
Seal (b) was discovered at Nippur, in Mesopotamia, where it is stylistically
unusual, leading to the inference that it was imported.

composition of clay, stone, and other materials. Analysts assemble archives of such
characterizations from samples of finished items and of raw materials acquired
from potential sources. By comparing the chemical and physical "signatures" of
possible imports to the archive, the sources of the materials can be determined.
Such identifications have been used productively in many parts of the world to
trace procurement and exchange of pottery, stone, and obsidian, a volcanic glass.

While human exchange systems involve the transfer of goods, services, and
ideas, by necessity archaeologists deal directly only with the tangible products
of trade, usually recovered as artifacts and ecofacts. These data are traditionally divided into two classes. The first category, utilitarian items, refers to food
items; tools for acquiring, storing, and processing food; and other useful materials such as weapons or clothing. The second category, nonutilitarian items,
includes the remainder of exchanged objects, including gifts, ritual items, and
prestige goods.

By considering such distinctions, the archaeologist attempts to reconstruct
both the inventory of trade goods and the mechanism of exchange. The goal is
to determine the sources, routes, destinations, and consumers of the trade goods.
These reconstructions are based on the archaeologist's ability to separate trade
goods from local goods in the archaeological record and to amplify the understanding of ancient acquisition, manufacture, and use behavior.

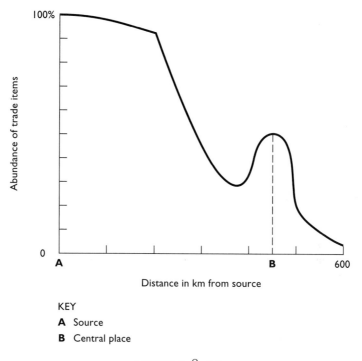

KEY
A Source
B Central place

FIGURE 8.13

The amount of an exchange item reaching a specific destination decreases with the distance of that destination from the source. But the rate of decrease is not completely constant, and the presence of redistribution centers in particular disrupts the distance decay curve.

These data allow the archaeologist to reconstruct ancient trade and its accompanying social interaction by examining spatial patterning from several perspectives, including the presence or absence of certain trade items and quantitative patterns in their occurrence, such as distance decay plots (Fig. 8.13). Simple presence-absence plots show the distributions for one or more categories of traded artifacts and their identified raw-material sources, suggesting the spatial range and even the routes used in ancient trade systems.

Ideological Systems

The final area of archaeological reconstruction, and certainly the most difficult to accomplish, deals with ideology. Ideological systems are the beliefs and practices by which human societies codify their beliefs about both the natural and the supernatural worlds. Through ideology, people structure their ideas about the order of the universe, their place in that universe, and their relationships with one another and with things and beings around them. Ancient ideologies are preserved through symbols and symboling practices, which are their material expression. The difficulty in reconstructing ideologies lies not in discovering symbolic representations but in recognizing them as such and in assigning them an appropriate meaning. For example, artifacts classed as ceremonial would appear to offer the kind of information needed to reconstruct ideologies; too often, however, that label is simply applied to artifacts whose function is unknown.

Archaeologists traditionally have given scant attention to ideology for two reasons. First, since the foundation of archaeology is material remains, it has often been assumed that the realm of ideas lies beyond the reach of archaeological inquiry. Second, since archaeology often emphasizes the processes of culture change, ideology, especially religious ideology, has usually been ignored because it is considered a conservative force that resists change.

Thus, even in cases in which this dimension of culture can be reconstructed archaeologically, ideologies are often seen as passive rather than causal forces in cultural change. It is often assumed that ideology can be safely disregarded because it is both difficult to deal with and not important to the concerns of archaeology. While the difficulty of inquiry into past ideologies is real, it has become clear that the assumption that ideology is unimportant is false. If ancient ideologies are ignored, our understanding of the past will remain woefully biased and incomplete.

The importance of research into this realm is attested by the expansion of archaeological interest in past ideological systems in recent years. This trend is closely linked to the development of feminist, Marxist, and postprocessual perspectives in archaeology discussed in Chapter 3. We briefly survey several areas of research into past ideologies, beginning with the core issue of recognizing and interpreting symbols.

Symbol systems may be preserved in the material remains that archaeologists deal with every day. Symbols are things that stand for something else; the relationship between the symbol and what it stands for is arbitrary. Symbols are thus shorthand ways of conveying messages about often complex subjects. It is this arbitrariness and complexity that makes symbols both rewarding to study and difficult to interpret, especially in the archaeological record. Even when an interpretation seems obvious, there may be no way of testing its appropriateness.

As an example, consider the rock art of southern Africa. The paintings come from areas once occupied by San hunter-gatherers, but the San of today have no surviving tradition of painting. Western analysts frequently interpret the pictures as representing life among the ancestral San, and the scene in Figure 8.14 is usually said to show people crossing a rope bridge similar to the bridge in Figure 8.6. J. D. Lewis-Williams argues, however, that if we can step outside our own culture for a moment and look from the perspective of San customs, the scene can be reinterpreted (and probably more accurately deciphered) as a curing ceremony like those known among the San today. Adopting this cultural perspective, the individuals depicted in the center of the scene have entered a trance; the lines above their heads represent their spirits leaving their bodies, while the dashed

FIGURE 8.14

Traditionally interpreted as people crossing a bridge, this San rock art scene has been reinterpreted, on the basis of ethnographic information, as a curing ritual.

lines in front of one figure symbolize an active nosebleed (a frequent side effect of trance). Other features of the painting likewise fit the trance scene interpretation. The so-called bridge probably represents two curers facing each other with outstretched arms, the exaggerated length and hairs of which correspond to sensations experienced in the trances. Whether these interpretations are completely correct in detail, they illustrate how easily misled we may be in interpreting archaeological symbols unless we can consider them within their own cultural context. Interpretation is possible, but it must be done with caution. Because rock art is so widespread across the world and is, in many places, thousands of years old, the study of this kind of symbolic communication has expanded tremendously in recent years, in both the number of investigations and the critical care with which their interpretation has been undertaken.

The rock art scene just discussed also illustrates the importance of ritual practices (in this case trance) as expressions of symbols and beliefs. A major instance of inferring symbol, belief, and practice comes from research on African American spiritual practices documented in 17th- and 18th-century Annapolis and the Chesapeake region. Bundles of meticulously selected items such as mirrors, crystals, and four-hole buttons have been encountered repeatedly in a limited range of carefully chosen locations. Crucial to their interpretation were the strong patterning in content and location of the finds, together with a fundamental analog source—insights about spirit practices gleaned from collective autobiographies of former slaves. Drawing from the combined evidence, Mark Leone writes of such caches found under house floors, and of their placement there as spiritual protection. Thomas Cuddy and Leone write of curative intent of caches. The symbols and practices attest to resistance of enslaved and free African Americans to the hostile, racist world around them.

One category of archaeological data frequently subjected to symbolic interpretation involves burial practices, including mortuary goods. Much attention has focused recently on funerary customs as indices of social organization: chiefs are frequently buried in areas separate from paupers, while grave goods in individual interments are often a gauge of the kinds of possessions the deceased had in life. John W. Hedges's study of Neolithic communal tombs in the Orkney Islands of Scotland identified possible prehistoric social symbols used by the ancient peoples of these islands. The best data came from the Isbister tomb, used repeatedly for almost 1000 years (ca. 3200–2400 B.C.), which contained more than three hundred individuals and the bones of birds and other animals. The animals are probably the result of offerings or mortuary feasting. In contrast, almost all of the bird bones were not from edible species, but from birds of prey, especially the white-tailed sea eagle. The presence of this species in such numbers suggested that it had a symbolic meaning for the people who buried their dead over the generations in this tomb. The distribution of various artifact styles suggested that Neolithic Orkney society was divided into a number of distinct groups, each with its own chambered tombs. Other tombs were associated with animal symbols different from the sea eagle. Hedges used general analogy, relating these practices to the widespread human custom of using animals as emblems to identify distinct social groups. Thus, the sea eagle was interpreted as the emblem or symbol of the people who had buried their dead in the Isbister tomb over 4000 years ago.

Writing systems provide the most regularized means of codifying symbols (Fig. 8.15). With writing, archaeologists enter the realm of historical documentation, which allows far more complete and accurate interpretations of ancient ideology. Writing systems were developed by many ancient societies all over the world; some, like Minoan Linear A script, have not yet been deciphered. Maya hieroglyphic inscriptions have only in recent years been read with any facility. The earliest writing in Southwest Asia dates to at least 3500 B.C., and people were carving inscriptions in stone in Mesoamerica by the first millennium B.C. In both cases, the earliest records archaeologists have unearthed pertain to counting —in the Middle East, to accounting records for commercial transactions, and in Mesoamerica, to counts of time.

Interestingly, Alexander Marshack has proposed that the oldest known notational records belong to a far earlier era. Marshack examined the scratches and marks on a series of Upper Paleolithic bone artifacts, marks usually ignored by other scholars. But Marshack detected regularity in such characteristics as angle of nicking and spatial patterning of groups of marks. From this, he argued that the

FIGURE 8.15

The earliest known written records are in cuneiform (wedge-shaped) characters, on clay tablets that first appeared in Southwest Asia in the fourth millennium B.C.

marks represent the beginnings of notation—the precursors of writing. Marshack further suggested that the subject of this Upper Paleolithic notation was time, the passage of lunar months, seasons, or other observable time periods. This theme raises an area of archaeological inquiry that has grown dramatically in recent years—**archaeoastronomy,** or the study of ancient astronomical knowledge from material remains. As noted in Chapter 6, a host of archaeological sites and features throughout the world have been identified as ancient astronomical observatories used to chart the cyclical movements of sun, moon, and other celestial bodies.

Archaeological features with astronomical associations are found throughout the world. In the Americas, astronomer Anthony Aveni and others have studied a variety of constructions in Mesoamerica to discover ancient astronomical alignments. At Cahokia, across the Mississippi from St. Louis, Warren Wittry identified postholes from a series of large circles of wooden posts, dubbed woodhenges, dated to about A.D. 1000. These circles range from 240 to almost 500 feet in diameter and may have served as observatories for tracking the seasonal movement of the sun. A variety of archaeoastronomical features identified in Chaco Canyon, New Mexico, date to about the same time. Puebloan peoples of the area today still observe daily changes in the position of the sunrise, and a number of Chacoan sites may preserve earlier traces of this custom. Several unusual corner windows in the apartmentlike site of Pueblo Bonito, for example, were probably used to observe sunrises (perhaps especially for the winter solstice).

Worldviews represent how people of different cultures define and categorize their social and natural environment, including everything from their attitudes about raising children to burying their dead. Through symbols, some of these beliefs and practices are expressed concretely. But, as we have already seen, there are numerous difficulties in interpreting symbols from the archaeological record.

The most reliable interpretations of symbols and worldviews, of course, can be made for situations in which ethnographic or historical records describe symbols and their meanings. As noted in Chapter 1, however, archaeology complements written texts in the kinds of data provided and balances the documentary bias toward affairs of only certain privileged social groups.

We have already mentioned the obvious difficulties in reconstructing ancient ideologies from material remains, which supported the assumption that these systems were unimportant in affecting the course of culture change. But this assumption has been successfully challenged in specific cases where archaeological evidence indicates that ideological systems played fundamental roles at times of momentous change. The dramatic florescence of Cahokia in the middle of the 11th century A.D. is a good example.

Located in today's Illinois across the Mississippi River from St. Louis, this imposing site includes hundreds of earthen platform mounds, expansive civic plazas, and public ritual facilities such as the woodhenges described earlier (see Fig. 5.10). Cahokia occupies extraordinarily fertile floodplains known today as American Bottom, and dominated an ancient crossroads for communication with much of eastern North America. It was a major political, economic, and ritual center between about A.D. 1050 and 1250. Although scholars differ in interpreting Cahokia's rise, explanations have long focused on local population growth, technological changes, and the unmistakable advantages of the site's location, which clearly benefited farming, long-distance communication, and exchange.

Abundant new data from both Cahokia and much of the surrounding countryside, however, combine with shifting theoretical approaches to suggest alternative interpretations for the sudden transformations that took place. Timothy Pauketat and Thomas Emerson are among those who argue that use of ideology and symbols was crucial to the rapid centralization of authority, in what had been previously a somewhat undistinguished place.

Before A.D. 1050 the countryside was dotted with small farming settlements, but the next few decades witnessed both an abrupt decline in the rural populace of the floodplain and an equally abrupt population explosion at Cahokia. Within a very few years—virtually "overnight" in archaeological terms—the center expanded from perhaps 1000–3000 people to at least five and perhaps ten times its former size. Such growth is not unique; it has been documented, for example, at places like Teotihuacan and Monte Albán, both in ancient Mexico. But in all these cases, the speed of expansion is far beyond what normal birthrates and small-scale migration would accomplish. And all such spurts accompanied major overhauls in societal organization. At Cahokia, as in these other places, rural farmers clearly moved to town in large numbers.

FIGURE 8.16

Modern visitors to Monk's Mound at Cahokia illustrate the monumental
size of this earthen platform, the largest construction in ancient America
north of Mexico (compare with Fig. 2.5).

Also important to that brief time span of Cahokia's emergence, farmers created the earliest parts of the town we know today. They built earthen platforms
and plazas, carrying out a well-organized plan under the careful supervision of
their new leaders. As we discussed in Chapter 6, one such early leader may have
been interred in Mound 72, a location that could also have been a key point in
the town plan. Thereafter, the builders made annual additions to the platform
mounds of Cahokia, including the largest, Monk's Mound (Fig. 8.16). South of
Monk's Mound, people had begun even earlier what became the Grand Plaza,
literally laying the "groundwork" by extensive leveling of uneven terrain.

Pauketat contends that ideology and symbols were important to the actions
of both commoners and chiefs at this critical time of social and cultural change.
Specifically, he sees mound and plaza construction at Cahokia as material traces of
how rulers and ruled negotiated their differing goals in the emergence of unprecedented new social arrangements. The farmers were not duped, but there is no evidence that they were forced labor crews either. Why, then, did they participate in the
construction work? Both commoners and chiefs contributed actively to establishing
a new community and creating prominent symbols of that community. They jointly
created arenas in which ritual gatherings and other events aimed at reinforcing
community solidarity could take place. Pauketat suggests that a Native American
song of much later times may parallel ancient Cahokian feelings of unity: "Behold
the wonderful work of *our* hands . . . and let *us* be glad" (Pauketat 2000:121).

Moreover, items recovered as refuse adjoining the Great Plaza strongly suggest that large-scale community feasts and other rituals took place in that publicly central location early in Cahokia's history. Prominent among the contents of the pit were the remains of choice cuts of meat and ritually important articles like cedar branches and tobacco, as well as broken pottery vessels used in serving the food to those assembled. Rulers also distributed distinctive pottery vessels to favored people, and these possessions likely became marks of prestige in the new social order.

Thus, new interpretations illustrate how central ideology can be in the organization of human society, and perhaps especially so at times of social and cultural change. This is not to say that ideology should be viewed as the only or even the prime cause of culture change. Economic and other factors played a role in both the rise and decline of Cahokia. But history is full of examples of ideologies that have made significant contributions to the direction and development of society, including the rise and fall of nations. Archaeologists must heed the lesson of these examples. They cannot ignore the role of ideology if they wish to reconstruct the past as fully as possible.

SUMMARY

Because past activities can never be directly observed, similarities between these data and the material correlates of living societies (either observed directly or recorded in historical or ethnographic accounts) are the basis for reconstructing the past. Reasoning by analogy has not always been correctly applied in archaeology, but use of logical guidelines can reduce or eliminate inaccuracies. For specific analogy, these guidelines are based on continuity of occupation, similarity of environmental setting, and comparability of cultural forms between the archaeological situation and the proposed analog. For general analogy, actualistic studies define links between particular behaviors and their material traces. The more analog links that can be established, using sources such as history, ethnography, and actualistic studies done by archaeologists, the more secure will be the proposed reconstruction.

Analogy is paired with examination of spatial order in archaeological data to reconstruct the varieties of ancient behavior. Human activities can be divided into three broad areas—technology, social systems, and ideology.

Technology refers to the behavior most closely related to the environment, best approached in archaeology through the concept of cultural ecology. This relationship is complex, for each environment provides a range of resources, and each culture defines, through capabilities and choices, which of these are actually used. As a result, understanding ancient technology requires study not only of cultural remains but also of the environment in which they were used.

Past social systems—the kinds of human organizations that channel human behavior—are reconstructed in various ways. Settlement archaeology relies on the spatial distribution of archaeological remains as reflections of the full range of human behavior, from single-activity areas to households, sites, and entire regions. At this broader end of the scale, archaeologists study ancient exchange systems—the means used by human societies to procure nonlocal goods and services. These studies attempt to determine which artifacts or ecofacts are nonlocal and thus may reflect exchanges with other places. Reconstruction of these organizations rests on analogies drawn from ethnography, economics, geography, and other sources.

Ideological systems, the means used by human societies to codify their knowledge and beliefs, are the most difficult of human activities to approach archaeologically, since this kind of behavior is often marked by relatively fewer and more enigmatic material remains. Identification and study of symbols provide one approach, but while the archaeological record is full of such symbols, their proper interpretation is often difficult. Writing systems, when present, can provide the most direct evidence of ideological systems for, if deciphered, they allow reading of messages. Other notational forms, such as counts of astronomical or other events, also offer clues to ancient ideologies. Worldviews furnish the underlying concepts about the universe that guide individual behavior and the course of human societies. In order to provide the most complete reconstruction of the past possible, archaeology attempts to understand the roles played by technology, social systems, and ideology.

FOR FURTHER READING

ANALOGY

Binford 1967, 2001; Bordes 1968; Brumfiel 2006; Crabtree 1972; David and Kramer 2001; Gould 1980; Keeley 1980; Lee and DeVore 1968; Longacre and Skibo 1994; Semenov 1964; Stone and Panel 1999

IDENTIFYING ACTIVITIES

Aveni 1982, 2000; Balter 2005; Battle-Baptiste 2011; Bender 1998; Binford and Binford 1969; Bordes 1968; Chang 1972; Chippindale and Taçon 1998; Cuddy and Leone 2008; Dalan et al. 2003; David and Thomas 2008; Ferguson and Colwell-Chanthaphonh 2006; Hastorf 1991; Hays-Gilpin 2004; Hedges 1984; Heggie 1982; Hodder 1982b, 1996; Holley, Dalan, and Smith 1993; Lambert 1997; Leone 2005; Lewis-Williams 1986, 2002; MacNeish et al. 1972; MacNeish, Patterson, and Browman 1975; Matthews et al. 1997; Mellaart 1967; Meskell 1998; Moseley and Mackey 1974; Pauketat 1998, 2000; Pauketat and Emerson 1997; C. Richards 1990; J. Richards 1999; Robin 2002; Rogers and Smith 1995; Rossignol and Wandsnider 1992; Sabloff and Ashmore 2001; Stone and Panel 1999; Tringham 1994; Wheatley and Gillings 2002; Yamin and Metheny 1996

ADDITIONAL SOURCES

Ambrose, Buikstra, and Krueger 2003; Andresen et al. 1981; Brain 1981; Brumfiel and Fox 1994; Butzer 1982; Feinman and Price 2001; Hodder and Hassal 1971; Hyslop 1984; Isaac 1984; Kehoe 2008; Marshack 1972; Renfrew 1975, 1983; Renfrew and Zubrow 1994; Trigger 1968; Ucko 1969; Wilk and Rathje 1982; Willey 1953; Wittry 1977; Zeder, Buikstra, and van der Leeuw 2010

9

Understanding the Past

IN THIS CHAPTER, WE complete the final step in archaeological research—the reconstruction and interpretation of the past. We began this process in Chapters 7 and 8, where we considered how the analyses of different data categories (artifacts, ecofacts, and features) are combined across time and space to interpret those data. Those chapters involved interpretation in a descriptive sense—attempts to answer questions such as *what* happened in the past, *when* it happened, and *where* it happened. In this chapter, we turn to a more explanatory aspect that addresses the questions of *how* and *why* it happened.

To illustrate the differences, let us examine the cultures that successively occupied the Great Plains of the United States, each of which exploited a different aspect of the region's varied resources. The *what* of our understanding of the sequence is provided by the analysis of the archaeological and historical data pertaining to these cultures. The same sources describe *when* and *where* the cultures existed and *where* they lived within the Great Plains. But *how* did a new culture take the place of the old? And *why?*

The prehistoric occupants of the Plains were limited in their day-to-day mobility. The remains of stone weapons, campsites, bones of game animals, and plants tell us that those who hunted and gathered for their food exploited a wide variety of food sources (hunting small game, occasionally hunting large game, gathering wild plant foods, and so on) in small, localized groups. Some groups took up cultivation of maize (originally derived from Mexico) and other plants late in the first millennium A.D. In the 17th century, some adopted a new technology by hunting on horseback (the horses had been introduced by the Spaniards) and thereby gained increased mobility, speed, and transport capabilities that enabled them to specialize in the hunting of large game animals (bison). Because of this specialization, these groups proved vulnerable to outside invaders (Euro-American colonists) who had a different technology. This new technology included the repeating rifle, which was used to decimate the herds of bison and thereby destroy the subsistence base of the mobile Plains societies, and the plow, which allowed the invading settlers to harness a previously unexploited portion of the environment for extensive agriculture. What had been a land of hunters and horticulturalists became first a land of hunters and then a land of plow farmers. Of course, in the 20th century, a still newer technology led to the industrialized exploitation of yet another portion of this same environment—the vast deposits of fossil fuel and water located beneath the surface of the Plains.

It is easy to describe the what, when, and where of this simplified sequence of Great Plains cultures. But how and why did the changes take place? Some of the mechanisms of change—the how—are evident: adoption of ideas from other cultures, invasion, migration. Interpreting why the ideas took hold in the new culture, however, or why the mass movement of people took place (either peacefully or with violence) is more difficult and controversial.

In this chapter, we will discuss the principal models archaeologists have used to answer the questions of how and why things happened as they did. Our discussion of archaeological interpretation will follow the three most prominent perspectives first introduced in Chapter 3, culture history, processualism, and emergent approaches. Although the three form a historical sequence in their development, they are also mutually complementary in questions they address. Through the use of all three approaches, archaeologists meet the general goals of their research: to reconstruct, describe, and explain past human behavior.

CULTURE HISTORICAL INTERPRETATION

In Chapter 3, we described the research goals and frameworks of culture history archaeology. The temporal and spatial synthesis of the archaeological data produced by this approach provides the foundation for interpretation. The analogs used for culture historical interpretation usually presuppose a normative view of culture, describing idealized rules for how things should be done—how pottery should be made, what house forms were prescribed, and so on. These models are primarily descriptive, not explanatory, in that they identify and describe the elements and trends of cultural change, but these models do not attempt to describe the relationships among elements or identify the causes of change.

Because the culture history approach emphasizes chronology and cultural change, most of the interpretive models used are diachronic, identifying and describing change in the archaeological record over time. A distinction can be made between those models that emphasize internal sources of change and those that focus on external stimuli (Fig. 9.1).

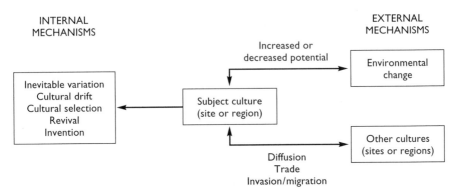

INTERNAL
MECHANISMS

EXTERNAL
MECHANISMS

Increased or
decreased potential

Environmental
change

Inevitable variation
Cultural drift
Cultural selection
Revival
Invention

Subject culture
(site or region)

Other cultures
(sites or regions)

Diffusion
Trade
Invasion/migration

FIGURE 9.1

Culture historical interpretation is based on models that describe cultural
change as proceeding from either internal or external mechanisms.

Internal cultural models describe mechanisms of change within a given
culture. The most general of these mechanisms is **inevitable variation,** which
follows the simple premise that all cultures inevitably change over time. One
particular version is that all cultures experience growth and development analogous to that of a living organism; they grow, mature, and eventually die (the
rise and fall of civilization). The inevitable variation model is so simplistic and
general that it is of little use in archaeological interpretation: we do not increase
our understanding by saying that Rome fell apart because it was destined to
do so. Of greater benefit to archaeological interpretation are internal cultural
models that identify specific variables with which to describe the mechanisms of
cultural change.

How does this change come about? The human species is inquisitive and
innovative. **Cultural invention** is the result of these human qualities; new ideas
originate within a culture, by either accident or design. But to attribute to invention the appearance of a given trait in the archaeological record at a particular
place, the archaeologist must demonstrate that the trait was not introduced from
outside by trade or some other external mechanism. An example is the controversy
over the early occurrence of bronze metallurgy in Southeast Asia. Proponents
of an independent-invention model point out that cast bronze artifacts found
in Thailand rival those of Southwest Asia in age. The counterargument is that
Southwest Asia exhibits a full range of evidence for the local development of
metallurgical technology, including evidence of workshops and of gradually
increasing sophistication in metalworking techniques. In order to establish that
Southeast Asia was indeed an independent center for the invention of metallurgy,
archaeological research is seeking equivalent evidence to that found in Southwest
Asia, enabling archaeologists to document the local prototypes and developmental steps leading to an independent invention of bronze metallurgy.

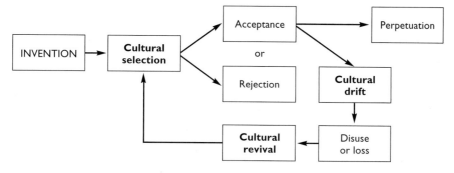

FIGURE 9.2

Internally induced cultural change is affected by the filtering mechanisms of cultural selection, cultural drift, and cultural revival.

To contribute to cultural change, an invention must be accepted in a culture. Two general models, both founded on loose analogies to biological evolution, have been offered to describe mechanisms of acceptance, perpetuation, or rejection of new cultural traits (Fig. 9.2). The first, **cultural selection,** mirrors the biological concept of natural selection. According to this model, those cultural traits that are advantageous to members of a society are accepted or retained while those that are useless or actively harmful tend to be discarded. This tendency results in gradual and cumulative change over time. Selection can act on any cultural trait, whether technological, social, or ideological. Whether a given trait is advantageous depends ultimately upon whether it contributes to—or hinders—the survival and well-being of those who adopt it. For example, investment of power in a central authority figure may increase efficiency in food production, resolution of disputes, and management of interactions with neighboring societies. If such centralization of authority leads the society in question to prosper, centralization is advantageous, and selection will favor its perpetuation. If, however, the society falls on hard times as a result of centralization —perhaps because of inept leadership—authority is likely to become more dispersed again.

Selection acts against innovative traits that are inconsistent with prevailing cultural values or norms. Generally, technological inventions are more likely to be accepted than social or ideological ones because they are less likely to conflict with value systems. A new form of axe head, for instance, usually has an easier path to acceptance than does a change in the authority hierarchy or an innovative religious belief.

A related model, often labeled **cultural drift** (see Fig. 9.2), describes a mechanism complementary to that of cultural selection. Like selection, this process results in change over time, but it is a random process. Cultural traits are transmitted from one generation to the next by learning. Cultural drift results from

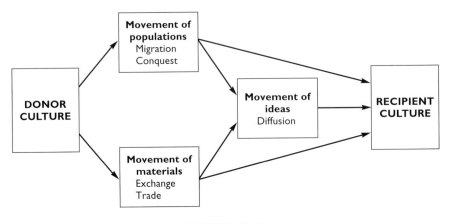

FIGURE 9.3

Externally induced cultural change includes the mechanisms of diffusion, trade, migration, invasion, and conquest.

the fact that cultural transmission is incomplete or imperfect; no individual ever learns all the information possessed by any other member of the society. Hence, cultural changes through time have a random aspect. Sally Binford and others have suggested that cultural drift may be responsible for some of the variations in artifacts of early Paleolithic tool assemblages. That is, the accumulation of minor changes gives a superficial impression of deliberate stylistic innovation, but only after about a million years of development in these tool traditions can consistent styles be discerned.

Another source for cultural change is the **cultural revival** of elements that have fallen into disuse (see Fig. 9.2). A number of stimuli may lead to the revival of old forms, including the chance rediscovery and reacceptance of old styles, reoccurrence of specific needs, and duplication of treasured heirlooms. One model relates revival to a coping response to stressful situations. Some kinds of stress elicit technological responses—for example, townspeople construct a fortification wall as a defense against siege. In other cases, societies deal with stress by social or ideological means. Cultural anthropologist Anthony F. C. Wallace developed a model that describes rapid and radical cultural change in the face of stress. This revitalization model refers to situations in which members of a society perceive their culture as falling apart, unable to provide them with an adequate standard of living. According to Wallace, a leader emerges who revives old symbols associated with earlier periods of well-being, squashes those identified with the stressful situation, inspires positive and prideful identification with the society, and promises renewed prosperity if people adhere to the new rules that are set down.

External cultural models describe change by the introduction of new customs from outside a particular society (Fig. 9.3). When a custom, such as that resulting from the acceptance of an invention, has become established within one society, its utility or prestige may allow it to spread far beyond its place of origin. The spread of new ideas and objects is a complex process. Various modes of dispersal are well documented by both history and ethnography; these are often used as models for culture historical interpretation. These include the spread of ideas (diffusion), the dispersal of material objects by exchange or trade, and the movement of human populations through migration or invasion and conquest.

Diffusion occurs under a variety of circumstances: any contact between individuals from different societies involves the potential transmission of new ideas from one culture to another. When a given society is exposed to a new idea, that idea may be accepted unchanged, reworked or modified to better fit the accepting culture, or completely rejected (governed by much the same factors that determine the fate of internal inventions).

The archaeological record contains numerous examples of ideas that have diffused over varying distances with varying degrees of acceptance. For example, the pre-Columbian 260-day ritual calendar of Mesoamerica is found in a wide range of cultural contexts. Although specific attributes such as day names vary from one society to the next, the essential unity of this calendrical system reflects a long-term exchange of ideas over a wide geographical area.

Diffusion is a well-documented mechanism of culture change in societies known from history and ethnography. Because diffusion is so common and because evidence of more specific mechanisms, such as trade, migration, invasion, and invention, is sometimes difficult to find, culture historical interpretations have relied heavily on this model. All too often, however, the concept is used uncritically, with *any* observed similarity between cultures attributed to diffusion. An extreme example of this kind of abuse is found in the diffusionist school of anthropology of the early 20th century, especially the branch that traced the roots of all world civilizations to dynastic Egypt. Proponents such as Sir Grafton Elliot Smith argued that the observed distribution of widespread traits of civilization, such as divine kingship and pyramid construction, resulted from diffusion from a single Egyptian source. When applied in more plausible ways, however, the concept of diffusion rests on documenting how and why the cultures involved were in communication with each other.

Although diffusion is often an elusive mechanism, easy to invoke and difficult to substantiate, contact and communication via **trade** can frequently be demonstrated. This is because trade involves the exchange of material objects; the less perishable of these may be recovered by the archaeologist as artifacts and ecofacts, as discussed in Chapter 8. Once trade goods have been identified, archaeologists may be able to reconstruct ancient trade routes by plotting both the distribution of sources of material and the observed distribution of products from these sources. The important implication of trade distributions for cultural change is that archaeologists can use them to demonstrate contact between groups. When an obsidian trade route is reconstructed, for example, a minimal inference is that obsidian thus became available to people who could add tools made from that material to their cultural inventory. More broadly, however, the observed distribution of obsidian is concrete evidence of contact between groups, which potentially allowed the transmission of a much greater array of materials and ideas, some of which may leave no material trace in the archaeological record.

Another mechanism of culture change is the movement of populations, both as **migrations** and as aggressive **conquests.** Culture historical interpretations often cite these movements to account for evidence of widespread and rapid change. Emil W. Haury listed four conditions that must be met for an archaeologist to argue that migration has occurred:

1. A number of new cultural traits must appear suddenly, too many to be feasibly accounted for by diffusion, invention, or trade, and none having earlier local prototypes.
2. Some local materials should be modified in form, style, or function by the newcomers.
3. A source for the immigrant population must be identified—a homeland where the intrusive cultural elements have prototypes.
4. The artifacts used as indices of population movement must exist in the same form at the same time level in both the homeland and the newly adopted home.

As an example, Haury noted that new architectural styles, both sacred and secular, along with very specific ceramic attributes, appear suddenly in one particular sector of the prehistoric site of Point of Pines, Arizona. At the same time level, some distinctively "foreign" design elements are found on locally made pottery vessels, also recovered in this same sector. These findings supply the first two kinds of evidence needed to postulate a migration. Looking for a source for these cultural traits, Haury found the same elements in association at sites in northern Arizona on an equivalent time level. Finally, Haury noted that independent evidence points to a population decline in the proposed homeland at the appropriate time.

Migration can be contrasted with its more violent counterpart, conquest. This also involves population movements, but with presumably more drastic effects on the way of life of the recipient society. Elements cited as evidence of conquest include massive burning or other destruction of buildings in a settlement, usually accompanied by large-scale loss of human life (Fig. 9.4).

The change brought about by conquest may, of course, be the annihilation of the existing population, sometimes with no replacement by the intruders. In many cases, however, part of the original population survives and stays on, often under the political domination of the invaders. The invaders may bring in new cultural elements, but even historically documented conquests show up rather inconsistently in the archaeological record. A case in point is the Spanish conquest of the Americas in the 16th century. Both European and native chronicles of the period

FIGURE 9.4

Evidence of cultural change through conquest can take dramatic forms.
This photograph shows human skeletal remains sprawled among the
remains of burned buildings in the walled palace compound of Hasanlu,
Iran, the result of the destruction of the city in the 9th century B.C.

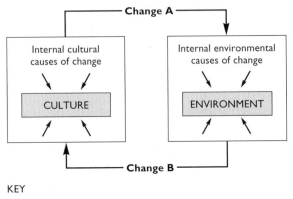

KEY

A   Environmental change caused by cultural factors

B   Cultural change caused by environmental factors

FIGURE 9.5

The culture historical approach stresses a simple interaction between culture and environment, based on the capability of each to modify the other (compare with Fig. 9.9).

attest to the extent and severity of the changes wrought by the Spaniards. Even so, archaeologists working in a number of the affected areas, including Mexico, Guatemala, and Peru, have sometimes had difficulty in identifying evidence of the Spanish arrival in the archaeological record. At some sites, European artifacts clearly appear, but local pottery and other traits often remain unchanged for long periods after the conquest. With reference to Haury's criteria, then, archaeologists can positively identify some prehistoric population movements, but the example just given argues rather strongly that not all such movements—violent or peaceful—can be accurately detected in the archaeological record.

Environmental change is used in culture historical interpretation as an external factor (see Fig. 9.1), independent of culture, that nonetheless may affect the destiny of human society. This model describes rather general environmental sources of cultural change. In most cases, culture history models of culture and environment hold that each has the potential to modify the other (Fig. 9.5). A dramatic example of the cultural impact of an environmental change can be seen in the effects of the eruption of the volcano that formed Sunset Crater, near Flagstaff, Arizona, sometime in the middle of the 11th century A.D. The initial effect of the eruption was to drive away all residents in the approximately 800 square miles blanketed by the black volcanic ash. A century later, however, the area was resettled by a diverse population that apparently took advantage of the rich mulching action of the volcanic soil. By A.D. 1300, however, the environment had changed again: wind had converted the ash cover to shifting dunes, exposing the original hard clay soil. Once again, the human settlers moved away.

In contrast, culture also changes environment. A change in technology may redefine the environment by increasing or decreasing the range of exploitable resources. Agricultural overuse may exhaust local soils; the clearing of trees on hillsides may foster erosion, landslides, and ultimately—by increasing the load deposited in a streambed by runoff—flooding. Alteration of the natural environment by cultural activities is not an exclusively modern phenomenon; the alterations today may be far more catastrophic and extensive than before, but they are part of a long, global tradition of cultural impact on the natural world.

PROCESSUAL INTERPRETATION

The second major approach to reconstructing the past is by using processual interpretation. As we saw in Chapter 3, this approach is based on ecological and materialist views of culture and uses both systems and multilinear evolutionary models to explain the past. Although the descriptive models discussed earlier are usually associated with culture history reconstruction, they may also be applied in processual interpretations. As we have noted, culture history models often generate hypotheses that are tested, modified, and advanced as explanations for prehistoric cultural processes. But just as some models are used more frequently in culture history reconstructions, certain others are primarily associated with processual explanations.

Systems models recognize that an organization represents more than a simple sum of its parts; in fact, they emphasize the study of the relations between these parts. Two kinds of systems can be defined: open and closed. Closed systems receive no matter, energy, or information from other systems; all sources of change are internal. Open systems exchange matter, energy, and information with other systems; change can come either from within or from outside. Living organisms and sociocultural systems are open systems. In order to understand how systems operate, we will examine systems models that are often applied in processual interpretations.

Let us begin with a simple closed-systems model. As an example, consider the components and relationships in a self-regulated temperature control system, such as those found in many modern buildings (Fig. 9.6). The components in the system are the air in the room or building, the thermometer, the thermostat, and the heater or air conditioner. In this case, a change in the air temperature acts as

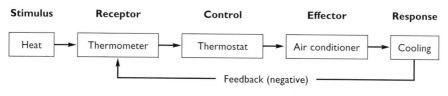

FIGURE 9.6

This diagram of a homeostatic temperature control system illustrates the operation of a closed system.

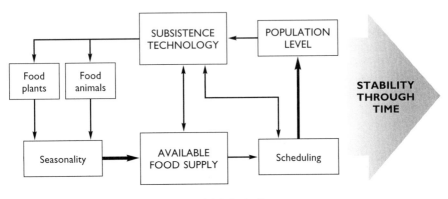

FIGURE 9.7

This simplified diagram shows a system characterized by negative
feedback mechanisms (→) that lead to population and cultural stability
over time; the diagram is based on data from prehistoric Mesoamerica
(ca. 8000–5000 B.C.). The larger arrow at the right indicates the trajectory
of the system as a whole.

a stimulus that is detected by the thermometer and transmitted to the thermostat. When the temperature rises above a predetermined level, the thermostat
triggers the air conditioner. The cooling response acts as **feedback** by stimulating the same interdependent components to shut down the air conditioner once
the temperature has gone below the critical level.

This closed system illustrates how certain systems operate to maintain a
stable condition, or steady state. When a specific change in one part of the system threatens the steady state, this stimulates a response from other component
parts. When the steady state has been restored, a feedback loop shuts down the
response. This is **negative feedback** in that it dampens or cuts off the system's
response and thus maintains a condition of dynamic equilibrium in which the
system's components are active, but the overall system is stable and unchanging.
Although they are useful for illustrating the operation of systems, such models
are applicable only to unchanging and stable aspects of human societies.

Since archaeologists are more often concerned with cultural change, we must
also consider dynamic systems models that can account for cumulative systemic
change. The most commonly applied model for this deals with **positive feedback,**
which stimulates change within the system. A good example of the application of
these concepts to an archaeological situation is Kent Flannery's systems model for
the development of food production in Mesoamerica. In setting forth the model,
Flannery first described the food procurement system used by peoples of highland Mexico between about 8000 and 5000 B.C. (Fig. 9.7). The components of this
system were the people themselves, their technology—including knowledge and
equipment—for obtaining food, and the plants and animals actually used for food.

People in the highland valleys lived in small groups, periodically coming
together into larger "macrobands" but not settling down in permanent villages.

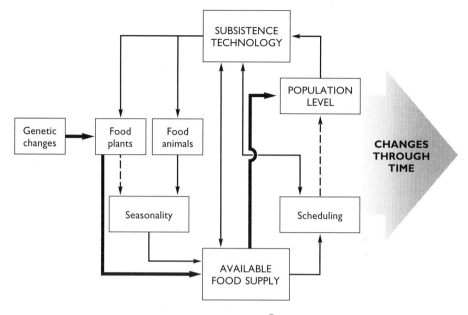

FIGURE 9.8

This simplified diagram shows a system characterized by positive feedback mechanisms (→) that both weaken the negative feedback mechanisms in Figure 9.7 and lead to population growth and cultural change stimulated by genetic changes; the diagram is based on data from prehistoric Mesoamerica (after 5000 B.C.).

The subsistence technology available to them included knowledge of edible plants and animals that could be procured by gathering and hunting techniques, as well as the implements and facilities for procurement. Among the food items actively used were cactus, avocado, white-tailed deer, and rabbits. Wild grasses related to maize were sometimes eaten but did not form a very important part of the diet.

This food procurement system was regulated and maintained by negative feedback acting through seasonality and scheduling. Seasonality refers to characteristics of the food resources themselves—some were available only during one season or another. To gather enough food, the people had to go where it was available. Periodic abundance of particular resources allowed people to form temporary macrobands, but the seasons of lean resources placed sharply defined limits on both total population and effective social group size. Scheduling, the other negative feedback mechanism, refers to the people's organizational response to seasonality. Seasonally scheduled population movement and diet diversity prevented exhaustion of resources by overexploitation, but it also kept population levels low.

This stable system persisted for several thousand years. But according to Flannery, sometime after 5000 B.C., genetic changes in some of the wild maize stimulated a positive feedback system (Fig. 9.8). Improved traits of the maize, such as larger cob size, induced people to reproduce the improved grass by sowing. As a result, scheduling patterns were gradually altered. For instance, planting and harvesting requirements increased the time spent in spring and autumn camps, precisely where larger population gatherings had been feasible before. The larger, stabler population groupings then invested more time and labor in improving the quality and quantity of crop yield; this positive feedback continued to induce change in the subsistence system. For example, irrigation technology was developed to extend agriculture and settlement into more arid zones. As Flannery says, the "positive feedback following these initial genetic changes caused one minor [sub]system to grow out of all proportion to the others, and eventually to change the whole ecosystem of the Southern Mexican Highlands" (Flannery 1968:212).

Although some cultural systems may maintain a state of dynamic equilibrium for long periods of time, all cultures do change. Not all change involves growth, however. Sometimes positive feedback results in cultural loss or decline, and ultimately in dissolution of the system. The modern case of the Ik of East Africa, described by ethnographer Colin Turnbull, provides an example of such decline. Disruption of traditional behavior patterns by such factors as forced migration from preferred lands led to apathy, intragroup hostility, a devaluation of human life, and population decline. The result in this case is as dramatically bleak as Flannery's is dramatically positive. Most cases of cultural change are less extreme, as cultural systems are affected simultaneously by both growth and decline of subsystems within them in a gradual and cumulative course of change.

Cultural ecology models are a category of systems models that provide a more sophisticated understanding of the interaction between culture and environment than do culture history models discussed previously (see Chapter 3). Whereas the culture history approach often treated environment as a single entity, cultural ecology considers a given culture as interacting with an environmental system composed of three complex subsystems: (1) the physical landscape, (2) the biological environment, and (3) the cultural environment, which refers to other, adjacent human groups (Fig. 9.9).

For any given society, the sum of specific interactions contained within its overall cultural ecology describes the nature of the society's **cultural adaptation.** Each society adjusts itself or adapts to its environment primarily through its technological system, but these adaptations are reinforced through the social and ideological systems. The technological system interacts directly with all three components of the environment—physical, biological, and cultural—by providing, for instance, the tools and techniques required for securing shelter, food, and defense. The social system adapts by integrating and organizing society. The relationship described earlier between band organization and seasonality and scheduling in preagricultural highland Mexican societies is an example of social system adaptation to the biological environment. The ideological system is adaptive in that it reinforces the organization and integration of society by providing motivation, explanation, and confidence in the appropriateness of the technological and social adaptations.

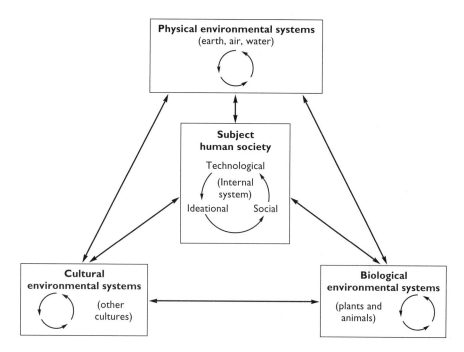

FIGURE 9.9

The cultural ecology system, illustrating the relationships between a given culture (the subject human society) and its environment, is composed of physical, cultural, and biological subsystems (compare with Fig. 9.5).

Of course, the full set of interactions within such a complex system is difficult to study all at once. As a result, archaeologists often begin by isolating one or more of the subordinate systems directly involved in cultural adaptation. The technological system is the obvious focus of studies seeking to understand the adaptive process. Fortunately for the prehistoric archaeologist, not only is the technological subsystem an obvious agent of cultural adaptation, but the remains of ancient technology are also usually the fullest part of the archaeological record. These technological data may be used to reconstruct a particular aspect of the technological system, such as subsistence. In one example of the adaptive process of a technological system, Robert Bettinger has described the impact of the bow and arrow on the foragers in the Americas. When the technology first appeared in this hemisphere, no more than 2000 years ago, it completely replaced spears and spear throwers, "as if New World hunter-gatherers had been waiting for [the bow and arrow] all their lives" (Bettinger 2001:152). From such detailed inferences about one or more subsystems, archaeologists then create complex integrated models of overall cultural adaptation, much as Flannery did in the example from Mexico described earlier.

Because of the mass of information involved in such models, computers are often used for information storage and processing. Computers also enable archaeologists to perform experimental manipulations of their models. After a hypothetical change is introduced in one component of a stable system, a **computer simulation** determines what kind of feedback would be induced by the change. Research using GIS, discussed in Chapters 5 and 8, provides growing opportunities for such simulation.

Some archaeologists measure the effectiveness of cultural adaptation by the rate of population growth and resultant population size. In this sense, population growth and size are a measurable response to the overall cultural ecology system (see Fig. 9.9). With regard to population increase, some societies are characterized by one or more positive feedback mechanisms. For example, changes in the technological system may provide more efficient food production and storage capabilities, resulting in an increase in population. Changes in the social or ideational system will follow to accommodate the population growth; these, in turn, may allow more efficient food distribution or expansion via conquest or colonization to open new areas for food production, resulting in still further population growth. This may place new stress on technology, which must respond with further changes to increase the food supply, and so forth. The result is an interrelated cycle of change and population growth, perhaps best illustrated by the phenomenon of recent world population growth.

However, successful adaptation (biological or cultural) can also be marked by stability of population size. Some societies maintain population stability by negative feedback mechanisms, including their own culturally acceptable population control methods (birth control, infanticide, warfare), migration, and social fissioning. Environmental mechanisms, including periodic famine or endemic disease, may also contribute to the maintenance of such systems.

Multilinear cultural evolutionary models constitute the final perspective of processual interpretation to be considered. These models combine the materialist view of culture and the adaptation concept of cultural ecology. In so doing, they view the evolution of culture as the cumulative changes in a system resulting from the continuous process of cultural adaptation over extensive periods of time. But how does the archaeologist reveal the causes of evolutionary change? Two schools of thought have emerged. The first emphasizes the identification of universal prime movers of cultural change; the second seeks multiple and variable causes.

The search for **prime movers** emphasizes the identification of a few specific, primary factors that underlie the process of cultural change and cultural evolution. It is based on the premise that the regularities and patterns in evolutionary change result from regularities of cause. Accordingly, this approach emphasizes the testing of broad hypotheses that seek the fundamental, far-reaching causes of all cultural change.

Population growth is often proposed as a fundamental cause of cultural change. This prime mover has been applied in various regions to explain the course of cultural evolution. For example, William T. Sanders and Barbara Price based their

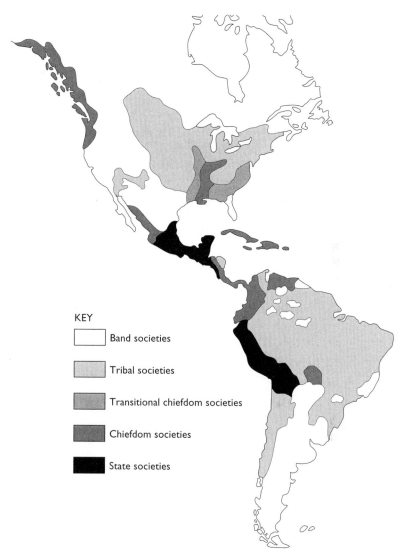

FIGURE 9.10

This map summarizes the distribution of New World societies in 1492,
classified by organizational complexity according to one version of a
multilinear evolutionary model.

thesis for the development of pre-Columbian Mesoamerican culture through
a succession of five evolutionary stages upon population growth and its effects
upon two secondary factors, competition and cooperation (Fig. 9.10). Other prime
movers, such as warfare or agriculture based on irrigation, have been proposed to
explain evolutionary developments such as the rise of complex state societies.

The **multivariate strategy** attempts to delineate the basic processes of cultural change by focusing on specific subsystems most directly involved in each instance of cultural adaptation. In order to identify the focus of change, research of this kind may test hypotheses concerned, for example, with a variety of alternative subsistence modes or with the acquisition and distribution of critical natural resources. Since each instance of change is considered unique, this model holds that no single factor or small group of prime movers causes all cultural change. Cultural evolution, the overall product of change, is thus viewed within each society as the product of a unique series of adaptive adjustments of the sort that are a constant feature of all cultural systems. It is this perspective that gives this model of culture change its name—*multivariate*. Specific examples, such as Flannery's models for the transformation from hunting-and-gathering subsistence to food production, build upon this premise and call for substantial cumulative cultural changes over a sufficient period of time.

The multivariate concept of cultural evolution is usually based on cultural ecology and systems models. This approach requires that the archaeologist identify the components of and understand the relationships among the specific subsystems crucial to cultural adaptation. This is not an easy task, especially given the inherent limitations of archaeological data. The archaeologist must formulate and test a series of sophisticated hypotheses, using data that are often difficult to collect. As in the case of the transformation to food production in Mesoamerica described earlier in this chapter, such research may show that multivariate causes effectively explain fundamental cultural change.

EMERGENT INTERPRETATIONS

Feminist, Marxist, and postprocessual archaeologists use a dynamic culture concept (see Chapter 3) in which people are active agents, constantly choosing how best to relate to those around them. This emphasizes the active role of individual actions in cultural stability and change. The past actions we study occurred within distinct cultural contexts and should not be expected or assumed to mirror actions adopted in the culture in which we live.

For example, certain artifacts in the archaeological record represent gender distinctions. As we have seen, the meaning of gender-related or other kinds of patterning is an area of increasing emphasis in postprocessual archaeology, one often subject to alternative interpretations, depending on the kinds of models being applied to the data. To illustrate this, imagine finding clusters of cooking utensils near hearths and woodworking tools in a corner of a house yard. This pattern would usually be explained as defining female and male activity areas, based on projecting our cultural expectations onto the archaeological record. But now assume that we have independent documentary evidence that this association between gender and activities is not correct for this society, and that both cooking and woodworking were in fact female activities. As a result, the meaning of the data patterning might be seen as reinforcing past concepts of female-ness within this society while challenging those of our own society. In other words, the definition of these activity areas allows two different interpretations that define both occupational roles and gender concepts, which, when combined, give a more complete meaning to the patterning in the archaeological record.

When dealing with cultural change, feminist, Marxist, and postprocessual interpretations are dominated by internal change models. Some of the latter apply concepts we have already discussed, such as diffusion and exchange. A major difference is viewing people of the past as active agents for change, rather than faceless and passive participants. Practice models also treat variability as reflecting actions by individuals or groups, rather than focusing, as do proces-sualists, on collective adaptations and comparing effects between whole societies. In these ways, emergent interpretations both depart from and integrate models used by cultural historians and processual archaeologists.

Practice models draw on observed changes in the archaeological record that are interpreted as the accumulation of adjustments—deliberate or unconscious—to customs within a particular cultural context and worldview. These models address very short-term fluctuations (and therefore are essentially synchronic), as well as longer time spans and culture change. Interpretation proceeds by iden-tifying the nature of the settings in which adjustments were made, the actors involved, and the implications for negotiating social relations. This attempt to integrate small-scale and large-scale phenomena can be illustrated by a specific example, which also shows how this approach differs from culture historical and processual approaches.

Consider the Aztec of Mexico: widely recognized as the empire encountered by the Spanish in A.D. 1519, Aztec culture is best known for its kings, its expan-sive warfare and tribute system, and its public rituals, especially human sacrifice. Beyond its leaders and the actions they directed, however, was a much larger society, notably diverse internally along ethnic, class, gender, and other social and cultural dimensions. Elizabeth Brumfiel has studied Aztecs in farming vil-lages beyond the imperial capital, with particular interest in how the expanding empire affected villagers' lives. How did individuals and groups respond? Her inferences about changes in women's roles were discussed in Chapter 3, especially how women shifted to making tortillas and other more portable foods in response to men's being called to serve the empire at greater distance from their homes. In other spheres of life, Brumfiel contends that village residents challenged impe-rial claims of women's subordination, at least within the contexts of their home communities. That is, dramatic public images officially depicted female Aztec dei-ties as weak or damaged (Fig. 9.11). Some were shown with fatal mutilations, but others knelt in subordination, and even women with trappings of authority (such as warriors) were portrayed as androgynous—ambiguous as to gender—and therefore not indicative of specifically *female* authority. Insofar as deities embody attitudes about ideal humans, these official portrayals thus publicly cast women as

FIGURE 9.11

Stone sculpture, 3.25 meters in diameter, depicting the dismembered body
of Coyolxauhqui, sister of the Aztec patron deity.

inferior. Craft specialists in Aztec villages, however, created clay figurines under-
scoring women's importance in community life, especially in matters of health
and fertility. Portrayed most often in standing poses, these clay images also frequently represent women holding one or two children in their arms. In Brumfiel's
view, then, villagers resisted official doctrines and insisted, through popular styles
of imagery, on women's fundamental contributions to everyday life.

The differences between this interpretation and culture historical or processual interpretation are marked. Though all approaches recognize interpretive
roles for style, culture history uses stylistic change to create time-space grids.
Feminist, Marxist, and postprocessual archaeologists draw on style as a means to
express ideas about culture, through which individuals and social groups nego-
tiate how they interact with each other. For processual archaeologists, on the
other hand, we have seen that interpretation emphasizes the adaptive aspects
of culture, usually by examining its most accessible parts—subsistence, technology, and (albeit indirectly) social organization—and seeks broad, cross-cultural

regularities. Emergent approaches in archaeology, however, look to the social meaning behind cultural forms and, to do so, stay within the context of individual cultural traditions or sets of related traditions.

As different as these frameworks are, they are not incompatible. They are different ways of looking at the data, and they ask different questions of the archaeological record. Most striking, however, is the difference in interpretive emphasis. Where culture history describes and processualism seeks to explain, emergent approaches seek to understand meanings and social impacts of peoples' actions in shaping the world around them. Each approach provides working interpretations, and each should be subjected to the kind of systematic examination we described in Chapter 2 that characterizes all pursuits of knowledge.

UNDERSTANDING THE PAST FROM MULTIPLE APPROACHES

The three basic approaches to the past that we have discussed offer different ways of interpreting archaeological evidence. But these different perspectives need not be contradictory or mutually exclusive. New evidence often corrects specific reconstructions of the past, but the broader perspectives offered by the culture historical, processual, and postprocessual approaches often complement one another. Archaeology allows us to improve our understanding of the past by constantly refining an array of different perspectives, not by adhering dogmatically to a single approach.

The way these multiple perspectives improve our understanding of the past is well illustrated by a single issue of major interest to archaeologists: the origins of agriculture, a subject raised earlier in this chapter. The shift from hunting and gathering to agriculture profoundly changed human society and our entire world. This shift is often revealed in the archaeological record in the subtle changes in plant remains that reflect domestication (such as increased seed size), with corresponding changes in tools, settlement patterns, and social organization.

Agriculture developed in various parts of the world (East Asia, Africa, Southwest Asia, North America, Mesoamerica, and South America) at roughly the same time (between 10,000 and 5000 years ago). Because domestication involved plants more often than animals, we focus on plant domestication here. The search for the causes of this development has led to many different interpretations of the archaeological record. We will look at some of these interpretations based on the culture historical, processual, and emergent approaches.

Agriculture and Culture History

Viewed from a culture historical perspective, the causes of agriculture can be seen as a result of both internal and external culture changes. Although the wild plants that were domesticated varied from region to region (for example, rice in

China, wheat in Southwest Asia, and maize in Mesoamerica), the steps leading to agriculture are seen as broadly similar.

The culture historical interpretation sees the causes for the shift to agriculture in a combination of internal and external culture changes (see Fig. 9.1). The internal changes include inevitable variation, invention, and cultural selection. Inevitable variation in this case refers specifically to long-term population increase, which led to the need to increase the food supply. The necessity of finding more food led to invention—in this case, the discovery that plant yields could be increased by interfering with the natural reproductive and growth cycles by weeding wild plants to reduce competition, watering to improve nutrition, and planting seeds to locate plants in the best growing areas. Cultural selection came into play once the benefits of the increased food supply were realized, thus explaining how agricultural societies expanded at the expense of nonagricultural societies.

According to culture history, the origins of agriculture were also due to external changes, especially environmental change, with farming spread subsequently by diffusion and trade. Environmental change—specifically, gradual drying conditions in several key regions where agriculture developed—is seen as a major incentive for the invention of plant domestication. That is, long-term decreases in rainfall reduced the supply of wild plants collected as food by human societies, forcing people to take measures to artificially boost the amount of wild plant food. This led to the same innovations in plant cultivation posited as responses to population increase. In other words, both long-term population growth and environmental change are seen as having the same effect—the invention of plant domestication. In addition, the selective advantages of agriculture led to its spread by diffusion as the knowledge of plant domestication and the trade in domesticated seeds spread agriculture to other societies.

Agriculture and Processualism

The processual approach has refined our understanding of the origins of agriculture. Some of the basic mechanisms remain the same—plant nurturing, seed storage, and planting in the best growing areas remain important—but cause-and-effect relationships have been reworked. And processual interpretations of the archaeological evidence often emphasize specific differences in the cause-and-effect relationships from one region to another. This highlights the importance of a multivariate strategy in archaeology to better understand the past.

In several regions, such as Southwest Asia and Mesoamerica, the prime mover of population growth has been advanced as the principal stimulus for the invention of agriculture. This, of course, recalls one of the internal changes advanced by culture historical interpretations. But in this case, the increase in population is seen as due not to inevitable growth but to conditions specific to each region. For example, in Southwest Asia population increase has been posited as a result of the concentration of people in the most favorable plant-growing areas. Thus, in these areas, a localized population pressure is seen as the impetus for increased reliance on planting and cultivating crops such as wheat.

We have already described one of the most detailed processual interpretations for the origins of agriculture, Flannery's ecological system model for Mesoamerica, which identified the components of early hunting and gathering and defined a stable, self-regulating system in which the scheduling of food procurement and the seasonality of food availability were in equilibrium (see Fig. 9.7). From this, it was posited that agriculture developed from disruption of the equilibrium caused by scheduling conflicts—such as an increasing emphasis on collecting wild maize. Further alterations in the system (including genetic changes in maize that produced larger cob size, along with changes in the size and mobility of society) led to reliance on agriculture (see Fig. 9.8).

Agriculture and Emergent Approaches

Feminist, Marxist, and postprocessual archaeologists have also contributed to our understanding of agricultural origins. Their work underscores the importance of individual decision making in the day-to-day events that led to domestication of plants. They pay particular attention to groups that have been unrecognized or ignored by most previous interpretations, especially the role of women in the cultivation of food plants.

When Europeans arrived in eastern North America, many Native American groups were horticulturalists, and maize was the single most important food crop grown. As we know, maize was originally domesticated in highland Mexico; it reached eastern North America by about A.D. 150–200 among societies that had by then practiced cultivation of local plants for well over 1500 years. Culture historians would see the introduction of maize as a clear case of diffusion, the result of recognition of the value of this productive crop among receptive new societies. Processual archaeologists would see this development as an evolutionary process, in which people gradually modified available food plants within the local ecological system. But a feminist interpretation by Patty Jo Watson and Mary C. Kennedy shows how considering the role of individual decision makers offers an expanded insight into this change. They point out that because maize was not native to eastern North America, it required active care and tending, which reflected a deliberate decision to include and encourage this crop, rather than simply a passive or accidental acceptance of a new cultigen. This implies purposeful behavior on the part of ancient individuals, almost certainly women, highlighting the potential importance of women in promoting this cultural change. Watson and Kennedy do not claim that their view has been demonstrated, but it provides an alternative perspective on eastern North American prehistory and suggestions (such as further study of native plant ecologies) for further research.

The interpretations based on both culture history and processualism almost always seem to be gender-neutral—that is, they do not specify whether men or women played the leading role in the origins of agriculture. There is nothing inherently wrong with this, except that by *not* considering the diversity of society's members along dimensions like gender, age, or class, we tend to presume that roles familiar in our own society were the most plausible for ancient times. In our own cultural context, we tend to think of agriculture as a male pursuit, so when we read about the reconstruction of agricultural origins, we might naturally assume that these early decision-makers, planters, and harvesters were men. This is why studies like that by Watson and Kennedy are so important—they take us out of our own specific cultural context and make us realize that there is plenty of ethnographic evidence to suggest, by analogy, that women were decision-makers, planters, and harvesters, or perhaps just as likely, that these activities were done by women and men working together.

In fact, the case of the origins of agriculture in eastern North America points out how the more established processual interpretation is complemented by more recent practice models being advanced for emergent approaches. The evidence shows that agriculture developed in several floodplain settings in what is now the eastern United States more than 4000 years ago. The established view seems gender-neutral in that it portrays small family groups as the key participants in the process of plant domestication. More recently, feminist, Marxist, and postprocessual archaeologists have sought to specify the kinds of individuals, such as women, who would have taken an active role in collecting and domesticating food plants. The evidence for domestication comes from increasing seed size in native plants such as gourds, marshelder, and sunflowers. The processual view describes this as the result of gradual human interference in the plant growth cycle, by weeding, nurturing plants, storing seeds, and then planting seeds in prepared locations. Views from emergent approaches differ from the others in emphasis; in the illustration discussed, they see planting as the most important step but go on to propose that women, because of their roles in society, were crucial actors in selecting the largest seeds and thereby accelerated the domestication process.

Combining Approaches

Given the complexity of human culture and the difficulties in dealing with the archaeological record, the most effective research avoids being confined to a single theoretical approach. Since no two research situations are the same, each requires a unique combination of theoretical approaches to yield the most productive results from the available archaeological data.

In one case, the need to establish a site chronology, combined with data reflecting details of craft specialization by women, may call for combining culture historical and postprocessual approaches. Elsewhere, the intertwined effects of climatic changes and historically documented events such as religious revivals or political revolts make combining processual and postprocessual approaches the most productive strategy.

These different approaches to the past have appeared sequentially as part of the history of archaeology. Processualism arose in the 1960s as a critique of culture history. Feminist, Marxist, and postprocessual approaches emerged at different times; all flourished as reactions to processualism in the 1980s. And although the initial aim of the processual approach was to critique culture history, it has developed into a mature and sophisticated vehicle to understanding the past in its own right. In a similar vein, the more eclectic set of emergent approaches has moved beyond a critique of processualism, developing an array of active and productive voices for understanding the past.

There have been disagreements over the utility of these approaches—especially, in recent times, between the advocates of processualism and postprocessualism—but most archaeologists see these divisions as harmful to archaeology. In 1989 Robert Preucel organized an international symposium at Southern Illinois University to bring together leaders of processual and postprocessual approaches. Since then, the dialogue has continued, and most archaeologists now agree that the use of all approaches with demonstrated merit benefits everyone. Above all, archaeology continues to grow from the interaction between field research and its diverse theoretical approaches.

SUMMARY

The past is reconstructed from its material remains by synthesizing all analyzed data and interpreting these data in light of the various research questions. Interpretation attempts to describe the what, when, and where of past events and to explain how and why they happened. Three prominent complementary approaches are used: culture history reconstructions set the foundation by identifying the what, when, and where; processual reconstructions follow (often using hypotheses generated from this descriptive reconstruction) to identify the how and why; and emergent feminist, Marxist, and postprocessual approaches seek more fine-grained understanding of people's actions.

These approaches to archaeological interpretation are guided by several alternative views of culture. Culture history reconstructions identify the events of the past based on temporal and spatial syntheses of data. Descriptive models based on the normative concept of culture are used to account for the similarities and differences observed in the data. Differences are usually emphasized and are seen as reflections of cultural change, ascribed to factors originating either inside (invention, selection, drift, and revival) or outside (diffusion, trade, migration, conquest, and environmental change) a particular culture.

Processual reconstruction is concerned with explaining the causes of cultural change based on testing a series of competing hypotheses. Explanatory models based on systems, ecological, or multilinear evolutionary concepts are most often used in such reconstructions. The systems and ecological perspectives emphasize reconstructions at one or more specific points in time, and seek causality from interactions within the system and of the system with its environment. The evolutionary perspective emphasizes reconstructions over time, seeking causality from the identification of single, universal (prime movers), or multiple (multivariate) factors.

Emergent approaches offer a finer-grained interpretation, emphasizing the active role of individuals in shaping the world around them. The perspective for interpretation is that of the culture under study, not that of the archaeologist's own culture. While feminist, Marxist, and postprocessual interpretations are often based on synchronic models (or short-term fluctuations), they can have implications for long-term change as the cumulative sum of these actions over time.

Finally, although archaeologists continue to debate the relative merits of the culture history, processual, and emergent approaches, all three complement each other in developing the most complete and accurate understanding of the past. In confronting the complexities of the past, combining relevant aspects of all available approaches offers the most comprehensive research strategy for the archaeologist.

FOR FURTHER READING

CULTURE HISTORICAL INTERPRETATION
Binford 1968; Flannery 1967, 1986; Haury 1958; Smith 1928; Willey and Phillips 1958; Willey and Sabloff 1993

PROCESSUAL INTERPRETATION
Bettinger 2001; Feinman and Price 2001; Flannery 1968, 1972, 1986; Johnson and Earle 1987; Marcus and Flannery 1996; Netting 1977; Sabloff 1992; Sanders and Price 1968; Turnbull 1972; Willey and Sabloff 1993

EMERGENT INTERPRETATIONS
Feminist interpretations: Brumfiel 1991, 1996, 2006; Conkey and Gero 1997; Conkey and Wylie 2007; Geller 2008; Gero and Conkey 1991; Nelson 2006; Watson and Kennedy 1991
Marxist interpretations: Leone 2005; McGuire 1992; Patterson 2004; Paynter 2000
Postprocessual interpretations: Balter 2005; Hodder 1999, 2000, 2001; Hodder and Hutson 2003; Preucel 1991, 1995

UNDERSTANDING THE PAST FROM MULTIPLE APPROACHES
Bender 1978; Flannery 1968, 1986; Franklin and Paynter 2010; Harris 1996; Pauketat and Meskell 2010; Preucel 1991; Rosenberg 1990; Smith 1993, 2001; Watson and Kennedy 1991

10

Archaeology Today

ARCHAEOLOGY TODAY FACES A challenge to its very existence: the accelerating destruction of the heritage of past societies. As we saw at the beginning of this book, the processes of transformation affect all forms of archaeological data, and among those processes is the impact of later societies. In recent decades, however, the toll of archaeological destruction has reached immense proportions. Critical information has already been lost forever, and many archaeologists fear that unless immediate action is taken, the bulk of the remains of most past societies will be completely destroyed in the near future (Fig. 10.1). In this chapter, we review such challenges and how archaeologists respond to them, and close by considering archaeology in the future.

Archaeologists attempt to stimulate public concern about physical threats to archaeological remains throughout the world. This is especially apparent in the United States, where public awareness and governmental protective action concerning archaeology have traditionally lagged behind other nations. There are encouraging signs that this situation is changing, most excitingly through new partnerships between archaeologists and local communities, and a growing concern with the ethics of archaeological practice (see Chapter 1). The risks remain real, however, and confronting them requires concerted efforts like those we discuss in this chapter.

There are three major sources of destruction. The first, and most senseless, is the looting that robs the remnants of ancient societies for artifacts or art to be sold to collectors. The second is the constant destructive effect of expanding societies all over the world. Everyday activities such as farming and construction, though not intended to obliterate archaeological information, nevertheless take

FIGURE 10.1

This aerial photograph shows Oldtown Village in New Mexico, one of the
many sites of the prehistoric Mimbres culture that have been transformed
by looters into cratered wastelands. Scenes like this are becoming all too
common in many areas of the world, as collectors increase their demand for
authentic archaeological specimens.

their toll. The third is theft of heritage through colonial subjugation or warfare;
here, damage may take the form of physical destruction, injurious interpretation,
or both.

LOOTING AND ANTIQUITIES COLLECTING

Antiquities collecting is fueled by the **looting** of archaeological sites—the illicit
and often illegal digging of sites by nonarchaeologists, who seek not information
about the past but only objects with prestige or aesthetic or economic value. The
weekend souvenir hunter does damage the archaeological record, but the biggest
cause of the rapid acceleration of archaeological site destruction by looting is the
voracious demand for ancient artifacts with commercial value. As long as collectors consider certain kinds of archaeological remains to be art worth collecting,
the economics of supply and demand will lead to the plundering of sites to find
such artifacts that have commercial value. But plundering, of course, destroys
all information about the archaeological association and context of these objects

and usually physically destroys that part of the archaeological record that lacks commercial value. Looting takes place in many contexts, including wartime. The war in Iraq, for example, has compounded catastrophic loss of lives by rampant destruction of irreplaceable cultural heritage. Collecting and commercial trade in antiquities also stimulates the making of counterfeit artifacts, some of which are extremely difficult to detect.

Most archaeologists recognize that the looting of sites can never be stopped completely. Under most circumstances, about all that can be done is to reduce the rate of looting. New laws that restrict domestic and international traffic in archaeological materials are needed, and present laws should be better enforced. International cooperation and standardization of import-export regulations would help, but customs laws alone cannot solve the problem.

Ultimately, however, the way to reduce archaeological looting is to discourage the collector. If collectors no longer sought art from archaeological contexts, there would be no market for archaeological items and thus no incentive for the plundering of sites. Paintings, sculptures, or other works produced for the art market or art patrons are not at issue, for they were never part of the archaeological record. But the line must be drawn at any item that derives from an archaeological context, be it a Maya vase from a tomb or a Greek sculpture dragged from the bottom of the sea. Archaeological remains lose their scientific value when they have been ripped from their archaeological context. Archaeologists and all concerned people must therefore direct their efforts to preventing further destruction of the archaeological record and increase their efforts to preserve archaeological sites (Fig. 10.2).

Collectors are a diverse group of individuals and institutions. Only a few decades ago, most museums acquired at least some of the objects in their archaeological collections by purchase, and thus (directly or indirectly) encouraged looting. Fortunately, that situation has changed: most anthropological museums have pledged to abide by international agreements prohibiting commercial dealings in archaeological materials. Unfortunately, many art museums with collections of so-called primitive art still purchase looted archaeological materials. Still, the individual collector remains the greatest problem, for although museum acquisitions often become public knowledge, purchases of archaeological materials by private individuals usually take place privately and remain secret. This does not mean that collectors are evil. Many may not even be aware of the destruction of knowledge that such collecting spawns. But they should be made aware that as long as they go on buying, looting will continue.

As we saw at the beginning of this book, the United States has problems in protecting its archaeological resources. Hundreds of Native American sites like Slack Farm (see Chapter 1) have been destroyed by looters. Historical sites, such as Civil War battlefields, are also targets of looters—in this case, collectors of military equipment and bullets. Shipwrecks are often considered fair game for treasure hunters, which has allowed many shipwrecks with unique archaeological and historical value to be destroyed by treasure seekers. For example, in

(a)

(b)

FIGURE 10.2

Valuable archaeological evidence is often destroyed because it is sought by collectors and commands a high price on the art market. (a) Stela 1 from Jimbal, Guatemala, was photographed shortly after its discovery in 1965. (b) Less than ten years later, looters had sawed off the top panel to steal the sculpted figures; in the process, they destroyed the head of the Maya ruler and the top of the hieroglyphic inscription.

FIGURE 10.3

The ransacked National Museum of Antiquities in Baghdad, Iraq, continues
to recover stolen artifacts.

Florida, the 1733 wreck of the *San Jose*, originally slated to become the world's
first underwater shipwreck park, is now completely looted, all of its contents
destroyed or scattered.

Unfortunately, there are dozens of such cases of destruction for every case
of proper archaeological investigation. The positive results of such research are
illustrated by the 1554 wreck of the *San Esteban*, excavated off the coast of Texas
in 1973 under the sponsorship of the Texas State Antiquities Committee. The
results of this effort include recovery of important new data on little-known
16th-century ship architecture and construction methods, conservation of the
remains of the ship and its contents, and publication of the results in book,
movie, and exhibition formats aimed at both public and professional audiences.

There is some hope that the destruction of underwater sites such as the
San Jose is a thing of the past. In 1988, Congress passed the Federal Abandoned
Shipwreck Act, and many states have enacted laws protecting historic shipwrecks.

The demand for prized archaeological specimens has grown so much that
collectors are turning to museum collections to satisfy their appetite for antiquities. Robberies of archaeological museums are becoming more commonplace. In
2003, some 13,000 objects were stolen from the National Museum of Antiquities
in war-torn Baghdad, Iraq (Fig. 10.3). These ranged from small clay tablets

(comparable to the one shown in Fig. 8.15) to monumental stone sculptures. Photos of the objects were posted on the Internet, and officials in a half-dozen different countries intercepted would-be smugglers with their goods. By October 2004, nearly half the stolen items had been retrieved and returned to Iraq; otherwise, the people of that nation—and the world—would have lost a priceless portion of their heritage.

The question still remains of how to discourage collectors from seeking and purchasing looted archaeological materials. Since the root of the problem is economic, the solution must be economic as well. One promising line of legal action, already implemented by some governments, involves changes in the inheritance laws so that individuals cannot bequeath archaeological collections to their heirs. Like legitimate art, most antiquities increase in value over time and thus represent an investment. But under this type of legislation, items defined as archaeological materials would pass instead to the state. Many collectors may think twice about purchasing material that ultimately will be appropriated by the government.

The antiquities problem is as complex as it is urgent. In formulating antiquities legislation, politics and patronage often weigh more heavily than the security of archaeological materials. Archaeologists and other interested people must therefore fight to protect the past, or we shall lose it forever.

DESTRUCTION IN THE NAME OF PROGRESS

Although done in the name of progress, the opening of new lands to agriculture, the construction of new roads and buildings, and the creation of flood-control projects inevitably destroy countless remains of past human activity. Almost any action that affects the earth's surface is a threat to the archaeological record. Even under the best of circumstances, we can never answer all our questions about past cultural development, but as the physical remains continue to be obliterated, our ability to ask any new questions at all is drastically reduced.

Obviously, we cannot simply stop population growth and end new construction, so archaeological sites are going to continue to be destroyed. In the face of this fact, an increasing number of archaeologists are adopting a conservationist attitude toward cultural remains. This attitude involves a heightened emphasis on planning and a restructuring of the relative roles of excavation and survey in archaeological research. As we discussed in Chapter 4, archaeologists have dual responsibilities: to the present, especially in relation to descendent communities, and to the future, when greater resources and more sophisticated techniques may allow a more effective recovery of data. Therefore, unthreatened sites should never be completely excavated; some should be left undisturbed for future archaeologists to investigate, and efforts should be made to ensure the preservation of those undisturbed remains. Even for sites threatened with imminent destruction, there has been a change of attitude. Traditionally, the archaeologist's response to such situations has been to excavate quickly and recover as much data as possible—sometimes literally one step ahead of construction crews. In recent decades, a growing array of supportive legislation has allowed archaeologists more often to take the time to assess the situation, reconnoiter the area concerned, and then, *if appropriate*, conduct excavations. The scope of support, of course, is subject to economic and political constraints, too. In the context of the 2012 federal budget, legislation known as MAP-21 (Moving Ahead in the 21st Century) tightened resources for CRM archaeology. As economic conditions improve, it will up to archaeologists and the public to restore funding levels.

CULTURAL RESOURCE MANAGEMENT

Archaeologists have always responded to the threat of destruction, but until recently, the general public and the governments in most nations have shown little such concern. Fortunately, after years of neglect and destruction, many countries have begun to enact protective legislation, based on the premise that the remains of the past, both historic and prehistoric, are a nonrenewable resource, like oil and other minerals, or a fragile resource, like rain forests.

The motives for such conservation efforts are both humanistic and scientific, but they also have a very practical basis. Knowledge of the past fosters not only self-esteem and national unity but also economic development. Tourism, founded at least in part upon a well-documented and spectacular past, is a multimillion-dollar business in some nations. Sites such as Teotihuacan in Mexico (Fig. 10.4), the Great Pyramids in Egypt, Machu Picchu in Peru, and Williamsburg in the United States not only serve as symbols of national heritage but also attract millions of tourists every year. In Egypt, the Aswan Dam salvage project, conducted in the 1960s, was organized by UNESCO to save the magnificent site of Abu Simbel (Fig. 10.5), one of the most visited sites in that country. The program also included work in less spectacular aspects of archaeology, such as locating prehistoric occupation sites that would otherwise have been lost.

In the United States, a series of federal laws dating back to 1906 have been enacted to conserve archaeological sites (Table 10.1). Until recently, however, other countries, including several in Europe and Latin America, were far ahead of the United States in providing legal protection for their archaeological resources. Fortunately, the last two decades have witnessed passage of an important series of laws that have helped the United States to catch up, although additional protective measures are still needed.

With continuing expansion in preservationist legislation, archaeologists have been needed in growing numbers to conduct the surveys and other work the new laws require. As a consequence, a new specialty has arisen within archaeology—**cultural resource management** (CRM). As noted in Chapter 1, this specialty has become the fastest-developing area within American archaeology. Private CRM consulting firms now rival colleges and government agencies as employment places for professional archaeologists.

FIGURE 10.4

Archaeological remains are recognized national symbols for many countries, as well as providing huge revenues from tourists. One of the most famous examples is Teotihuacan, Mexico.

FIGURE 10.5

The spectacular remains of the temple of Abu Simbel were saved from the rising waters behind the Aswan Dam by being cut apart, moved, and reassembled on higher ground at a cost of over $40 million.

TABLE 10.1

Major U.S. Federal Legislation for the Protection of Archaeological Resources

Antiquities Act of 1906	Protects sites on federal lands
Historic Sites Act of 1935	Provides authority for designating National Historic Landmarks and for conducting archaeological surveys before destruction by development programs
National Historic Preservation Act of 1966 (amended 1976 and 1980)	Strengthens protection of sites via the National Register; integrates state and local agencies into the national program for site preservation
National Environmental Policy Act of 1969	Requires all federal agencies to specify the impact of development programs on cultural resources
Archaeological Resources Protection Act of 1979	Provides criminal and civil penalties for looting or damaging sites on public and Native American lands
Convention on Cultural Property Implementation Act of 1982	Authorizes U.S. participation in the 1970 UNESCO convention to prevent illegal international trade in cultural property
Cultural Property Act of 1983	Provides sanctions against U.S. import or export of illicit antiquities
Federal Abandoned Shipwreck Act of 1988	Removes sunken ships of archaeological interest from marine salvage jurisdiction; provides for protection under state jurisdiction
Native American Graves Protection and Repatriation Act of 1990	Specifies the return of Native American remains and cultural property by U.S. museums to Native American groups

This development has not been without growing pains, which have stemmed chiefly from two related issues. First, the increase in both available funds and the demand for archaeologists to conduct studies created some confusion related to complexities of the federal laws, regulations, and bureaucratic procedures and led to a shortage of qualified archaeologists able to undertake the flood of new contracts. Second, archaeologists had to reexamine seriously the ethics and professional standards appropriate for this kind of work, such as resolving competing priorities between preservation and excavation.

These growing pains led to some very positive responses: establishment of ROPA (see Chapter 1) and an increasingly positive attitude of archaeologists in general toward CRM as an opportunity for creative research. As evidence of this,

FIGURE 10.6

Atkeson Pueblo at Oak Creek Pueblo is one of two important Sinagua
culture ruins acquired for preservation by the Archaeological Conservancy
in 1985. This ruin is located on Oak Creek in the Verde Valley of central
Arizona and dates to A.D. 1200–1450. At one time, there were about forty
Sinagua culture ruins in the area, but most have been destroyed by looters
and by development. The Sinagua are thought to be ancestors of the
modern Hopi.

an expanding number of archaeologists are actively trying to coordinate with local
descendent communities as well as government officials, such as heads of state historic preservation offices, to formulate broad regional research goals and priorities.
Though flexible, such plans increase the applicability of data collected under CRM
projects to questions of broader and more general theoretical interest.

But CRM does not solve all the problems of archaeological destruction. The
laws providing for such work pertain only to sites on public land or those threatened by government-sponsored projects. Many sites, however, especially in the
eastern United States, where far less land is under public control, are on privately owned property. To preserve these sites, threatened just as often by looting, construction development, or simple neglect, archaeologists Mark Michel
and Steven LeBlanc created a private organization modeled on the successful
Nature Conservancy. Incorporated in 1979, the Archaeological Conservancy
seeks to identify archaeological sites worthy of protection, secure their preservation through purchase or donation, and educate the public about the need to
preserve our cultural heritage (Fig. 10.6).

Once a site has been secured, the Archaeological Conservancy ensures its short-term protection but eventually donates or sells it to institutions able to undertake long-term conservation. For example, the Conservancy has donated the Fort Craig site in New Mexico to the Bureau of Land Management and two other sites—Savage Cave in Kentucky and Powers Fort in Missouri—to local universities as centers for both environmental and archaeological research. As its resources grow, the Archaeological Conservancy is now a major factor for the protection of archaeological sites in the United States. And this illustrates wonderfully the kinds of effective action NGOs can pursue for protecting the past, as we noted in Chapter 1.

Archaeologists cannot preserve or excavate all sites, and some sites have more to tell us than others. Clearly, then, increased attention should be paid to improving the means by which decisions are made between protection, immediate investigation, and sometimes-necessary sacrifice. The question is not whether the past should be protected, but how best to protect it in the context of a rapidly growing and changing world.

EFFECTS OF NATIONALISM, COLONIALISM, AND WAR

As George Orwell once said, "Who controls the present controls the past, and who controls the past controls the future." Recent events in Iraq and elsewhere have highlighted how ancient monuments and archaeological remains can become weapons (and simultaneously victims) in modern social conflict. As discussed in Chapters 8 and 9, scholars recognize increasingly how material culture expresses and reinforces social identity for ethnic, national, religious, and other groups. And the preceding section called attention to the role of places like Teotihuacan, Machu Picchu, and Williamsburg in symbolizing national identity and heritage. It should not surprise us, then, that groups in conflict with one another often see destruction of key historical or archaeological items as a means of obliterating emblems valued by "the enemy." For example, malicious vandals desecrate shrines and temples with hateful graffiti; religious icons are stolen or destroyed. More publicly dramatic is capture or destruction of whole buildings. In Aleppo, Syria, in 2012, the walled medieval city as well as the people in it have suffered in ferocious battles for control of its historic location. The effect of such conflicts can be demoralizing, but it can also galvanize victims to impassioned resistance or retaliation.

Less overtly dramatic but often equally devastating have been the effects of colonialism on the archaeological heritage of the colonized. The legacy of colonial attitudes toward subjugated peoples lingers in colonists' accounts of the precolonial past of those peoples. And too often, as we saw in Chapter 2, those accounts provided justification for continued subjugation, by portraying the indigenous

societies as inferior to the colonizers or by assuming they were and so attribut-
ing creation of their monuments to others. A particularly infamous example—
but, unfortunately, not unique—is the archaeology of Great Zimbabwe, in the
modern African nation of Zimbabwe. This imposing ruin is now interpreted as
the political, economic, and religious capital of a 13th- to 15th-century kingdom,
prominent for its far-flung exchange of gold and other materials in and beyond
southeastern Africa. For decades, however, when Zimbabwe was first a colony and
then a nation known as Rhodesia, archaeologists and other members of ruling-
class society commonly presumed that such a place must have been built and governed by earlier colonists, perhaps Phoenicians. Only late in the 20th century was
Great Zimbabwe "restored" to its rightful creators, the Shona and related peoples
who still live in this part of Africa.

Certainly, not all colonists' accounts of the past are as problematic as those
of Great Zimbabwe. But just as individual archaeologists' interests and questions are shaped by their personal and national backgrounds, so are traditions
of archaeological interpretation shaped by the *collective* backgrounds of those
who do the interpreting. Since at least the early explorers of Renaissance times,
described in Chapter 2, archaeologists have come more often from colonizing
rather than colonized societies. In recent years, however, descendent groups in
many parts of the world have claimed quite active roles in determining how their
past is portrayed and in controlling access to the archaeological traces of their
past. Native American and Australian Aboriginal groups have been particularly
vocal and effective, and African American voices are being heard more often as
well.

WORKING WITH DESCENDENT COMMUNITIES

A growing number of former colonies and ethnic or other minorities are
actively pursuing preservation of their traditions and heritage. In Chapter 1,
we linked this activism to the growth of indigenous archaeologies. Often the
activism involves alliances with archaeologists to protect against common
foes—depredations of looting or runaway development, as in the community-
based archaeology discussed in Chapter 1. In several instances, however,
archaeologists have been a target of protest. Some archaeologists have been
accused of being unconcerned about the rights of native groups, and some
native peoples have demanded the return or reburial of excavated artifacts
and human remains. A federal law enacted in 1990 provides for the repatriation of Native American materials in the United States and for the new
National Museum of the American Indian, which opened in September 2004
as part of the Smithsonian Institution in Washington, D.C.

Despite this U.S. law, not all cases between archaeologists and native
peoples are resolved quickly or easily. Controversies surrounding the Ancient

One, also known as "Kennewick Man," have been particularly contentious. The well-preserved human skeleton was discovered by accident near Kennewick, Washington, in 1996. Although his features did not seem similar to those of Native Americans, the recognized style of a projectile point embedded in the man's hipbone appeared to be consistent with the radiocarbon age of a small bone fragment, suggesting the man had died more than 9000 years ago. The Umatilla and other Native American tribes together protested strenuously that destructive analyses must stop and the bones be reburied; multiple archaeologists argued, however, that the extraordinary skeleton merited careful examination. Bitter dispute raged for a decade before federal courts ultimately permitted the examination. Although the Ancient One has been housed in Seattle's Burke Museum since 2004, his ultimate resting place remains unresolved.

Christina Garza and Shirley Powell call the case over Kennewick Man "the first serious legal challenge to NAGPRA [Native American Graves Protection and Repatriation Act] since its passage" (Garza and Powell 2001:51). They go on, nevertheless, as follows:

> The bottom line . . . is that archaeologists *have* accepted reburial and are still able to do archaeology . . . [and it is likely that] a "new" archaeology will evolve that studies ancient populations with their descendants' consent and collaboration.

This kind of collaboration is definitely on the increase, reflecting concerns worldwide for more inclusive and ethical research. Community-based and indigenous archaeologies introduced in Chapter 1 illustrate the trend. As archaeologist and member of the Choctaw tribe Joe Watkins phrases it, the central question is: "to whom does the past belong?" Archaeologists and concerned descendent communities recognize that the greatest agent of destruction of cultural resources is the looter motivated by monetary greed rather than interest in, knowledge of, or respect for the past. The solution is already at hand when archaeologists and descendent communities collaborate to protect cultural resources from looting and increase understanding of the past. Under such agreements, professional archaeologists, including a growing number of Native American archaeologists, conduct research to gain knowledge for both science and the living descendants of ancient societies. More and more research is designed from the outset to respect the concerns of living descendants, where all involved are committed both to understanding the fragile archaeological record and to protecting it from wanton destruction.

The New York African Burial Ground is a prominent case in point. Before a new office building was constructed in downtown Manhattan, the federal government hired CRM archaeologists to investigate the cultural remains that would be affected. Although a late-17th- and 18th-century African and African-American cemetery was known from historical maps, excavators vastly underestimated the number of burials that would be encountered, as well as their importance both interpretively and spiritually to living descendants and the community at large.

Pressed by construction deadlines, archaeologists unearthed more than 400 skeletons in 1991 and 1992, despite mounting public protest from members of New York's African-American communities that they had never been consulted and were adamantly opposed to what was happening. Not only was the exhumation of the burials viewed as sacrilege, but little or no analysis had been planned of a sort that would justify removal of the skeletons under any circumstances, and the anticipated destination of the remains was murky. After much heated public confrontation, excavations were halted in 1992 when

> the Mayor of New York (the first African American elected to that office), New York State Legislators, and other members of the Congressional Black Caucus in Washington were empowered to step in and, despite opposition, brought a halt to construction on behalf of the ground-swell of community concern in New York and in keeping with Federal law.
>
> (BLAKEY 1998:54)

As a direct result of insistence by the local African-American communities and influential individuals at the local and national level, a new research staff was named with Michael L. Blakey as its scientific director. In 1993, the African Burial Ground was designated a National Historic Landmark. After much public consultation, a new research design was drawn up to focus subsequent analyses directly on the lives of the enslaved populace interred in the cemetery. Issues include identifying specific African cultural ancestry, changes involved in enslavement, quality of life, and forms of resistance. Dialogue linking researchers, the New York African-American communities, and the wider public has remained prominent, through a newsletter, public education programs, documentary films, and other means of communication. In October 2003, the ancestral remains were respectfully re-interred in New York, in the African Burial Ground Memorial Site.

Lessons from the New York African Burial Ground have intensified the attention paid to ethics in archaeological research. As community-based and indigenous archaeologies grow in strength around the world, this attention increases. More diverse perspectives are represented effectively in research questions and design, and all participants benefit from the knowledge gained. Partnership between Cochiti Pueblo and the University of Pennsylvania Museum was cited in Chapter 1, illustrating the diverse perspectives fostered in collaborative study, in this case community response to the Pueblo Revolt of 1680. Oral histories complement both written documents and archaeological mapping of the hilltop refuge at Kotyiti. In the San Pedro Ethnohistory Project, introduced in Chapter 8, Chip Colwell-Chanthaphonh and T. J. Ferguson collaborate with official representatives of four tribal governments in Arizona to consider findings from a century of archaeological documentation in the area jointly with tribal oral accounts of the past. Resultant links between indigenous perspectives and archaeological culture history "expand the humanistic understanding of scientific findings of San Pedro history" (2004:9).

THE RESPONSIBILITIES OF ARCHAEOLOGY

The archaeological profession has assumed certain responsibilities for the cultural resources that all peoples of the world have inherited from the past:

1. To preserve the world's archaeological resources.

2. To prevent the destruction of archaeological sites and resources. Toward this end, it is unethical for archaeologists to maintain personal collections of archaeological materials or engage in any commercial activity—including purchase, sale, or evaluation—involving artifacts or other archaeological material.

3. To conduct their research in a manner consistent with the standards of archaeology and ensure that their research records and data are available for examination by qualified scholars.

4. To publish the results of their research, ensuring that all research reports are accurate and unbiased and are available to all who would benefit from such knowledge, including both professional and public audiences.

5. To respect the rights of the living descendants of the ancient populations that created the archaeological record.

6. To work toward future improvements and the continuity of the archaeological profession.

These ethical standards highlight the archaeologist's prime obligations—to protect and preserve the archaeological record, to conduct research to the highest standards, to share as widely as possible the information gained from that research, to respect the rights of people descended from those who created that record, to improve the field, and to educate new generations of archaeologists.

It is especially appropriate in this concluding chapter to stress the responsibilities that archaeologists have toward the future. Like all scientists, archaeologists must ensure that their research is accurate and unbiased and that its results are available to future generations of both scholars and the general public. The dissemination of valid archaeological information is crucial to public awareness of the value of understanding our past and of the tragic loss of heritage caused by the wanton destruction of cultural resources.

Archaeological information is made available by a variety of means, ranging from public lectures and museum exhibits to the publication of both popular and scholarly articles and books. Most archaeologists recognize the obligation to make the results of their research available to their professional colleagues, but, unfortunately, not all see the need to provide this information to a more general audience. Because archaeologists are uniquely able to address the full range of the human past, they have an obligation to educate as many people as possible about the richness of our human heritage. The communication of archaeological information to the general public is not only an ethical responsibility but also wise policy, as it stimulates the recruitment of future archaeologists. Most important, perhaps, knowledge is the most powerful weapon against the destructive forces that threaten to rob all of us of our past cultural heritage.

ARCHAEOLOGY FOR TOMORROW

Archaeology in the future promises exciting advances on many fronts. As scholars such as Margaret Conkey, James Snead, and Jeremy Sabloff have noted, some developments in archaeology in the 21st century were anticipated well. Other developments, however, weren't envisioned in the 1980s and 1990s. At this point, even without a crystal ball, we can estimate that decades to come will see advances in technologies of survey, excavation, and analysis that will continue to enhance the precision and clarity of archaeological evidence and inference, as suggested earlier in Chapters 5 through 8. These will include conservation techniques as well as ones for the field research that often precedes conservation, whether in museums, field laboratories, or specialized laboratories like the Smithsonian Institution. For some future investigations, field research will rely more on remote sensing and other relatively noninvasive methods for ethical, conservation, or cost reasons. Still, excavation will remain invaluable in many if not most other cases. As foreshadowed in Chapters 1, 3, 4, 9, and 10, growth in collaborative research will increase understanding among all who have stakes in understanding and protecting the human past, including descendent communities and archaeologists. Moreover, collaboration among archaeologists and other scientists will enable more sophisticated interpretations of such modern concerns as health and illness, or establishment of reliable food supplies. And importantly, archaeology will continue to contribute significantly to improving lives in the modern world.

In this and previous chapters, we have seen that archaeological research is often relevant to life today. Investigating and conserving such places as Teotihuacan or Williamsburg foster pride in one's heritage. As often, archaeology can benefit living people in ecological, economic, and social ways. For instance, a growing number of scholars urge that archaeology can contribute much to understanding current issues of human-environment relations, a topic raised in Chapter 6. Sander van der Leeuw and Charles Redman argue that the long-term dynamics documented archaeologically in diverse geographic and cultural settings provide invaluable depth of time for understanding what they call socio-natural relations, between people and the world around them. No single discipline alone can solve such complex modern issues as desertification, hunger, and sustainability in food and water, but increasing collaboration among varied social, biological, and natural scientists offers the best hope for effective change. In part toward realizing these goals, Arizona State University has established a School of Sustainability, with Redman as its director.

In his book, *Archaeology Matters: Action Archaeology in the Modern World*, Sabloff highlights four important themes in archaeology's relevance to people today: sustainability, as already mentioned, plus warfare (is it inevitable or not?), understanding cities and how they work, and protection of the world's cultural heritage. Again, the sweep of archaeological evidence across time is invaluable for examining what has worked for each of these challenges, and what hasn't. Two additional specific cases will highlight diverse other ways in which archaeology is relevant to modern life.

The first example focuses on homelessness. Innovative work by Larry Zimmerman and others uses techniques of archaeological survey to document systematically the material traces of homeless people's activities. The team has identified "stopping places" for eating or hanging out; short-term places for sleeping, with no hint of permanency; and campsites, with some shelter construction, cooking facilities, and evidence of meals. These patterns are similar to traces of practices in mobile, foraging groups elsewhere in time and space. One instance of objects found illustrates inferences drawn:

> Small, unused bottles of shampoo and hair conditioner of the type found in hotels rooms were relatively common. Why they were there at all was puzzling until investigators discovered that local churches provided them, asking parishioners to collect such items when they stayed in hotels so that the church could distribute them. The problem is that in their camps, the homeless rarely had access to enough water to use them. (Little and Zimmerman 2010:145)

The archaeologists' aim is not to criticize the churches and shelters, but to identify the mismatch between aid policies and how they are received. From these studies, archaeologists found that behaviors of homeless people were similar to those of mobile, foraging societies elsewhere—locating key food and other resources and finding safe places to live. The goal of the research is not simply to identify these and other patterns, but also to engage constructively those who set and implement public policy toward the homeless.

A second example involves applying archaeological skills in response to human disasters. Richard Gould writes of rigorous scientific archaeological techniques and their contributions to survivors, family, and investigators in the aftermath of such devastating events as 9/11 at the World Trade Center, the 2003 Station Nightclub fire in Rhode Island, mass killings in Bosnia in the early 1990s, and Hurricane Katrina in and around New Orleans in 2005. Careful recording of physical remains, forensic studies of the scene and the deceased, and ethnoarchaeological examination of spontaneous memorials have all assisted in prosecuting those responsible and in giving some preliminary answers toward closure—never complete—for survivors, families, and witnesses. Members of the Society for American Archaeology can volunteer to help the Forensic Archaeology Recovery (FAR) team in a mass-fatality disaster.

SUMMARY

Archaeology today faces an unprecedented crisis from rapidly increasing destruction of archaeological sites, which causes loss of the nonrenewable cultural resources of humankind. Some of this destruction is an inevitable result of activities such as farming and construction, and some is a by-product of social conflict. But the greatest and most troubling toll is taken by looting. Most of this intentional destruction is generated to supply an illicit worldwide market in antiquities. Although there is no easy solution to this destruction, there is reason for cautious optimism. Protective laws in the United States and in many other countries address the issues, together with nongovernmental preservation initiatives such as the Archaeological Conservancy and the efforts of descendent communities. These measures have fostered new attitudes about the past, mobilizing concerned individuals and organizations to protect and preserve the cultural heritage of all peoples. Archaeologists are central to this effort, for they have a professional responsibility to protect the record of the past, partnering with descendent communities around the world, and, through training and publication, collectively ensuring that the knowledge acquired from their research is preserved and passed on to future generations.

FOR FURTHER READING

LOOTING AND ANTIQUITIES COLLECTING
Atwood 2004; Barkan and Bush 2002; Fagan 1988; Giesecke 1987; LeBlanc 1983

DESTRUCTION IN THE NAME OF PROGRESS
Harmon, McManamon, and Pitcaithley 2006; Wendorf 1973

CULTURAL RESOURCE MANAGEMENT
Cleere 1984, 1989, 1995; Ford 1983; Harmon, McManamon, and Pitcaithley 2006; King 1998, 2002; Lipe 1974, 1984; Michel 1981; Neumann and Sanford 2001; Pwiti 1996; Sebastian 2010; Sebastian and Lipe 2008

EFFECTS OF NATIONALISM, COLONIALISM, AND WAR
Arnold 1990; Atwood 2004; Gero and Root 1990; Gosden 2004; Kohl and Fawcett 1995; Kuklick 1991; Leone 2005; Liebmann and Rizvi 2008; McIntosh 1999; Pwiti 1996; Schmidt and Patterson 1995

COLLABORATIONS WITH DESCENDANT COMMUNITIES
Blakey 1998, 2001; Bray 2001; Bruchac, Hart, and Wobst 2012; Chatters 2001; Colwell-Chanthaphonh and Ferguson 2004; Ferguson 1996; Ferguson and Colwell-Chanthaphonh 2006; Franklin and McKee 2004; Garza and Powell 2001; Harrington 1993; Kehoe 2008; Killion 2008; King 1998; La Roche and Blakey 1997; Layton 1989a, 1989b; Leone 2005; Little 2002, 2007; Marshall 2002; Shackel and Chambers 2004; Silliman 2008; Silliman and Ferguson 2010; Society for American Archaeology 1986; Swidler et al. 1999; Thomas 2001; Watkins 2000, 2003; Watkins et al. 2000

THE RESPONSIBILITIES OF ARCHAEOLOGY

Allen and Joyce 2010; Altschul and Patterson 2010; Bender and Smith 2000; Blakey 1998; Burke and Smith 2007; Carroll 2001; Champe et al. 1961; Fowler 1987; Harmon, McManamon, and Pitcaithley 2006; Hubert 1989; King 1998; Little 2002, 2007; Lynott and Wylie 2000; J. Sabloff 1998, 2008; Zimmerman et al. 2003

ARCHAEOLOGY FOR TOMORROW

Albertson 2009; Allen and Joyce 2010; Battle-Baptiste 2011; Blau and Ubelaker 2009; Conkey 2010; Dawdy 2006; Franklin and Paynter 2010; Gould 2007; Lanata and Drennan 2010; Little and Shackel 2007; Little and Zimmerman 2010; Reitz and Shackley 2012; Sabloff 2008; Scarborough and Lucero 2010; Silliman 2008; Snead and Sabloff 2010; van der Leeuw and Redman 2002; Zeder, Buikstra, and van der Leeuw 2010; Zimmerman and Welch 2006

Bibliography

Note: This brief bibliography is designed to introduce the student to the vast literature on archaeology and the human past. The works listed include books and articles, both recent publications and classics. A fuller bibliography can be found in *Archaeology: Discovering Our Past*, 3rd ed. (Sharer and Ashmore, 2003). Of course, we would also recommend that the interested reader explore libraries for other works, including new books and issues of magazines and journals. In general, periodicals such as *Archaeology, National Geographic, Natural History, Scientific American*, and *Smithsonian* publish articles for the broadest audience. Such journals as *American Antiquity, American Scientist, Journal of Field Archaeology, Nature*, and *Science* are more technical in content and language.

Agurcia Fasquelle, R. 1986. Snakes, jaguars, and outlaws: Some comments on Central American archaeology. In *Research and Reflections in Archaeology and History. Essays in Honor of Doris Stone*, ed. E. W. Andrews V, pp. 1–9. New Orleans: Middle American Research Institute, Tulane University.

Aitken, M. J. 1990. *Science-Based Dating in Archaeology*. London: Longman.

Albertson, N. 2009. Archaeology of the homeless. *Archaeology* 62 (6): 42–43.

Allen, K. M. S., S. W. Green, and E. B. W. Zubrow, eds. 1990. *Interpreting Space: GIS and Archaeology*. London: Taylor & Francis.

Allen, M., and R. A. Joyce. 2010. Communicating archaeology in the 21st century. In *Voices in American Archaeology*, eds. W. Ashmore, D. T. Lippert, and B. J. Mills, pp. 270–290. Washington, D.C.: SAA Press.

Altschul, J. H., and T. C. Patterson. 2010. Trends in employment and training in American archaeology. In *Voices in American Archaeology*, eds. W. Ashmore, D. T. Lippert, and B. J. Mills, pp. 291–316. Washington, D.C.: SAA Press.

Alva, W., and C. B. Donnan. 1993. *Royal Tombs of Sipán*. Los Angeles: Fowler Museum of Cultural History, UCLA.

Ambrose, S. H., J. Buikstra, and H. W. Krueger. 2003. Status and gender differences in diet at Mound 72, Cahokia, revealed by isotopic analysis of bone. *Journal of Anthropological Archaeology* 22 (3): 217–226.

Andrén, A. 1998. *Between Artifacts and Texts: Historical Archaeology in Global Perspective*. New York: Plenum Press.

Andresen, J. M., B. F. Byrd, M. D. Elson, R. H. McGuire, R. G. Mendoza, E. Staski, and J. P. White. 1981. The deer hunters: Star Carr reconsidered. *World Archaeology* 13: 31–46.

Appelbaum, Barbara. 2011. *Conservation Treatment Methodology*. Seattle, WA: CreateSpace Independent Publishing Platform.

Arden, H. 1989. Who owns our past? *National Geographic* 175 (3): 376–392.

Arnold, B. 1990. The past as propaganda: Totalitarian archaeology in Nazi Germany. *Antiquity* 64: 464–478.

Ashmore, W., D. T. Lippert, and B. J. Mills, eds. 2010. *Voices in American Archaeology*. Washington, D.C.: SAA Press.

Atwood, R. 2004. *Stealing History: Tomb Raiders, Smugglers, and the Looting of the Ancient World*. New York: St. Martin's Press.

Aveni, A. F., ed. 1982. *Archaeoastronomy in the New World*. Cambridge: Cambridge University Press.

———. 2000. *Between the Lines: The Mystery of the Ancient Ground Drawings of Nazca, Peru*. Austin: University of Texas Press.

Bahn, P. G. 1995. Last days of the Iceman. *Archaeology* 48 (3): 66–70.

———. ed. 2003. *Written in Bones: How Human Remains Unlock the Secrets of the Dead.* Toronto and Buffalo: Firefly Books.

Baillie, G. L. 1995. *A Slice Through Time: Dendrochronology and Precision Dating.* London: Batsford.

Balter, M. 2005. *The Goddess and the Bull: Çatalhöyük: An Archaeological Journey to the Dawn of Civilization.* New York: Free Press.

Bannister, B. 1970. Dendrochronology. In *Science in Archaeology*, 2nd ed., ed. D. Brothwell and E. S. Higgs, pp. 191–205. New York: Praeger.

Barfield, L. 1994. The Iceman reviewed. *Antiquity* 68: 10–26.

Barkan, E., and R. Bush, eds. 2002. *Claiming the Stones/Naming the Bones: Cultural Property and the Negotiation of National and Ethnic Identity.* Los Angeles: Getty Research Institute.

Bass, G. F., ed. 2005. *Beneath the Seven Seas: Adventures with the Institute of Nautical Archaeology.* London: Thames & Hudson.

Battle-Baptiste, W. 2011. *Black Feminist Archaeology.* Walnut Creek, CA: Left Coast Press.

Beck, C., and G. T. Jones. 2000. Obsidian hydration dating, past and present. In *It's about Time: A History of Archaeological Dating in North America*, ed. S. E. Nash, pp. 124–151. Salt Lake City: University of Utah Press.

Bender, B. 1998. *Stonehenge: Making Space.* Oxford: Berg.

Bender, S. J., and G. S. Smith, eds. 2000. *Teaching Archaeology in the 21st Century.* Washington, D.C.: Society for American Archaeology.

Bettinger, R. 2001. Holocene hunter-gatherers. In *Archaeology at the Millennium: A Sourcebook*, ed. G. M. Feinman and T. D. Price, pp. 137–195. New York: Kluwer Academic/Plenum.

Billman, B., and G. M. Feinman, eds. 1999. *Settlement Pattern Studies in the Americas: Fifty Years since Virú.* Washington, D.C.: Smithsonian Institution Press.

Binford, L. R. 1962. Archaeology as anthropology. *American Antiquity* 28: 217–225.

———. 1964. A consideration of archaeological research design. *American Antiquity* 29: 425–441.

———. 1967. Smudge pits and hide smoking: The use of analogy in archaeological reasoning. *American Antiquity* 32: 1–12.

———. 1972. *An Archeological Perspective.* New York: Seminar Press.

———. 1981. *Bones: Ancient Men and Modern Myths.* New York: Academic Press.

———. 1982. The archaeology of place. *Journal of Anthropological Archaeology* 1: 5–31.

———. 1983. *In Pursuit of the Past: Decoding the Archaeological Record.* New York: Thames & Hudson.

———. 1989. *Debating Archaeology.* San Diego: Academic Press.

———. 2001. *Constructing Frames of Reference: An Analytical Method for Archaeological Theory Building Using Hunter-Gatherer and Environmental Data Sets.* Berkeley: University of California Press.

Binford, L. R., and S. R. Binford. 1969. Stone tools and human behavior. *Scientific American* 220 (4): 70–84.

Binford, S. R. 1968. Ethnographic data and understanding the Pleistocene. In *Man the Hunter*, ed. R. B. Lee and I. DeVore, pp. 274–275. Chicago: Aldine.

Biscott, J. L., and R. J. Rosenbauer. 1981. Uranium series dating of human skeletal remains from the Del Mar and Sunnyvale sites, California. *Science* 213: 1003–1006.

Black, S. L., and K. Jolly. 2003. *Archaeology by Design.* Walnut Creek, Calif.: AltaMira Press.

Blakey, M. L. 1998. The New York African Burial Ground Project: An examination of enslaved lives, a construction of ancestral ties. *Transforming Anthropology* 7: 53–58.

———. 2001. Bioarchaeology of the African Diaspora in the Americas: Its origins and scope. *Annual Review of Anthropology* 30: 387–422.

Blau, S., and D. H. Ubelaker, eds. 2009. *Handbook of Forensic Archaeology and Anthropology. World Archaeological Congress Research Handbooks in Archaeology.* Walnut Creek, Calif.: Left Coast Press.

Blinman, E. 2000. The foundations, practice, and limitations of ceramic dating in the American Southwest. In *It's about Time: A History of Archaeological Dating in North America*, ed. S. E. Nash, pp. 41–59. Salt Lake City: University of Utah Press.

Bordes, F. 1968. *The Old Stone Age*. New York: McGraw-Hill.

Boutin, A., A. Baadsgaard, and J. Buikstra, eds. 2011. *Breathing New Life into the Evidence of Death: Contemporary Approaches to Bioarchaeology*. Santa Fe, N.M.: SAR Press.

Boyd, D. C. 1996. Skeletal correlates of human behavior in the Americas. *Journal of Archaeological Method and Theory* 3: 189–251.

Brain, C. K. 1981. *The Hunters or the Hunted? An Introduction to African Cave Taphonomy*. Chicago: University of Chicago Press.

Bray, T. L., ed. 2001. *The Future of the Past: Archaeologists, Native Americans, and Repatriation*. New York: Garland.

Brew, J. O. 1968. *One Hundred Years of Anthropology*. Cambridge, Mass.: Harvard University Press.

Bruchac, M., S. M. Hart, and H. M. Wobst, eds. 2010. *Indigenous Archaeologies: A Reader on Decolonization*. Walnut Creek, Calif.: Left Coast Press.

Brumfiel, E. M. 1991. Weaving and cooking: Women's production in Aztec Mexico. In *Engendering Archaeology*, ed. J. M. Gero and M. W. Conkey, pp. 224–251. Oxford: Blackwell.

———. 1992. Breaking and entering the ecosystem—Gender, class, and faction steal the show. *American Anthropologist* 94: 551–556.

———. 1996. Figurines and the Aztec state: Testing the effectiveness of ideological domination. In *Gender and Archaeology*, ed. R. P. Wright, pp. 143–166. Philadelphia: University of Pennsylvania Press.

———. 2006. Cloth, gender, continuity, and change: Fabricating unity in anthropology. *American Anthropologist* 108: 862–877.

Brumfiel, E. M., and J. W. Fox, eds. 1994. *Factional Competition and Political Development in the New World*. Cambridge, U.K.: Cambridge University Press.

Buikstra, J. E., ed. 1981. *Prehistoric Tuberculosis in the Americas*. Northwestern University Archaeological Program, Scientific Papers 5. Evanston, Ill.: Northwestern University.

Buikstra, J. E., and L. E. Beck, eds. 2006. *Bioarchaelogy: The Contextual Analysis of Human Remains*. Boston: Academic Press.

Bunn, H. T., J. W. K. Harris, G. Isaac, Z. Kaufulu, E. Kroll, K. Schick, N. Toth, and A. K. Behrensmeyer. 1980. FxJj50: An early Pleistocene site in northern Kenya. *World Archaeology* 12: 109–136.

Burke, H., and C. Smith, eds. 2007. *Archaeology to Delight and Instruct: Active Learning in the University Classroom*. Walnut Creek, Calif.: Left Coast Press.

Cahan, D., L. H. Keeley, and F. L. Van Noten. 1979. Stone tools, toolkits, and human behavior in prehistory. *Current Anthropology* 20: 661–683.

Carmichael, D. L., R. H. Lafferty, and B. L. Molyneaux. 2003. *Excavation*. Walnut Creek, Calif.: AltaMira Press.

Carroll, M. S. 2001. *Delivering Archaeological Information Electronically*. SAA Monographs. Washington, D.C.: Society for American Archaeology.

Catsambis, A., B. Ford, and D. L. Hamilton, eds. 2011. *The Oxford Handbook of Maritime Archaeology*. New York: Oxford University Press.

Champe, J. L., D. S. Byers, C. Evans, A. K. Guthe, H. W. Hamilton, E. B. Jelks, C. W. Meighan, S. Olafson, G. I. Quimby, W. Smith, and F. Wendorf. 1961. Four statements for archaeology. *American Antiquity* 27: 137–138.

Chang, K. C. 1972. *Settlement Patterns in Archaeology*. Modules in Anthropology 24. Reading, Mass.: Addison-Wesley.

Chase, A. F., D. Z. Chase, J. F. Weishampel, J. B. Drake, R. L. Shrestha, K. C. Slatton, J. J. Awe, and W. E. Carter. 2011. Airborne LiDAR, archaeology, and the ancient Maya landscape at Caracol, Belize. *Journal of Archaeological Science* 38: 387–398.

Chatters, J. C. 2001. *Ancient Encounters: Kennewick Man and the First Americans.* New York: Simon & Schuster.

Chippindale, C., and P. S. C. Taçon, eds. 1998. *The Archaeology of Rock Art.* Cambridge, U.K.: Cambridge University Press.

Christenson, A. L., ed. 1989. *Tracing Archaeology's Past: The Historiography of Archaeology.* Carbondale: Southern Illinois University Press.

Clark, J. G. D. [1954] 1971. *Excavations at Star Carr.* Reprint. Cambridge: Cambridge University Press.

Clarke, D. L., ed. 1972. *Models in Archaeology.* London: Methuen.

Cleere, H., ed. 1984. *Approaches to the Archaeological Heritage: A Comparative Study of World Cultural Resource Management Systems.* Cambridge, U.K.: Cambridge University Press.

———, ed. 1989. *Archaeological Heritage Management in the Modern World.* London: Unwin Hyman.

———. 1995. Cultural landscapes as world heritage. *Conservation and Management of Archaeological Sites* 1: 63–68.

Coles, B., and J. M. Coles. 1986. *Sweet Track to Glastonbury: The Somerset Levels in Prehistory.* New York: Thames & Hudson.

Coles, J. M. 1984. *The Archaeology of Wetlands.* Edinburgh: Edinburgh University Press.

———. 1989. The world's oldest road. *Scientific American* 261 (5): 100–106.

Collins, J. M., and B. L. Molyneaux. 2003. *Archaeological Survey.* Walnut Creek, Calif.: AltaMira Press.

Colwell-Chanthaphonh, C., and T. J. Ferguson. 2004. Virtue ethics and the practice of history: Native Americans and archaeologists along the San Pedro Valley of Arizona. *Journal of Social Archaeology* 4: 5–27

———, eds. 2008. *Collaboration in Archaeological Practice: Engaging Descendant Communities.* Lanham, Md.: AltaMira Press.

Conkey, M. W. 2010. Re-visioning archaeology, or, the future matters as much as the past. In *Voices in American Archaeology*, eds. W. Ashmore, D. T. Lippert, and B. J. Mills, pp. 8–26. Washington, D.C.: SAA Press.

Conkey, M. W., and J. M. Gero. 1997. Programme to practice: Gender and feminism in archaeology. *Annual Review of Anthropology* 26: 411–437.

Conkey, M. W., and J. D. Spector. 1984. Archaeology and the study of gender. In *Advances in Archaeological Method and Theory*, vol. 7, ed. M. B. Schiffer, pp. 1–38. Orlando, Fla.: Academic Press.

Conkey, M. W., and A. Wylie, eds. 2007. Doing archaeology as a feminist. *Journal of Archaeological Method and Theory* 14 (3): whole issue.

Cowgill, G. L. 1974. Quantitative studies of urbanism at Teotihuacan. In *Mesoamerican Archaeology: New Approaches*, ed. N. Hammond, pp. 363–397. Austin: University of Texas Press.

Crabtree, D. E. 1972. *An Introduction to Flintworking: Part I. An Introduction to the Technology of Stone Tools.* Occasional Papers 28. Pocatello: Idaho State University.

Crown, P. L., and W. J. Hurst. 2009. Evidence of cacao use in the prehispanic American Southwest. *Proceedings of the National Academy of Sciences* 106 (7): 2110–2113.

Crumley, C. L., ed. 1994. *Historical Ecology: Cultural Knowledge and Changing Landscapes.* Santa Fe, N.M.: School of American Research Press.

Cuddy, T. W., and M. P. Leone. 2008. New Africa: Understanding the Americanization of African descent groups through archaeology. In *Collaboration in Archaeological Practice: Engaging*

Descendant Communities, ed. C. Colwell-Chanthaphonh and T. J. Ferguson, pp. 203–223. Lanham, Md.: AltaMira Press.

Dalan, R., G. R. Holley, W. I. Woods, H. Watters, Jr., and J. Koepke. 2003. *Envisioning Cahokia: A Landscape Perspective.* De Kalb: Northern Illinois University Press.

Daniel, G., and C. Chippindale, eds. 1989. *The Pastmasters: Eleven Modern Pioneers of Archaeology.* London: Thames & Hudson.

David, B., and J. Thomas, eds. 2008. *Handbook of Landscape Archaeology.* Walnut Creek, Calif.: Left Coast Press.

David, N., and C. L. Kramer. 2001. *Ethnoarchaeology in Action.* Cambridge, U.K.: Cambridge University Press.

Davis, E. L. 1975. The "exposed archaeology" of China Lake, California. *American Antiquity* 40: 39–53.

Dawdy, S. L. 2006. The taphonomy of disaster and the (re)formation of New Orleans. *American Anthropologist* 108 (4): 719–730.

Deetz, J. F. 1967. *Invitation to Archaeology.* Garden City, N.Y.: Natural History Press.

———. 1977. *In Small Things Forgotten: The Archaeology of Early American Life.* Garden City, N.Y.: Doubleday/Anchor.

Deetz, J. F., and E. Dethlefsen. 1967. Death's head, cherub, urn and willow. *Natural History* 76 (3): 28–37.

Derry, L., and M. Malloy, eds. 2003. *Archaeologists and Local Communities: Partners in Exploring the Past.* Washington, D.C.: Society for American Archaeology.

Drooker, P. B., ed. 2001. *Fleeting Identities: Perishable Material Culture in Archaeological Research.* Center for Archaeological Investigations, Occasional Papers 28. Carbondale: Southern Illinois University.

Ebert, J. I. 1984. Remote sensing applications in archaeology. In *Advances in Archaeological Method and Theory*, vol. 7, ed. M. B. Schiffer, pp. 293–362. Orlando, Fla.: Academic Press.

Eighmy, J. L. 2000. Thirty years of archaeomagnetic dating. In *It's about Time: A History of Archaeological Dating in North America*, ed. S. E. Nash, pp. 105–123. Salt Lake City: University of Utah Press.

Ellis, L., ed. 2000. *Archaeological Method and Theory: An Encyclopedia.* New York: Garland.

Erickson, C. L. 2000. The Lake Titicaca basin: A precolumbian built landscape. In *Imperfect Balance: Landscape Transformations in the Precolumbian Americas*, ed. D. Lentz, pp. 311–356. New York: Columbia University Press.

Estes, J. E., J. R. Jensen, and L. R. Tinney. 1977. The use of historical photography for mapping archaeological sites. *Journal of Field Archaeology* 4: 441–447.

Fagan, B. M. 1985. *The Adventure of Archaeology.* Washington, D.C.: National Geographic Society.

———. 1988. Black day at Slack Farm. *Archaeology* 41 (8): 15–16, 73.

———. 2010. *Writing Archaeology: Telling Stories about the Past.* 2nd ed. Walnut Creek, Calif.: Left Coast Press.

Farnsworth, P., J. E. Brady, M. J. DeNiro, and R. S. MacNeish. 1985. A re-evaluation of the isotopic and archaeological reconstructions of diet in the Tehuacán Valley. *American Antiquity* 50: 102–116.

Feathers, J. K. 2000. Luminescence dating and why it deserves wider application. In *It's about Time: A History of Archaeological Dating in North America*, ed. S. E. Nash, pp. 152–166. Salt Lake City: University of Utah Press.

Feder, K. L. 2010. *Frauds, Myths, and Mysteries: Science and Pseudoscience in Archaeology*, 7th ed. Mountain View, Calif.: Mayfield.

Feinman, G. M., and T. D. Price, eds. 2001. *Archaeology at the Millennium: A Sourcebook.* New York: Kluwer Academic/Plenum.

Ferguson, T. J. 1996. Native Americans and the practice of archaeology. *Annual Review of Anthropology* 25: 63–79.

Ferguson, T. J., and C. Colwell-Chanthaphonh. 2006. *History Is in the Land: Multivocal Tribal Traditions in Arizona's San Pedro Valley.* Tucson: University of Arizona Press.

Fish, S. K., and S. A. Kowalewski, eds. 1990. *The Archaeology of Regions: A Case for Full-Coverage Survey.* Washington, D.C.: Smithsonian Institution Press.

Flannery, K. V. 1967. Culture history vs. cultural process: A debate in American archaeology. *Scientific American* 217 (2): 119–122.

———. 1968. Archeological systems theory and early Mesoamerica. In *Anthropological Archeology in the Americas*, ed. B. J. Meggers, pp. 67–87. Washington, D.C.: Anthropological Society of Washington.

———. 1972. The cultural evolution of civilizations. *Annual Review of Ecology and Systematics* 2: 399–426.

———, ed. 1976. *The Early Mesoamerican Village.* New York: Academic Press.

———. 1986. A visit to the master. In *Guila Naquitz, Archaic Foraging and Early Agriculture in Oaxaca, Mexico*, ed. K. V. Flannery, pp. 511–519. Orlando, Fla.: Academic Press.

Ford, J. A. 1954. The type concept revisited. *American Anthropologist* 56: 42–53.

Ford, R. I. 1983. The Archaeological Conservancy, Inc.: The goal is site preservation. *American Archaeology* 3: 221–224.

Fowler, B. 2001. *Iceman: Uncovering the Life and Times of a Prehistoric Man Found in an Alpine Glacier.* Chicago: University of Chicago Press.

Fowler, D. D. 1987. Uses of the past: Archaeology in the service of the state. *American Antiquity* 52: 229–248.

Franklin, M., and L. McKee, eds. 2004. Transcending boundries, transforming the discipline: African diaspora archaeologies in the new millennium. *Historical Archaeology* 38(1): whole issue.

Franklin, M., and R. Paynter. 2010. Inequality and archaeology. In *Voices in American Archaeology*, eds. W. Ashmore, D. T. Lippert, and B. J. Mills, pp. 94–130. Washington, D.C.: SAA Press.

Friedman, I., and F. W. Trembour. 1983. Obsidian hydration dating update. *American Antiquity* 48: 544–547.

Friedman, I., F. W. Trembour, and R. E. Hughes. 1997. Obsidian hydration dating. In *Chronometric Dating in Archaeology*, ed. R. Taylor and M. J. Aitken, pp. 297–322. New York: Plenum.

Frink, D. S. 1984. Artifact behavior within the plow zone. *Journal of Field Archaeology* 11: 356–363.

Funari, P. P., A. Zarankin, and E. Stovel, eds. 2005. *Global Archaeological Theory: Contextual Voices and Contemporary Thoughts.* New York: Kluwer Academic/Plenum.

Garza, C. E., and S. Powell. 2001. Ethics and the past: Reburial and repatriation in American archaeology. In *The Future of the Past: Archaeologists, Native Americans, and Repatriation*, ed. T. L. Bray, pp. 37–56. New York: Garland.

Geller, P. L. 2008. Conceiving sex: Fomenting a feminist bioarchaeology. *Journal of Social Archaeology* 8 (1): 113–138.

Gero, J. M. 1991. Genderlithics: Woman's roles in stone tool production. In *Engendering Archaeology: Women and Prehistory*, ed. J. M. Gero and M. W. Conkey, pp. 163–193. Oxford: Basil Blackwell.

Gero, J. M., and M. W. Conkey, eds. 1991. *Engendering Archaeology: Women and Prehistory.* Oxford: Basil Blackwell.

Gero, J. M., and D. Root. 1990. Public presentations and private concerns: Archaeology in the pages of *National Geographic*. In *The Politics of the Past*, ed. P. Gathercole and D. Lowenthal, pp. 19–37. London: Unwin Hyman.

Giddings, J. L. 1967. *Ancient Men of the Arctic.* New York: Knopf.

Giesecke, A. G. 1987. The Abandoned Shipwreck Bill: Protecting our threatened cultural heritage. *Archaeology* 40 (4): 50–53.

Glob, P. V. 1969. *The Bog People: Iron-Age Man Preserved,* trans. R. Bruce-Mitford. Ithaca, N.Y.: Cornell University Press.

Gosden, C. 1999. *Anthropology and Archaeology: A Changing Relationship.* London: Routledge.

———. 2004. *Archaeology and Colonialism: Cultural Contact from 5000 BC to the Present.* Cambridge, U.K.: Cambridge University Press.

Gould, R. A. 1980. *Living Archaeology.* Cambridge, U.K.: Cambridge University Press.

———. 2007. *Disaster Archaeology.* Salt Lake City: University of Utah Press.

Gould, S. J. 1985. *The Flamingo's Smile.* New York: Norton.

Hall, R. L. 1977. An anthropomorphic perspective for eastern United States prehistory. *American Antiquity* 42: 499–518.

Hamilton, S. L., and R. Woodward. 1984. A sunken 17th-century city: Port Royal, Jamaica. *Archaeology* 37 (1): 38–45.

Hardesty, D. L., and D. D. Fowler. 2001. Archaeology and environmental changes. In *New Directions in Anthropology and Environment,* ed. C. L. Crumley, with A. E. van Deventer and J. J. Fletcher, pp. 72–89. Walnut Creek, Calif.: AltaMira Press.

Hardesty, D. L., and B. J. Little. 2000. *Assessing Site Significance: A Guide for Archaeologists and Historians.* Walnut Creek, Calif.: AltaMira Press.

Harmon, D., F. P. McManamon, and D. T. Pitcaithley, eds. 2006. *The Antiquities Act: A Century of American Archaeology, Historic Preservation, and Nature Conservation.* Tucson: University of Arizona Press.

Harrington, S. P. M. 1993. Bone and bureaucrats: New York's great cemetery imbroglio. *Archaeology* 46 (2): 28–38.

Harris, D., ed. 1996. *The Origins and Spread of Agriculture and Pastoralism in Eurasia.* Washington, D.C.: Smithsonian Institution Press.

Harris, E. C. 1989. *Principles of Archaeological Stratigraphy,* 2nd ed. London: Academic Press.

Hastorf, C. A. 1991. Gender, space, and food in prehistory. In *Engendering Archaeology: Women and Prehistory,* ed. J. M. Gero and M. W. Conkey, pp. 132–159. Oxford: Blackwell.

———. 2001. Making the invisible visible: The hidden jewels of archaeology. In *Fleeting Identities: Perishable Material Culture in Archaeological Research,* ed. P. B. Drooker, pp. 27–42. Center for Archaeological Investigations, Occasional Papers 28. Carbondale: Southern Illinois University.

Hastorf, C. A., and S. Johannessen. 1991. Understanding changing people/plant relationships in the prehispanic Andes. In *Processual and Postprocessual Archaeologies: Multiple Ways of Knowing the Past,* ed. R. W. Preucel, pp. 140–155. Center for Archaeological Investigations, Occasional Papers 16. Carbondale: Southern Illinois University.

Haury, E. W. 1958. Evidence from Point of Pines for a prehistoric migration from northern Arizona. In *Migrations in New World Culture History,* ed. R. H. Thompson, pp. 1–6. Social Science Bulletin 27. Tucson: University of Arizona.

Haven, S. F. 1856. *Archaeology of the United States.* Smithsonian Contributions to Knowledge 8. Washington, D.C.: Smithsonian Institution.

Haviland, W. A. 1967. Stature at Tikal, Guatemala: Implications for ancient demography and social organization. *American Antiquity* 32: 316–325.

Hawkins, G. S. 1965. *Stonehenge Decoded.* New York: Doubleday.

Hays-Gilpin, K. 2004. *Ambiguous Images: Gender and Rock Art.* Walnut Creek, Calif.: AltaMira Press.

Hedges, J. W. 1984. *Tomb of the Eagles: Death and Life in a Stone Age Tribe.* New York: New Amsterdam.

Hedges, R. E. M., and J. A. J. Gowlett. 1986. Radiocarbon dating by accelerator mass spectrometry. *Scientific American* 254 (1): 101–107.

Hill, J. N. 1970. *Broken K Pueblo: Prehistoric Social Organization in the American Southwest.* Anthropological Paper 18. Tucson: University of Arizona Press.

Hill, J. N., and R. K. Evans. 1972. A model for classification and typology. In *Models in Archaeology*, ed. D. L. Clarke, pp. 231–273. London: Methuen.

Hodder, I. 1982a. *Symbols in Action: Ethnoarchaeological Studies of Material Culture.* Cambridge, U.K.: Cambridge University Press.

———, ed. 1982b. *Symbolic and Structural Archaeology.* Cambridge, U.K.: Cambridge University Press.

———. 1985. Postprocessual archaeology. In *Advances in Archaeological Method and Theory*, vol. 8, ed. M. B. Schiffer, pp. 1–26. Orlando, Fla.: Academic Press.

———. 1990. *The Domestication of Europe: Structure and Contingency in Neolithic Societies.* Oxford: Basil Blackwell.

———, ed. 1996. *On the Surface: Çatalhöyük 1993–95.* Monograph No. 22. Cambridge and London: McDonald Institute for Archaeological Research/British Institute of Archaeology at Ankara.

———. 1997. "Always momentary, fluid and flexible": Towards a reflexive excavation methodology. *Antiquity* 71: 691–700.

———. 1999. *The Archaeological Process: An Introduction.* Oxford: Blackwell.

———, ed. 2000. *Towards Reflexive Method in Archaeology: The Example at Çatalhöyük.* Cambridge: McDonald Institute for Archaeological Research.

———, ed. 2001. *Archaeological Theory Today.* Cambridge, U.K.: Polity Press.

Hodder, I., and M. Hassal. 1971. The non-random spacing of Romano-British walled towns. *Man* 6: 391–407.

Hodder, I., and S. Hutson. 2003. *Reading the Past: Current Approaches to Interpretation in Archaeology*, 3rd ed. Cambridge, U.K.: Cambridge University Press.

Holley, G. R., R. A. Dalan, and P. A. Smith. 1993. Investigations in the Cahokia site Grand Plaza. *American Antiquity* 58: 306–319.

Hosler, D. 1994. *The Sounds and Colors of Power, The Sacred Metallurgical Technology of Ancient West Mexico.* Cambridge, Mass.: MIT Press.

Hubert, J. 1989. First World Archaeological Congress Inter-Congress, Vermillion, South Dakota, USA. *World Archaeological Bulletin* 4: 14–20.

Hyslop, J. 1984. *The Inca Road System.* Orlando, Fla.: Academic Press.

Isaac, G. L. 1984. The archaeology of human origins: Studies of the Lower Pleistocene in East Africa 1971–1981. In *Advances in World Archaeology*, ed. F. Wendorf and A. E. Close, pp. 1–87. Orlando, Fla.: Academic Press.

Jackson, T. L. 1991. Pounding acorn: Woman's production as social and economic focus. In *Engendering Archaeology: Women and Prehistory*, ed. J. M. Gero and M. W. Conkey, pp. 301–325. Oxford: Basil Blackwell.

Johnson, A. W., and T. Earle. 1987. *The Evolution of Human Societies: From Foraging Group to Agrarian State.* Stanford, Calif.: Stanford University Press.

Jovanovic, B. 1980. The origins of copper mining in Europe. *Scientific American* 242(5): 152–167.

Katzenberg, M. A., and R. G. Harrison. 1997. What's in a bone? Recent advances in archaeological bone chemistry. *Journal of Archaeological Research* 5: 265–293.

Keeley, L. H. 1980. *Experimental Determination of Stone Tool Uses: A Microwear Analysis.* Chicago: University of Chicago Press.

Kehoe, A. B. 1998. *The Land of Prehistory: A Critical History of American Archaeology*. London: Routledge.

———. 2008. *Controversies in Archeology*. Walnut Creek, Calif.: Left Coast Press.

Kelley, J. H., and M. P. Hanen. 1988. *Archaeology and the Methodology of Science*. Albuquerque: University of New Mexico Press.

Kelly, R. L. 2000. *The Foraging Spectrum: Diversity in Hunter-Gatherer Lifeways*. Washington, D.C.: Smithsonian Institution Press.

Kepecs, S., and M. J. Kolb, eds. 1997. New approaches to combining the archaeological and historical records. *Journal of Archaeological Method and Theory* 4 (3/4): whole issue.

Kidder, A. V. [1924] 1962. *An Introduction to the Study of Southwestern Archaeology*. Reprint with introduction, Southwestern archaeology today, by I. Rouse. New Haven, Conn.: Yale University Press.

Killion, T. W., ed. 2008. *Opening Archaeology: Repatriation's Impact on Contemporary Research and Practice*. Santa Fe, N.M.: School for Advanced Research Press.

King, T. F. 1998. *Cultural Resource Laws and Practice: An Introductory Guide*. Walnut Creek, Calif.: AltaMira Press.

———. 2002. *Thinking about Cultural Resource Management: Essays from the Edge*. Walnut Creek, Calif.: AltaMira Press.

Kipfer, B. A. 2007. *The Archaeologist's Fieldwork Companion*. Malden, Mass.: Blackwell.

Klein, R. G., and K. Cruz-Uribe. 1984. *The Analysis of Animal Bones from Archaeological Sites*. Chicago: University of Chicago Press.

Knapp, A. B., V. C. Pigott, and E. W. Herbert, eds. 1998. *Social Approaches to an Industrial Past: The Archaeology and Anthropology of Mining*. London: Routledge.

Kohl, P. 1981. Materialist approaches in prehistory. *Annual Review of Anthropology* 10: 89–118.

Kohl, P. L., and C. Fawcett, eds. 1995. *Nationalism, Politics, and the Practice of Archaeology*. Cambridge, U.K.: Cambridge University Press.

Kolata, A. 1987. Tiwanaku and its hinterland. *Archaeology* 40 (1): 36–41.

Kuklick, H. 1991. Contested monuments: The politics of archeology in Southern Africa. In *Colonial Situations: Essays on the Contextualization of Ethnographic Knowledge*, ed. G. W. Stocking, Jr., pp. 135–169. Madison: University of Wisconsin Press.

Lambert, J. B. 1997. *Traces of the Past: Unraveling the Secrets of Archaeology Through Chemistry*. Reading, Mass.: Addison-Wesley.

La Motta, V., and M. B. Schiffer. 2001. Behavioral archaeology: Toward a new synthesis. In *Archaeological Theory Today*, ed. I. Hodder, pp. 14–64. Cambridge, U.K.: Polity Press.

Lanata, J. L., and R. D. Drennan. 2010. Crossing boundaries and academic fair trade. In *Voices in American Archaeology*, eds. W. Ashmore, D. T. Lippert, and B. J. Mills, pp. 73–93. Washington, D.C.: SAA Press.

La Roche, C. J., and M. L. Blakey. 1997. Seizing intellectual power: The dialogue at the New York African Burial Ground. *Historical Archaeology* 31: 84–106.

Lasaponara, E., and N. Masini. 2011. Satellite remote sensing in archaeology: past, present, and future perspectives. *Journal of Archaeological Science* 38: 1995–2002.

LeBlanc, S. A. 1983. *The Mimbres People: Ancient Pueblo Painters of the American Southwest*. New York: Thames & Hudson.

Lee, R. B., and I. DeVore, eds. 1968. *Man the Hunter*. Chicago: Aldine.

Leone, M. P. 2005. *The Archaeology of Liberty in an American Capital: Excavations in Annapolis*. Berkeley: University of California Press.

Levin, A. M. 1986. Excavation photography: A day on a dig. *Archaeology* 39 (1): 34–39.

Lewis-Williams, J. D. 1986. Cognitive and optical illusions in San rock art research. *Current Anthropology* 27: 171–178.

———. 2002. *The Mind in the Cave: Consciousness and the Origins of Art.* London: Thames & Hudson.

Liebmann, M., and U. Z. Rizvi, eds. 2008. *Archaeology and the Postcolonial Critique.* Lanham, Md.: AltaMira Press.

Lipe, W. D. 1974. A conservation model for American archaeology. *The Kiva* 39: 213–245.

———. 1984. Value and meaning in cultural resources. In *Approaches to the Archaeological Heritage: A Comparative Study of World Cultural Resource Management Systems,* ed. H. Cleere, pp. 1–11. Cambridge, U.K.: Cambridge University Press.

Little, B. J., ed. 2002. *Public Benefits of Archaeology.* Gainesville: University Press of Florida.

———. 2007. *Historical Archaeology: Why the Past Matters.* Walnut Creek, Calif.: Left Coast Press.

Little, B. J., and P. A. Shackel, eds. 2007. *Archaeology as a Tool of Civic Engagement.* Lanham, Md.: AltaMira Press.

Little, B. J., and L. J. Zimmerman. 2010. In the public interest: Creating a more activist, civically engaged archaeology. In *Voices in American Archaeology,* eds. W. Ashmore, D. T. Lippert, and B. J. Mills, pp. 131–159. Washington, D.C.: SAA Press.

Longacre, W. A., and J. M. Skibo, eds. 1994. *Kalinga Ethnoarchaeology: Expanding Archaeological Method and Theory.* Washington, D.C.: Smithsonian Institution Press.

Loy, T. H. 1983. Prehistoric blood residues: Detection on tool surfaces and identification of species of origin. *Science* 220: 1269–1271.

Lucas, G. 2012. *Understanding the Archaeological Record.* Cambridge, U.K.: Cambridge University Press.

Lyman, R. L., M. J. O'Brien, and R. C. Dunnell, eds. 1997. *Americanist Culture History: Fundamentals of Time, Space, and Form.* New York: Plenum.

Lynott, M. J., and A. Wylie, eds. 2000. *Ethics in American Archaeology,* 2nd ed. Washington, D.C.: Society for American Archaeology.

McGuire, R. H. 1992. *A Marxist Archaeology.* San Diego: Academic Press.

McIntosh, R. J. 1999. Africa's storied past. *Archaeology* 52 (3): 54–58, 60.

MacNeish, R. S., M. L. Fowler, A. G. Cook, F. A. Peterson, A. Nelken-Terner, and J. A. Neely. 1972. *Excavations and Reconnaissance: The Prehistory of the Tehuacán Valley,* vol. 5. Austin: University of Texas Press.

MacNeish, R. S., T. C. Patterson, and D. L. Browman. 1975. *The Central Peruvian Interaction Sphere.* Andover, Mass.: Phillips Academy.

Man, J. 2008. *The Terra Cotta Army: China's First Emperor and the Birth of a Nation.* Cambridge, Mass.: Da Capo Press.

Marcus, J., and K. V. Flannery. 1996. *Zapotec Civilization: How Urban Society Evolved in Mexico's Oaxaca Valley.* London: Thames & Hudson.

Marquardt, W. H. 1985. Complexity and scale in the study of fisher-gatherer-hunters: An example from the eastern United States. In *Prehistoric Hunter-Gatherers: The Emergence of Cultural Complexity,* ed. T. D. Price and J. A. Brown, pp. 59–98. Orlando, Fla.: Academic Press.

Marshack, A. 1972. Upper Paleolithic notation and symbol. *Science* 178: 817–827.

Marshall, Y., ed. 2002. Community archaeology. *World Archaeology* 34 (2): whole issue.

Matero, F. G. 2000. The conservation of the excavated past. In *Towards Reflexive Method in Archaeology: The Example at Çatalhöyük,* ed. I. Hodder, pp. 71–88. Cambridge, U.K.: McDonald Institute for Archaeological Research.

Matthews, W., C. A. I. French, T. Lawrence, D. F. Cutler, and M. K. Jones. 1997. Micro-stratigraphic traces of site formation processes and human activities. *World Archaeology* 29: 281–308.

Matthews, W., and C. Hastorf, with P. Andrews, T. Molleson, et al. 2000. Integrating archaeological science. In *Towards Reflexive Method in Archaeology: The Example at Çatalhöyük*, ed. I. Hodder, pp. 37–50. Cambridge, U.K.: McDonald Institute for Archaeological Research.

Mellaart, J. 1967. *Çatal Hüyük: A Neolithic Town in Anatolia*. New York: Thames & Hudson.

Meltzer, D. J., D. D. Fowler, and J. A. Sabloff, eds. 1986. *American Archaeology Past and Future: A Celebration of the Society for American Archaeology 1935–1985*. Washington, D.C.: Smithsonian Institution Press.

Meskell, L. 1998. Twin peaks: The archaeologies of Çatalhöyük. In *Ancient Goddesses*, ed. L. Goodison and C. Morris, pp. 46–62. London: British Museum Press.

Michael, H. N. 1985. Correcting radiocarbon dates with tree ring dates at MASCA. *University Museum Newsletter* (University of Pennsylvania) 23 (3): 1–2.

Michel, M. 1981. Preserving America's prehistoric heritage. *Archaeology* 34 (2): 61–63.

Michels, J. W. 1973. *Dating Methods in Archaeology*. New York: Academic Press.

Moseley, M. E. 1975. Prehistoric principles of labor organization in the Moche valley, Peru. *American Antiquity* 40: 190–196.

Moseley, M. E., and C. J. Mackey. 1974. *Twenty-four Architectural Plans of Chan Chan, Peru: Structure and Form at the Capital of Chimor*. Cambridge, Mass.: Harvard University, Peabody Museum Press.

Nash, S. E. 2000a. Seven decades of archaeological tree-dating. In *It's about Time: A History of Archaeological Dating in North America*, ed. S. E. Nash, pp. 60–82. Salt Lake City: University of Utah Press.

———, ed. 2000b. *It's about Time: A History of Archaeological Dating in North America*. Salt Lake City: University of Utah Press.

Nelson, S. M., ed. 2006. *Handbook of Gender in Archaeology*. Walnut Creek, Calif.: AltaMira Press.

Neumann, T. W., and R. M. Sanford. 2001. *Practicing Archaeology: A Training Manual for Cultural Resources Archaeology*. Walnut Creek, Calif.: AltaMira Press.

Noël Hume, I. 1969. *Historical Archaeology*. New York: Knopf.

———. 1979. *Martin's Hundred: The Discovery of a Lost Colonial Virginia Settlement*. New York: Knopf.

Numbers, R. L. 1982. Creationism in 20th-century America. *Science* 218: 538–544.

Oakley, K. P. 1956. *Man the Tool-Maker*, 3rd ed. London: British Museum.

———. 1970. Analytical methods of dating bones. In *Science in Archaeology*, 2nd ed., ed. D. Brothwell and E. S. Higgs, pp. 35–45. New York: Praeger.

O'Brien, M. 1996. *Evolutionary Archaeology: Theory and Application*. Salt Lake City: University of Utah Press.

O'Brien, M. J., R. L. Lyman, and M. B. Schiffer. 2005. *Archaeology as a Process: Processualism and Its Progeny*. Salt Lake City: Univ. of Utah Press.

Olsen, S. J. 1964. *Mammal Remains from Archaeological Sites*. Papers of the Peabody Museum 56. Cambridge, Mass.: Harvard University.

Orme, B., ed. 1982. *Problems in Case Studies in Archaeological Dating*. Atlantic Highlands, N.J.: Humanities Press.

Parcak, S. H. 2009. *Satellite Remote Sensing for Archaeology*. London and New York: Routledge.

Patterson, T. C. 1995. *Toward a Social History of Archaeology in the United States*. Fort Worth, Tex.: Harcourt Brace.

———. 2001. *A Social History of Anthropology in the United States*. Oxford: Berg.

———. 2003. *Marx's Ghost: Conversations with Archaeologists*. Oxford: Berg.

———. 2004. Social archaeology and Marxist social thought. In *A Companion to Social Archaeology*, ed. L. Meskell and R. W. Preucel, pp. 66–81. Oxford: Blackwell.

———. 2005. *The Theory and Practice of Archaeology: A Workbook*, 3rd ed. Upper Saddle River, N.J.: Pearson Prentice-Hall.

Patterson, T. C., and C. E. Orser, eds. 2004. *Foundations of Social Archaeology: Selected Writings of V. Gordon Childe*. Walnut Creek, Calif.: AltaMira Press.

Pauketat, T. R. 1998. Refiguring the archaeology of greater Cahokia. *Journal of Archaeological Research* 6: 45–89.

———. 2000. The tragedy of the commoners. In *Agency in Archaeology*, ed. M. A. Dobres and J. Robb, pp. 113–129. London: Routledge.

Pauketat, T. R., and T. E. Emerson, eds. 1997. *Cahokia: Domination and Ideology in the Mississippian World*. Lincoln: University of Nebraska Press.

Pauketat, T. R., and L. Meskell. 2010. Changing theoretical directions in American archaeology. In *Voices in American Archaeology*, eds. W. Ashmore, D. T. Lippert, and B. J. Mills, pp. 193–219. Washington, D.C.: SAA Press.

Paynter, R. 2000. Historical archaeology and the post-Columbian world of North America. *Journal of Archaeological Research* 8: 169–217.

Pearce, S. M. 1990. *Archaeological Curatorship*. Washington, D.C.: Smithsonian Institution Press.

Pearsall, D. M. 1989. *Paleoethnobotany: A Handbook of Procedures*. San Diego: Academic Press.

Petrie, W. M. F. 1901. *Diospolis Parva*. Memoir 20. London: Egyptian Exploration Fund.

Potts, R., and P. Shipman. 1981. Cutmarks made by stone tools on bones from Olduvai Gorge, Tanzania. *Nature* 291: 577–580.

Preucel, R. W., ed. 1991. *Processual and Postprocessual Archaeologies: Multiple Ways of Knowing the Past*. Center for Archaeological Investigations, Occasional Papers 16. Carbondale: Southern Illinois University.

———. 1995. The postprocessual condition. *Journal of Archaeological Research* 3: 147–175.

———. 1999. Review of *Evolutionary Archaeology: Theory and Application*. *Journal of Field Archaeology* 26: 93–99.

———. 2000. Making Pueblo communities: Architectural discourse at Kotyiti, New Mexico. In *The Archaeology of Communities: A New World Perspective*, ed. M. A. Canuto and J. Yaeger, pp. 58–77. London: Routledge.

———, ed. 2002. *Archaeologies of the Pueblo Revolt: Identity, Meaning, and Renewal in the Pueblo World*. Albuquerque: University of New Mexico Press.

Pwiti, G. 1996. Let the ancestors rest in peace? New challenges for cultural heritage management in Zimbabwe. *Conservation and Management of Archaeological Sites* 1: 151–160.

Rakita, G. F. M., J. E. Buikstra, L. A. Beck, and S. R. Williams, eds. 2005. *Interacting with the Dead: Perspectives on Mortuary Archaeology for the New Millennium*. Gainesville: University Press of Florida.

Ramenofsky, A. F., and A. Steffen, eds. 1998. *Unit Issues in Archaeology: Measuring Time, Space, and Material*. Salt Lake City: University of Utah Press.

Rapp, G., Jr., and C. L. Hill. 1998. *Geoarchaeology: The Earth-Science Approach to Archaeological Interpretation*. New Haven, Conn.: Yale University Press.

Rathje, W. L. 1978. The ancient astronaut myth. *Archaeology* 31 (1): 4–7.

Redman, C. L., and P. J. Watson. 1970. Systematic, intensive surface collection. *American Antiquity* 35: 279–291.

Reitz, E. J., and M. Shackley. 2012. *Environmental Archaeology (Manuals in Archaeological Method, Theory and Technique)*. New York: Springer.

Renfrew, C. 1971. Carbon 14 and the prehistory of Europe. *Scientific American* 225 (4): 63–72.

———. 1973. *Before Civilization: The Radiocarbon Revolution and Prehistoric Europe*. New York: Knopf.

———. 1975. Trade as action at a distance: Questions of integration and communication. In *Ancient Civilization and Trade*, ed. J. A. Sabloff and C. C. Lamberg-Karlovsky, pp. 3–59. School of American Research. Albuquerque: University of New Mexico Press.

————. 1983. The social archaeology of megalithic monuments. *Scientific American* 249 (5): 152–163.

Renfrew, C., and E. B. W. Zubrow, eds. 1994. *The Ancient Mind: Elements of Cognitive Archaeology.* Cambridge, U.K.: Cambridge University Press.

Rice, P. M. 1987. *Pottery Analysis: A Sourcebook.* Chicago: University of Chicago Press.

————. 1996a. Recent ceramic analysis: 1. Function, style, and origins. *Journal of Archaeological Research* 4: 133–163.

————. 1996b. Recent ceramic analysis: 2. Composition, production, and theory. *Journal of Archaeological Research* 4: 165–202.

————. 1999. On the origins of pottery. *Journal of Archaeological Method and Theory* 6: 1–54.

Richards, C. 1990. The Late Neolithic house in Orkney. In *The Social Archaeology of Houses*, ed. R. Samson, pp. 111–124. Edinburgh: Edinburgh University Press.

Richards, J. E. 1999. Conceptual landscapes in the Egyptian Nile Valley, in W. Ashmore and A. B. Knapp (eds.), *Archaeologies of Landscape: Contemporary Perspectives*, pp. 83–100. Oxford: Blackwell.

Robin, C. 2002. Outside of houses: The practices of everyday life at Chan Nòohol, Belize. *Journal of Social Archaeology* 2: 245–268.

Rogers, J. D., and B. D. Smith, eds. 1995. *Mississippian Communities and Households.* Tuscaloosa: University of Alabama Press.

Rosenberg, M. 1990. The mother of invention: Evolutionary theory, territoriality, and the origins of agriculture. *American Anthropologist* 92: 399–415.

Roskams, S. 2001. *Excavation.* Cambridge Manuals in Archaeology. Cambridge, U.K.: Cambridge University Press.

Rossignol, J., and L. Wandsnider, eds. 1992. *Space, Time, and Archaeological Landscapes.* New York: Plenum.

Sabloff, J. A. 1975. *Ceramics: Excavations at Seibal*, no. 2. Memoirs of the Peabody Museum of Archaeology and Ethnology, vol. 13. Cambridge, Mass.: Harvard University, Peabody Museum.

————. 1982. Introduction. In *Archaeology: Myth and Reality: Readings from Scientific American*, ed. J. A. Sabloff, pp. 1–26. San Francisco: Freeman.

————. 1992. Interpreting the collapse of Classic Maya civilization: A case study of changing archaeological perspectives. In *Metaarchaeology: Reflections by Archaeologists and Philosophers*, ed. L. Embree, pp. 99–119. Dordrecht and Boston: Kluwer Academic.

————. 1998. Distinguished Lecture in Archaeology: Communication and the future of American archaeology. *American Anthropologist* 100: 869–875.

————. 2008. *Archaeology Matters: Action Archaeology in the Modern World.* Walnut Creek, Calif.: Left Coast Press.

Sabloff, J. A., and W. Ashmore. 2001. An aspect of archaeology's recent past and its relevance in the new millennium. In *Archaeology at the Millennium*, ed. T. D. Price and G. M. Feinman, pp. 11–32. New York: Kluwer Academic/Plenum.

Sabloff, P. L. W. 1998. *Conversations with Lew Binford: Drafting the New Archaeology.* Norman: University of Oklahoma Press.

Sanders, W. T., and B. J. Price. 1968. *Mesoamerica: The Evolution of a Civilization.* New York: Random House.

Scarborough, V. L., and L. J. Lucero. 2010. The non-hierarchical development of complexity in the semitropics: Water and cooperation. *Water History* 2: 185–205.

Schick, K., and N. Toth. 2001. Paleoanthropology at the millennium. In *Archaeology at the Millennium*, ed. T. D. Price and G. M. Feinman, pp. 39–108. New York: Kluwer Academic/Plenum.

Schiffer, M. B. 1987. *Formation Processes of the Archaeological Record.* Albuquerque: University of New Mexico Press.

Schliemann, H. [1881] 1968. *Ilios, the City and Country of the Trojans.* Reissue. New York: Benjamin Blom.

Schmidt, P. R. 1997. *Iron Technology in East Africa: Symbolism, Science, and Archaeology.* Bloomington: Indiana University Press.

Schmidt, P. R., and T. C. Patterson, eds. 1995. *Making Alternative Histories: The Practice of Archaeology and History in Non-Western Settings.* Santa Fe, N.M.: SAR Press.

Schortman, E., P. Urban, W. Ashmore, and J. Benyo. 1986. Interregional interaction in the southeast Maya periphery: The Santa Bárbara Archaeological Project 1983–1984 seasons. *Journal of Field Archaeology* 13: 259–272.

Sebastian, L. 2010. Archaeology and historic preservation law: Twenty-five years of interesting times. In *Voices in American Archaeology*, eds. W. Ashmore, D. T. Lippert, and B. J. Mills, pp. 160–177. Washington, D.C.: SAA Press.

Sebastian, L., and W. D. Lipe, eds. 2010. *Archaeology and Cultural Resource Management: Visions for the Future.* Santa Fe, N.M.: School for Advanced Research.

Sekaquaptewa, E., and D. Washburn. 2004. They go along singing: Reconstructing the Hopi past from ritual metaphors in song and image. *American Antiquity* 69: 457–486.

Semenov, S. A. 1964. *Prehistoric Technology.* New York: Barnes & Noble.

Shackel, P. A., and E. J. Chambers, eds. 2004. *Places in Mind: Public Archaeology as Applied Anthropology.* New York: Routledge.

Sharer, R. J. 2006. *The Ancient Maya* (with L. P. Traxler) 6th ed. Stanford, Calif.: Stanford University Press.

Sharer, R. J., and W. Ashmore. 2003. *Archaeology: Discovering Our Past*, 3rd ed. New York: McGraw-Hill.

Sheets, P. D. 2006. *The Cerén Site: An Ancient Village Buried by Volcanic Ash in Central El Salvador*, 2nd ed. Belmont, Calif.: Thomson Wadsworth.

Shennan, S. 2008. Evolution in archaeology. *Annual Review of Anthropology* 37: 75–91.

Shennan, S. J., ed. 1988. *Quantifying Archaeology.* San Diego: Academic Press.

Silliman, S., ed. 2008. *Collaborating at the Trowel's Edge: Teaching and Learning in Indigenous Archaeology.* Tucson: University of Arizona Press.

Silliman, S., and T. J. Ferguson. 2010. Consultation and collaboration with descendant communities. In *Voices in American Archaeology*, eds. W. Ashmore, D. T. Lippert, and B. J. Mills, pp. 48–72. Washington, D.C.: SAA Press.

Smith, B. D. 1993. Reconciling the gender-credit critique and the floodplain weed theory of plant domestication. In *Archaeology of Eastern North America: Papers in Honor of Stephen Williams*, ed. J. B. Stoltman, pp. 111–125. Archaeological Report 25. Jackson: Mississippi Department of Archives and History, Jackson.

———. 2001. The transition to food production. In *Archaeology at the Millennium: A Sourcebook*, ed. G. M. Feinman and T. D. Price, pp. 199–229. New York: Kluwer Academic/Plenum.

Smith, C., and H. M. Wobst, eds. 2005. *Indigenous Archaeologies: Decolonizing Theory and Practice.* London: Routledge.

Smith, G. E. 1928. *In the Beginning: The Origin of Civilization.* New York: Morrow.

Smith, G. S., and J. E. Ehrenhard, eds. 1991. *Protecting the Past.* Boca Raton, Fla.: CRC Press.

Snead, J., and J. A. Sabloff. 2010. Professional societies and the lives of American archaeologists. In *Voices in American Archaeology*, eds. W. Ashmore, D. T. Lippert, and B. J. Mills, pp. 27–47. Washington, D.C.: SAA Press.

Society for American Archaeology. 1986. Statement concerning the treatment of human remains. *Bulletin of the Society for American Archaeology* 4 (3): 7–8.

Spaulding, A. C. 1953. Statistical techniques for the discovery of artifact types. *American Antiquity* 18: 305–313.

Spector, J. D. 1993. *What This Awl Means: Feminist Archaeology at a Wahpeton Dakota Village.* St. Paul: Minnesota Historical Society Press.

Squier, E. G., and E. H. Davis. 1848. *Ancient Monuments of the Mississippi Valley.* Smithsonian Contributions to Knowledge 1. Washington, D.C.: Smithsonian Institution.

Steadman, S. R. 1996. Recent research in the archaeology of architecture: Beyond the foundations. *Journal of Archaeological Research* 4: 51–93.

Stein, J. K. 2000. Stratigraphy and archaeological dating. In *It's about Time: A History of Archaeological Dating in North America*, ed. S. E. Nash, pp. 14–40. Salt Lake City: University of Utah Press.

Stein, J. K., and W. R. Farrand, eds. 2001. *Sediments in Archaeological Context*. Salt Lake City: University of Utah Press.

Stephens, J. L. [1843] 1963. *Incidents of Travel in Yucatan*. 2 vols. New York: Harper Reprint.

———. [1841] 1969. *Incidents of Travel in Central America, Chiapas, and Yucatan*. 2 vols. New York: Harper Reprint.

Sternberg, R. S. 1997. Archaeomagnetic dating. In *Chronometric Dating in Archaeology*, ed. R. E. Taylor and M. J. Aitken, pp. 323–356. New York: Plenum.

Steward, J. H. 1955. *Theory of Culture Change*. Urbana: University of Illinois Press.

Stone, P. G., and P. G. Panel, eds. 1999. *The Constructed Past: Experimental Archaeology, Education, and the Public*. London: Routledge.

Stottman, M. J., S. E. Miller, and A. G. Henderson. 2007. Culture of litterbugs. In *Archaeology to Delight and Instruct: Active Learning in the University Classroom*, eds. H. Burke and C. Smith, pp. 180–200. Walnut Creek, Calif.: Left Coast Press.

Sullivan, L. P., and S. T. Childs. 2003. *Curating Archaeological Collections: From the Field to the Repository*. Walnut Creek, Calif.: AltaMira Press.

Swidler, N., K. Dongoske, R. Anyon, and A. Downer, eds. 1999. *Native Americans and Archaeologists: Stepping Stones to Common Ground*. Walnut Creek, Calif.: AltaMira Press.

Taylor, R. E. 2000. The introduction of radiocarbon dating. In *It's about Time: A History of Archaeological Dating in North America*, ed. S. E. Nash, pp. 84–104. Salt Lake City: University of Utah Press.

Taylor, R. E., and M. J. Aitken, eds. 1997. *Chronometric Dating in Archaeology*. New York: Plenum.

Taylor, W. W. [1948] 1967. *A Study of Archeology*. American Anthropological Association Memoir 69. Reprint. Carbondale: Southern Illinois University Press.

Thomas, D. H. 1973. An empirical test for Steward's model of Great Basin settlement patterns. *American Antiquity* 38: 155–176.

———. 2001. *Skull Wars: Kennewick Man, Archaeology, and the Battle for Native American Identity*. New York: HarperCollins.

Torrence, R., ed. 1989. *Time, Energy and Stone Tools*. Cambridge, U.K.: Cambridge University Press.

Toth, N. 1987. The first technology. *Scientific American* 256 (4): 112–121.

Towner, R. H. 2000. Dendrochronology and historical records: Concordance and conflict in Navajo archaeology. In *It's about Time: A History of Archaeological Dating in North America*, ed. S. E. Nash, pp. 168–185. Salt Lake City: University of Utah Press.

Trigger, B. G. 1968. The determinants of settlement patterns. In *Settlement Archaeology*, ed. K. C. Chang, pp. 53–78. Palo Alto, Calif.: National Press.

———. 1984. Archaeology at the crossroads: What's new? *Annual Review of Anthropology* 13: 275–300.

———. 2006. *A History of Archaeological Thought*. 2nd ed. Cambridge, U.K.: Cambridge University Press.

Tringham, R. 1991. Households with faces: The challenge of gender in prehistoric architectural remains. In *Engendering Archaeology: Women and Prehistory*, ed. J. M. Gero and M. W. Conkey, pp. 93–131. Oxford: Blackwell.

———. 1994. Engendered places in prehistory. *Gender, Place and Culture* 1: 169–203.

Turnbull, C. 1972. *The Mountain People*. New York: Simon & Schuster.

Tylor, E. B. 1871. *Primitive Culture*. London: Murray.

Ucko, P. J. 1969. Ethnography and archaeological interpretation of funerary remains. *World Archaeology* 1: 262–280.

———. 1987. *Academic Freedom and Apartheid: The Story of the World Archaeological Congress*. London: Duckworth. (Free download from WAC website: http://www.worldarchaeologicalcongress.org/)

van der Leeuw, S., and C. L. Redman. 2002. Placing archaeology at the center of socio-natural studies. *American Antiquity* 67: 597–605.

van der Merwe, N. J. 1982. Carbon isotopes, photosynthesis, and archaeology. *American Scientist* 70: 596–606.

van der Merwe, N. J., and P. Avery. 1982. Pathways to steel. *American Scientist* 70: 146–155.

Van Noten, F., D. Cahan, and L. Keeley. 1980. A Paleolithic campsite in Belgium. *Scientific American* 242 (4): 48–55.

VanPool, T. L., and C. S. VanPool, eds. 2003. *Essential Tensions in Archaeological Method and Theory*. Salt Lake City: University of Utah Press.

Verano, J. W., and D. H. Ubelaker, eds. 1992. *Disease and Demography in the Americas*. Washington, D.C.: Smithsonian Institution Press.

Villa, P. 1982. Conjoinable pieces and site formation processes. *American Antiquity* 47: 276–290.

Walker, W. H. 2000. Ceremonial trash? In *Expanding Archaeology*, ed. J. M. Skibo, W. H. Walker, and A. E. Nielsen, pp. 67–79. Salt Lake City: University of Utah Press.

Watkins, J. 2000. *Indigenous Archaeology: American Indian Values and Scientific Practice*. Walnut Creek, Calif.: AltaMira Press.

———. 2003. Beyond the margin: American Indians, First Nations, and archaeology in North America. *American Antiquity* 68: 273–285.

———. 2010. Politicae et publicae: Aspects of influence. In *Voices in American Archaeology*, eds. W. Ashmore, D. T. Lippert, and B. J. Mills, pp. 317–323. Washington, D.C.: SAA Press.

Watkins, J., K. A. Pyburn, and P. Cressey. 2000. Community relations: What the practicing archaeologist needs to know to work effectively with local and/or descendant communities. In *Teaching Archaeology in the Twenty-First Century*, ed. S. J. Bender and G. Smith, pp. 73–81. Washington, D.C.: Society for American Archaeology.

Watson, P. J., and M. C. Kennedy. 1991. The development of horticulture in the Eastern Woodlands of North America: Woman's role. In *Engendering Archaeology: Women and Prehistory*, ed. J. M. Gero and M. W. Conkey, pp. 255–275. Oxford: Basil Blackwell.

Watson, P. J., S. A. LeBlanc, and C. L. Redman. 1984. *Archaeological Explanation: The Scientific Method in Archaeology*. New York: Columbia University Press.

Weiner, S. 2010. *Microarchaeology: Beyond the Visible Archaeological Record*. Cambridge, U.K.: Cambridge University Press.

Wendorf, F. 1973. "Rescue" archaeology along the Nile. In *In Search of Man: Readings in Archaeology*, ed. E. L. Green, pp. 39–42. Boston: Little, Brown.

Wertime, T., and S. Wertime, eds. 1982. *Early Pyrotechnology*. Washington, D.C.: Smithsonian Institution Press.

Whallon, R., and J. A. Brown, eds. 1982. *Essays on Archaeological Typology*. Evanston, Ill.: Center for American Archeology Press.

Wheat, J. B. 1972. *The Olsen-Chubbuck Site: A Paleo-Indian Bison Kill*. Society for American Archaeology Memoir 26. Washington, D.C.

Wheatley, D., and M. Gillings. 2002. *Spatial Technology and Archaeology: The Archaeological Applications of GIS*. London and New York: Taylor & Francis.

Wheeler, M. 1954. *Archaeology from the Earth*. Harmondsworth, U.K.: Penguin Books.

Wilcox, M. 2010. NAGPRA and indigenous peoples: The social context and controversies, and the transformation of American archaeology. In *Voices in American Archaeology*, eds. W. Ashmore, D. T. Lippert, and B. J. Mills, pp. 178–192. Washington, D.C.: SAA Press.

Wilk, R. R., and W. L. Rathje, eds. 1982. Archaeology of the household: Building a prehistory of domestic life. *American Behavioral Scientist* 25 (6).

Willey, G. R. 1953. *Prehistoric Settlement Patterns in the Virú Valley, Peru*. Bureau of American Ethnology, Bulletin 155. Washington, D.C.: Smithsonian Institution.

———, ed. 1974. *Archaeological Researches in Retrospect*. Cambridge, Mass.: Winthrop.

Willey, G. R., and P. Phillips. 1958. *Method and Theory in American Archaeology*. Chicago: University of Chicago Press.

Willey, G. R., and J. A. Sabloff. 1993. *A History of American Archaeology*, 3rd ed. San Francisco: Freeman.

Williams, S. 1991. *Fantastic Archaeology: The Wild Side of North American Prehistory*. Philadelphia: University of Pennsylvania Press.

Williams-Thorpe, O., and R. S. Thorpe. 1992. Geochemistry, sources and transport of the Stonehenge bluestones. In *New Developments in Archaeological Science*, ed. A. M. Pollard, pp. 133–161. *Proceedings of the British Academy*, vol. 77. Oxford: Oxford University Press.

Windes, T. C., and P. J. McKenna. 2001. Going against the grain: Wood production in Chacoan society. *American Antiquity* 66: 119–140.

Wing, E. S., and A. R. Brown. 1980. *Paleonutrition: Method and Theory in Prehistoric Foodways*. New York: Academic Press.

Wiseman, J. R. 2001. Declaration of independence. *Archaeology* 54 (4): 10–12.

Wittry, W. L. 1977. The American Woodhenge. In *Explorations in Cahokia Archaeology*, ed. M. L. Fowler, pp. 43–48. Illinois Archaeological Survey, Bulletin 7. Urbana: University of Illinois.

Wolfman, D. 1984. Geomagnetic dating methods in archaeology. In *Advances in Archaeological Method and Theory*, vol. 7, ed. M. B. Schiffer, pp. 363–458. Orlando, Fla.: Academic Press.

Woolley, C. L. 1934. *Ur Excavations*. Vol. II: *The Royal Cemetery*. Oxford and Philadelphia: British Museum and University Museum, University of Pennsylvania.

Wylie, A. 1992. The interplay of evidential constraints and political interests: Recent archaeological research on gender. *American Antiquity* 57: 15–35.

———. 2002. *Thinking from Things: Essays in the Philosophy of Archaeology*. Berkeley: University of California Press.

Yamin, R., and K. B. Metheny, eds. 1996. *Landscape Archaeology: Reading and Interpreting the American Historical Landscape*. Knoxville: University of Tennessee Press.

Zeder, M. 1999. Animal domestication in the Zagros: A review of past and current research. *Paléorient* 25: 11–25.

Zeder, M., J. Buikstra, and S. van der Leeuw. 2010. Interdisciplinary studies in archaeology. In *Voices in American Archaeology*, eds. W. Ashmore, D. T. Lippert, and B. J. Mills, pp. 220–269. Washington, D.C.: SAA Press.

Zeuner, F. E. 1958. *Dating the Past: An Introduction to Geochronology*. London: Methuen.

Zimmerman, L. J. 2003. *Presenting the Past*. Walnut Creek, Calif.: AltaMira Press.

Zimmerman, L. J., K. D. Vitelli, and J. Hollowell-Zimmer, eds. 2003. *Ethical Issues in Archaeology*. Walnut Creek, Calif.: AltaMira Press.

Zimmerman, L. J., and J. Welch. 2006. Toward an archaeology of homelessness. *Anthropology News* 47 (2): 54.

Credits

LINE ART Chapter 1 **Fig. 1.6a** From Cartographic Computer Lab/National Geographic Image Collection, National Geographic June 1993, p. 41. © 1993 National Geographic Society. **Fig. 1.6b** From Mainz: Egg M., Spindler, K, Die Gletschermumie vom Ende der Steinzeit aus der Otztaler Alpen, 1993. Reprinted with permission of the Romiscb Germanisches Zentralmuseum Images Archives.

Chapter 3 **Fig. 3.1** From Rouse, I., Introduction to revised edition of *An Introduction to Southwestern Archaeology* by A. V. Kidder.© 1962 Yale University Press. Reprinted by permission of Yale University **Press. Fig. 3.3** From Willey, G. R., and P. Phillips. 1958. Method *and Theory* in *American Archaeology*. Chicago: University of Chicago Press. Reprinted by permission. **Fig. 3.4** After Thomas, reproduced by permission of The Society for American Archaeology, adapted from *American Archaeology* 38: 159, 1973. **Fig. 3.5** From Brumfiel "Weaving and Cooking: Women's Production in Aztec, Mexico" from Codex Mendoza (1964 Lám. LXI) in *Engendering Archaeology*, Conkey & Gero eds., © 1991 Blackwell. Reprinted with permission of Brumfiel. **Fig. 3.6** after Hall, reproduced by permission of Robert L. Hall and The Society for American Archaeology from *American Antiquity* 42: 4, 1997.

Chapter 4 **Fig. 4.13** by permission from Broken K Pueblo, *Prehistoric Social Organization in the American Southwest*, by James N. Hill, University of Arizona Anthropological Paper no. 18, Tucson: University of Arizona Press, copyright 1970. **Fig. 4.14** after Redman and Watson, reproduced by permission of The Society for American Archaeology, adapted from *American Antiquity* 35:281–282, 1970.

Chapter 5 **Fig. 5.1** From MacNeish, R. S., M. L. Fowler, A. G. Cook, F. A. Peterson, A. Nelken-Turner, and J. A. Neeley. 1972. *Excavations and Reconnaissance: The Prehistory of the Tebuacan Valley*, vol. 5. Austin:University of Texas Press. Reproduced by permission of the Phillips Academy. **Fig. 5.10a & 5.10b** after Fowler 1989, courtesy of Melvin Fowler and the Illinois State Archaeological Survey. **Fig. 5.11** after Davis 1975, reproduced by permission of The Society for American Archaeology, adapted from American Antiquity 40: 51, 1975. **Fig. 5.12** From Cowgill, G. L. 1974. Quantitative studies of urbanization at Teotihuacan. Lt *Mesoamerican Archaeology: New Approaches*, ed. N. Hammond, pp. 363–397. Austin: University of Texas Press. Reproduced by permission of the Phillips Academy. **Fig. 5.16** Harris, E. C. 1989. *Principles of Archaeological Stratigraphy*, 2e. London: Academic Press. Reprinted with permission. **Fig. 5.25** From INVITATION TO ARCHAEOLOGY by James Deetz, copyright © 1967 by James Deetz. Used by permission of Doubleday, a division of Random House, Inc.

Chaptet 6 **Fig. 6.1** ©The Natural History Museum, London. Reprinted with permission. **Fig. 6.3** Courtesy of Payson D. Sheets. **Fig. 6.5** Jeremy A. Sabloff, "Ceramics," in *Excavations at Seibal, Department of Peten, Guatemala*, Gordon R. Willey, General Editor, Memoirs of the Peabody Museum of Archaeology and Ethnology, Harvard University, vol. 13, no.2. Copyright 1975 by the President and Fellows at Harvard College. **Fig. 6.7** Stylistic types of bronze fibulae from an Iron Age grave at Münsingen-Rain, canton of Berne, Switzerland. Reprinted by permission of the Bernese Historical Museum. courtesy of Arizona State Museum Collections, University of Arizona. **Fig. 6.12** From Blakely 1971, courtesy of Robert L. Blakely and the *American Journal of Physical Anthropology*. From *American Journal of Physical Anthropology*, April 28, 2005, pp. 43–53. Copyright © 2005 by John Wiley and Sons. Reprinted by permission of John Wiley and Sons via the Copyright Clearance Center.

Chapter 7 **Fig. 7.3** From INVITATION TO ARCHAEOLOGY by James Deetz, copyright © 1967 by James Deetz. Used by permission of Doubleday, a division of Random House, Inc. **Fig. 7.4** From ANCIENT MEN OF THE ARCTIC by J. Louis Giddings, copyright © 1967 by Alfred A. Knopf, Inc. Used by permission of Alfred A. Knopf, a division of Random House, Inc. Used by permission of Alfred A. Knopf, a division of Random House, Inc. **Fig. 7.6** From W S. Stallings, Jr., *Dating Prehistoric Ruins by Tree-Rings*, 1949 (revised ed.). Courtesy of Laboratory of Tree-Ring Research, The University of Arizona. **Fig. 7.8** Redrawn from R. E. Taylor, *Radiocarbon Dating: An Archaeological Perspective*. Copyright © 1987 by R. E. Taylor. Reprinted by permission of the author.

Chapter 8   Fig. 8.4 Plana of Mexico City, Mexico and Cusco City from before the conquest. Used with permission of Bridgeman Art Library International, New York. **Fig. 8.7** redrawn from *The Central Peruvian Interaction Sphere* by R. MacNeish, T. Patterson, and D. Brownman, Papers of the R. S. Peabody Foundation No. 7, 1975. **Fig. 8.8** From *Focus*, September 1995, p. 94. **Fig. 8.9** Michael Edward Moseley and Carol J. Mackey, *Twenty-Four Architectural Plans of Chan Chan, Peru*. Peabody Museum Press. Copyright 1974 by the President and Fellows of Harvard College. **Fig, 8.10** From Settlement Patterns in Archaeology by K C. Chang; copyright © 1972 by The Benjamin/Cummings Publishing Company. Reprinted with permission. **Fig. 8.11a & 8.11b** After Hodder and Hassal, 1971, by permission of Royal Anthropological Institute of Great Britain and Ireland. **Fig. 8.14** From Lewis-Williams, CURRENT ANTHROPOLOGY 27:2 (1986), p. 173. Reprinted by permission of The University of Chicago Press.

Chapter 9   Fig. 9.10 From *Mesoamerica: The Evolution of a Civilization* by Sanders and Price. © 1968 McGraw-Hill. Reprinted with permission. **Fig. 9.11** From *The Aztecs* by Michael E. Smith, published by Blackwell Publishers. © 1996 by Smith. Drawing by Emily Umberger. Reprinted by permission of Umberger.

Photo Credits

Chapter 1

Fig. 1.1: Courtesy of the Kentucky Archaeological Survey. Photo by Kenny Barkley.; Fig. 1.2: Courtesy of David Pollack, Kentucky Heritage Council and Cheryl Ann Munson, Indiana University, Bloomington; Fig. 1.3: © Martha Cooper/1988 National Geographic Image Collection; Fig. 1.4: © O. Louis Mazzatenta/National Geographic Society/Corbis; Fig. 1.5: © Griffith Institute, University of Oxford; Fig. 1.7: © Merle Greene Robertson, 1976.

Chapter 2

Fig. 2.1: © Fox Photos/Getty Images; Fig. 2.2: Courtesy Kenneth L. Feder; Fig. 2.3: © Alinari/Art Resource, NY; Fig. 2.4: From Stephens, John L. Incidents of Travel in Central America, Chiapas, and Yucatan. Copyright © 1949 by the Trustees of Rutgers College in New Jersey. Reprinted by permission of Rutgers University Press.; Fig. 2.5: © University/AFP/Getty Images.

Chapter 4

Fig. 4.1: Image Archives, Denver Museum of Nature & Science. All rights reserved.; Fig. 4.2: Courtesy of the Wendy Ashmore; Fig. 4.3: © Robert Harding World Imagery/Getty Images; Fig. 4.4: © The Institute of Nautical Archaeology; Fig. 4.8: © Christian Kober/JAI/Corbis; Fig. 4.9 (both): Otis Imboden, © 1972 National Geographic Image Collection; Fig. 4.10: © Massimo Vidale; Fig. 4.11: Courtesy of the Estate of Robert F. Heizer; Fig. 4.16: Courtesy of the Instituto Hondureño de Antropología e Historia and the Proyecto Arqueológico Acrópolis de Cópan.

Chapter 5

Fig. 5.2a: © Brand X Pictures/PunchStock; Fig. 5.2b: © Matt Champlin/Getty Images; Fig. 5.3: Courtesy of Centro Studie Scavi Archeologici in Asia of IsMEO, Rome; Fig. 5.4: © Julian Whittlesey; Fig. 5.5: Courtesy of the UCF Caracol Archaeological Project; Fig. 5.6: © European Space Imaging/DLR; Fig. 5.7 (both): © Nicolas Hartmann, MASCA, University of Pennsylvania Museum; Fig. 5.8, Fig. 5.9: Courtesy of the Museum of Applied Science Center for Archaeology, University of Pennsylvania Museum; Fig. 5.13: Courtesy of Payson D. Sheets; Fig. 5.17: Verapaz Project, University of Pennsylvania Museum; Fig. 5.18: Courtesy of Alan McPherron; Fig. 5.21: News and Information, University of Texas, Austin, photo by Larry Murphy; Fig. 5.22 (all): Courtesy of Martin Biddle, © Winchester Excavations Committee.

Chapter 6

Fig. 6.4a: Courtesy of the Wendy Ashmore; Fig. 6.4b: © Alan Gignoux/Alamy; Fig. 6.4c: © The Field Museum, Chicago, IL. Neg. #82515 (17); Fig. 6.4d: Courtesy of the Wendy Ashmore; Fig. 6.6: Courtesy of the Gordion Project, University of Pennsylvania Museum; Fig. 6.10: Courtesy University of Colorado Museum, J.B. Wheat; Fig. 6.13: Courtesy Dr. Frank P. Saul, Medical College of Ohio; Fig. 6.14a: Courtesy of the Wendy Ashmore; Fig. 6.14b: Courtesy of M. Thompson, Arizona State Museum, University of Arizona; Fig. 6.15: Courtesy of the Wendy Ashmore; Fig. 6.16a: © Patricia J. Wynne; Fig. 6.16b: © Somerset Levels Project. Photo by J.M. Coles.

Chapter 7

Fig. 7.5: Joseph W. Michels, Pennsylvania State University; Fig. 7.9b: Photo by Henry N. Michael. Courtesy of the Museum of Applied Science Center for Archaeology, University of Pennsylvania Museum; Fig. 7.10a: Courtesy Santa Bárbara Project, Honduras. Photo by Wendy Ashmore; Fig. 7.10b: © Manuel Leon Lopez and Helga Teiwes/National Geographic Image Collection.

Chapter 8

Fig. 8.1: © Carol Kramer, courtesy of Cambridge University Press; Fig. 8.3a: © The Field Museum, Chicago, IL. Neg. #CSA1185. Photograph by Charles Carpenter; Fig. 8.3b: © The Field Museum, Chicago, IL. Neg. #CSA246; Fig. 8.4: © Giraudon/Art Resource, NY; Fig. 8.5: Courtesy of the Wendy Ashmore; Fig. 8.6: © James Brunker/Alamy; Fig. 8.8: © Çatalhöyük Research Project. Photo by John G. Swogger.; Fig. 8.12a: Courtesy of George Dales; Fig. 8.12b: Courtesy of McGuire Gibson; Fig. 8.15: © The Bridgeman Art Library/Getty Images; Fig. 8.16: Courtesy of the Wendy Ashmore.

Chapter 9

Fig. 9.4: Courtesy of Robert H. Dyson, Jr., and the Hasanlu Project, University of Pennsylvania Museum.

Chapter 10

Fig. 10.1: Photo after The Mimbres People: Ancient Pueblo Painters of the American Southwest, by Steven A. LeBlanc; Fig. 10.2a: Courtesy of the Tikal Project, the University of Pennsylvania Museum; Fig. 10.2b: Courtesy Joya Hairs; Fig. 10.3: © Lucian Perkins/The Washington Post; Fig. 10.4: © Glow Images; Fig. 10.5: © Flickr RF/Getty Images; Fig. 10.6: Courtesy of The Archaeological Conservancy.

Glossary

Terms in italics are defined elsewhere in the glossary.

absolute dating or **chronometric dating**   Determination of age using a specific time scale, as in years before present (*B.P.*) or according to a fixed calendar (compare with *relative dating*). (Chapter 7)

acquisition   The first stage of *behavioral processes*, in which raw materials are procured (see *manufacture*, *use*, and *deposition*). (Chapter 4)

actualistic studies   Detailed observations of the actual use of materials like those found in the *archaeological record* (*artifacts*, *ecofacts*, and *features*), used to produce reliable *general analogies* for *interpretation*. (Chapter 8)

alloy   A mixture of two or more metals, such as bronze (copper and tin), used in *metallurgy*. (Chapter 6)

analogy   A process of reasoning in which similarity between two entities in some characteristics is taken to imply similarity in other characteristics as well; the basis of most archaeological *interpretation* (see *general analogy* and *specific analogy*). (Chapter 8)

analysis   A stage in archaeological *research design* in which data are isolated, described, and structured, usually via typological *classification*, and chronological, functional, technological, and constituent determinations are made. (Chapter 4)

annealing   Application of heat in the *manufacture* of metal *artifacts*. (Chapter 6)

anthropology   The comprehensive study of the human species from biological, social, and cultural perspectives using both *synchronic* and *diachronic* views; in the United States, it comprises the subdisciplines of biological or physical anthropology, cultural anthropology, linguistic anthropology, and archaeology, usually including both *historical* and *prehistoric archaeology*. (Chapter 1)

antiquarian   A nonprofessional who studies the past for its artistic or cultural value (compare with *archaeologist* and *looter*). (Chapter 2)

arbitrary sample unit   A unit of archaeological investigation; a subdivision of the *data universe* with no cultural relevance, such as a *sample unit* defined by a site grid (compare with *nonarbitrary sample unit*). (Chapter 4)

archaeoastronomy   Inference of ancient astronomical knowledge through study of astronomy-related aspects of the *archaeological record*; it combines perspectives of *archaeology* and astronomy. (Chapter 8)

archaeological culture   The maximum grouping of all *assemblages* assumed to represent the sum of human activities carried out within a single ancient *culture*. (Chapter 5)

archaeological record   The physical remains produced by past human activities, which are sought, recovered, studied, and interpreted by *archaeologists* to reconstruct the past (see also *artifact*, *ecofact*, and *feature*). (Chapter 1)

archaeological survey   A method of *data gathering* in which data are gathered and evaluated from the surface of archaeological *sites*, usually by mapping of *features* and surface collection of *artifacts* and *ecofacts*. (Chapter 5)

archaeologist   A professional scholar who studies the human past through its physical remains (compare with *antiquarian* and *looter*). (Chapter 1)

archaeology   The study of the human past through material remains, with the aim of ordering and describing the events of the past and explaining their meaning. (Chapter 1)

archaeomagnetic dating   Measurement of magnetic alignments within undisturbed *features*, such as hearths and kilns; comparison is then made to known schedules of past magnetic alignments within a region to yield an absolute age for the feature. (Chapter 7)

argon-argon dating   A *radiometric dating* technique, a refinement of *potassium-argon dating*, that measures argon isotopes in mineral samples. (Chapter 7)

artifact   A discrete and portable object in the archaeological record whose characteristics result wholly or in part from human activity; artifacts are individually assignable to *ceramic*, lithic, metal, *organic*, or other categories (see also *industry, lithic technology*, and *metallurgy*). (Chapter 4)

assemblage   A gross grouping of all *subassemblages* assumed to represent the sum of human activities carried out within an ancient community (see *archaeological culture*). (Chapter 5)

association   Occurrence of an item of archaeological data adjacent to another and in or on the same *matrix*. (Chapter 4)

attribute   The minimal characteristic used as a criterion for grouping artifacts into classes; includes *stylistic, form*, and *technological attributes* (see also *classification*). (Chapter 5)

augering   A *subsurface survey* technique using a drill run by either human or machine power to determine the depth and characteristics of archaeological or natural deposits. (Chapter 5)

battleship-shaped curve   A lens-shaped graph representing changes in *artifact* type frequencies over time, from origin to expanding popularity, decline, and, finally, disappearance. (Chapter 7)

behavioral archaeology   Study of the relationship between human behavior and material data, in the past and in the present. (Chapter 3)

behavioral processes   Human activities, including *acquisition, manufacture, use*, and *deposition* behavior, that produce tangible archaeological remains (compare with *transformational processes*). (Chapter 4)

bioarchaeology   Joint biological and cultural study of human remains and burial sites to investigate how people in a society lived, including their social organization, health, diet, division of labor, and population structure. (Chapter 6)

blade   A long, thin, parallel-sided *flake* usually made from a cylindrical *core* (see *lithic technology*). (Chapter 6)

bone chemistry   Several *relative dating* techniques applicable to bone material, including measurements of the depletion of nitrogen and the accumulation of fluorine and uranium. (Chapter 7)

B.P.   Before present; used in age determinations; in calculating radiocarbon dates, present means 1950 (a fixed reference date). (Chapter 7)

central place theory   The theory that human settlements will space themselves evenly across a landscape depending on the availability of resources and communication routes, and that these settlements will become differentiated, forming a hierarchy of controlling centers called central places (see *locational analysis*). (Chapter 8)

ceramics   *Artifacts* of fired clay belonging to *pottery*, figurine, or other ceramic *industries*. (Chapter 6)

chronometric dating   See *absolute dating.*

classification   The ordering of phenomena into groups (classes) based on the sharing of *attributes.* (Chapters 2 and 5)

clearing excavations   *Excavations* that reveal the horizontal dimensions of archaeological *sites* to define the extent, distribution, and patterning of archaeological data (compare with *penetrating excavations*). (Chapter 5)

cold hammering   A technique for making metal *artifacts* in which the metal is shaped by percussion without heating. (Chapter 6)

community-based archaeology   Research and interpretation planned and implemented by archaeologists and a local community, usually the people whose past is the subject of study. (Chapter 1)

computer simulation studies   Reconstructions of the past based on *models* that describe ancient conditions and variables and then use computers to generate a sequence of events in order to compare the results against the known *archaeological record,* thus refining and testing *hypotheses* about the past. (Chapter 9)

conjoining studies   The refitting of fragments of artifacts and ecofacts to evaluate the integrity of an archaeological deposit; such studies allow definition of *cumulative features,* such as lithic debris scatters; they sometimes allow reconstruction of ancient *manufacture* and *use* behavior. (Chapter 5)

conquest   Aggressive movement of human groups from one area to another resulting in the subjugation of the native society. (Chapter 9)

constructed feature   A *feature* deliberately built to provide a setting for one or more activities, such as a house, storeroom, or burial chamber (compare with *cumulative feature*). (Chapter 6)

context   Characteristics of archaeological data that result from combined *behavioral* and *transformational processes,* which are evaluated by means of recorded *association, matrix,* and *provenience* (see *primary context* and *secondary context*). (Chapter 4)

coprolites   Preserved ancient feces, studied because they contain food residues that can be used to reconstruct ancient diet and subsistence activities. (Chapter 6)

core   A lithic *artifact* from which *flakes* are removed; it is used as a tool or a blank from which other tools are made (see *lithic technology*). (Chapter 6)

coring   A *subsurface survey* technique using a hollow metal tube driven into the ground to lift a column of earth for stratigraphic study. (Chapter 5)

cultural adaptation   The sum of the adjustments of a human society to its environment (see *cultural ecology*). (Chapter 9)

cultural drift   Gradual cultural change due to the imperfect transmission of information between generations; it is analogous to genetic drift in biology. (Chapter 9)

cultural ecology   The study of the dynamic interaction between human society and its environment, which views *culture* as the primary adaptive mechanism in the relationship. (Chapters 8 and 9)

cultural evolution   The theory that human societies change via a process analogous to the evolution of biological species (see *unilinear cultural evolution* and *multilinear cultural evolution*). (Chapter 2)

cultural invention   The origin of new cultural forms within a society whether by accident or design. (Chapter 9)

cultural process approach   Archaeological *interpretation* aimed at delineating the inter-actions and changes in cultural *systems* by the application of both descriptive and explana-tory *models* based on ecological and materialist views of *culture*. (Chapters 3 and 9)

cultural resource management (CRM)   The conservation and selective investigation of prehistoric and historic remains; specifically, the development of ways and means, in-cluding legislation, to safeguard the past. (Chapters 1 and 10)

cultural revival   Reuse of abandoned cultural elements. (Chapter 9)

cultural selection   The process that leads to differential retention of cultural traits, which increases a society's potential for successful *cultural adaptation* while eliminating maladaptive traits. (Chapter 9)

culture   The concept that both underlies and unites the discipline of *anthropology* and, in its various definitions, acts as a central *model* by which archaeological data are interpreted; a definition suited to archaeology sees culture as the cumulative resource of human society that provides the means for nongenetic adaptation to the envi-ronment by regulating behavior in three areas—*technology*, *social systems*, and *ideology*. (Chapter 1)

culture area   A spatial unit defined by *ethnographically* observed cultural similarities within a given geographical area; used archaeologically to define spatial limits to *archaeo-logical cultures* (see also *time-space grids*). (Chapter 3)

culture history approach   Archaeological *interpretation* based on temporal and spatial syntheses of data and the application of general descriptive *models* usually derived from a normative view of *culture*. (Chapters 3 and 9)

cumulative feature   A *feature* without evidence of deliberate construction but which results instead from accretion, as a *midden*, or subtraction, as a quarry (compare with *constructed feature*). (Chapter 6)

data gathering   A stage in archaeological *research design* in which data are gathered, normally by *surface survey* and *excavation*. (Chapter 4)

data processing   A stage in archaeological *research design* usually involving, in the case of *artifacts*, cleaning, conserving, labeling, inventorying, and cataloging. (Chapter 4)

data universe   A defined area of archaeological investigation, often a *region* or *site*, bounded in time and space. (Chapter 4)

debitage   Workshop debris. (Chapter 6)

dendrochronology   The study of tree-ring growth patterns, which are linked to de-velop a continuous chronological sequence. (Chapter 7)

deposition   The last stage of *behavioral processes*, in which *artifacts* are discarded (see *acquisition*, *manufacture*, and *use*). (Chapter 4)

diachronic   Pertaining to phenomena as they occur or change over a period of time; a chronological perspective (compare with *synchronic*). (Chapter 1)

diffusion   Transmission of ideas from one culture to another. (Chapter 9)

direct dating   Determination of the age of archaeological data by analysis of the *artifact*, *ecofact*, or *feature* itself (compare with *indirect dating*). (Chapter 7)

direct percussion   A technique used for the manufacture of chipped-stone *artifacts* in which *flakes* are produced by striking a *core* with a hammer stone or striking the core against a fixed stone or anvil (compare with *indirect percussion* and *pressure flaking*). (Chapter 6)

documentary history   The study of the past through written records, which are compared, judged for accuracy, placed in chronological sequence, and interpreted in light of preceding, contemporary, and subsequent events. (Chapter 1)

ecofact   Nonartifactual evidence from the past that has cultural relevance; the category includes both inorganic and organic objects. (Chapter 4)

ethnoarchaeology   *Ethnographic* studies designed to aid archaeological *interpretation*, such as descriptions of *behavioral processes*, especially the ways material items enter the *archaeological record* (see *analogy*). (Chapter 8)

ethnocentrism   An observational bias in which other societies are evaluated by standards relevant to the observer's *culture*. (Chapters 2 and 9)

ethnography   The description of contemporary cultures; part of the subdiscipline of cultural *anthropology*. (Chapter 1)

ethnology   The comparative study of contemporary cultures; part of the subdiscipline of cultural *anthropology*. (Chapter 1)

evolutionary archaeology   A neo-Darwinian approach that sees culture change produced by evolutionary processes similar to those of biological evolution. (Chapter 3)

excavation   *Data gathering* by removal of *matrix* to reveal the three-dimensional structure of the data and matrix, both vertically (see *penetrating excavations*) and horizontally (see *clearing excavations*). (Chapter 5)

exchange systems   Systems for trade or transfer of goods, services, and ideas between individuals and societies. (Chapter 8)

experimental archaeology   Studies designed to aid archaeological *interpretation* by attempting to duplicate *behavioral processes* experimentally under carefully controlled conditions (see *analogy*). (Chapter 8)

feature   Nonportable archaeological remains that cannot be recovered from *matrix* without destroying their integrity (see *constructed feature* and *cumulative feature*). (Chapter 4)

feedback   A response to a stimulus that acts within a *system* (see *negative feedback* and *positive feedback*). (Chapter 9)

fission-track dating   A *radiometric dating* technique based on the number of fission tracks left by the decay of trace elements such as ^{238}U in mineral samples. (Chapter 7)

flake   A lithic *artifact* detached from a *core*, either as waste or as a tool (see *lithic technology*). (Chapter 6)

form attributes   *Attributes* based on the physical characteristics of an *artifact*, including overall shape, the shape of parts, and measurable dimensions; leads to form *classification*. (Chapter 5)

form types   Classes of *artifacts* based on *form attributes*. (Chapter 5)

formulation   The first stage in archaeological *research design*; involves definition of the research problem and goals, background investigations, and feasibility studies. (Chapter 4)

frequency seriation   A *relative dating* technique in which artifacts or other archaeological data are chronologically ordered by ranking their relative frequencies to conform with *battleship-shaped curves* (see *seriation*). (Chapter 7)

general analogy   An *analogy* used in archaeological *interpretation* based on broad and generalized comparisons that are documented across many cultural *traditions* (see *actualistic studies*). (Chapter 8)

geochronology   Determining age by studying the *association* of archaeological data with geological formations. (Chapter 7)

glaze   A specialized *slip*, applied to *pottery*, that produces an impermeable and glassy surface when fired at high temperatures (see *vitrification*). (Chapter 6)

ground truth   Determination of the causes of patterns revealed by *remote sensing*, such as by examining, on the ground, features identified by aerial photography. (Chapter 5)

half-life   The period required for one-half of a radioactive isotope to decay and form a stable element; this decay rate, expressed as a statistical constant for each isotope with a specified range of error, provides the measurement scale for *radiometric dating*. (Chapter 7)

historical archaeology   That area of *archaeology* concerned with literate societies and often allied with *history*. In the United States, both historical archaeology and *prehistoric archaeology* are usually considered part of *anthropology*. (Chapter 1)

horizon   Cross-cultural regularities at one point in time; the spatial baseline of the New World *culture history approach* synthesis proposed by Willey and Phillips (1958) (compare with *tradition*). (Chapter 3)

horizontal stratigraphy   Chronological sequences based on successive horizontal displacements, such as sequential beach terraces; analogous to *stratigraphy*. (Chapter 7)

hydration   See *obsidian hydration*.

hypothesis   A proposition, often derived from a broader generalization or law, which postulates relationships between two or more variables based on specified assumptions and which makes predictions that are tested by further research. (Chapter 1)

ideology   One of three components of *culture;* the knowledge or beliefs used by human societies to understand and cope with their existence (see also *technology* and *social systems*). (Chapter 8)

implementation   The second stage in archaeological *research design*, which involves obtaining permits, raising funds, and making logistical arrangements. (Chapter 4)

indigenous archaeologies   Archaeological research conducted by, and emphasizing perspectives, issues, and techniques of most interest to, the descendants of past peoples being studied. (Chapter 1)

indirect dating   Determining the age of archaeological data by using its *association* with a *matrix* or object of known age (compare *direct dating*). (Chapter 7)

indirect percussion   A technique used to manufacture chipped-stone *artifacts* in which *flakes* are produced by striking a punch, usually made of wood or bone, placed against a *core* (compare with *direct percussion* and *pressure flaking*). (Chapter 6)

industry   A category of *artifacts* defined by shared material and *technology*, such as the chipped-stone or *pottery* industries. (Chapter 6)

inevitable variation   The premise that all cultures vary and change over time without specific cause; a general and unsatisfactory descriptive *model* sometimes implied in *culture historical interpretation*. (Chapter 9)

interpretation   A stage in archaeological *research design* involving the synthesis of results of data *analysis* and the explanation of their meaning in order to reconstruct the past. (Chapter 4)

law of superposition   The principle that the sequence of observable *strata* from bottom to top reflects the order of *deposition* from earliest to latest (see *stratigraphy*). (Chapter 5)

LiDar   Light Detection and Ranging, an airborne remote sensing technique that can "see through" even dense vegetation to reveal architecture and other modifications to the landscape. (Chapter 5)

lithic technology   *Artifacts* made from stone, including the chipped-stone and ground-stone *industries*. (Chapter 6)

locational analysis   Techniques from geography used to study locations of human settlement and to infer the determinants of these locations (see *central place theory*). (Chapter 8)

looter   An individual who plunders archaeological *sites* to find *artifacts* of commercial value, at the same time destroying the evidence that archaeologists rely on to understand the past (compare with *antiquarian* and *archaeologist*). (Chapters 1 and 10)

magnetometer   A device used in *subsurface survey* that measures minor variations in the earth's magnetic field, which may reveal archaeological *features* as magnetic anomalies. (Chapter 5)

manufacture   The second stage of *behavioral processes*, in which raw materials are modified to produce *artifacts* (see *acquisition, use,* and *deposition*). (Chapter 4)

matrix   The physical medium that surrounds, holds, or supports archaeological data. (Chapter 4)

metallurgy   The group of *industries* involved in extracting metals from ore and using them to make *artifacts;* includes the copper, bronze, and iron industries. (Chapter 6)

metate   A common New World term for ground-stone basins used to process grains (see also *quern*). (Chapter 6)

micromorphology   The microscopic study of soils and sediments in thin sections cut from *matrix*. (Chapters 5 and 8)

midden   An accumulation of debris resulting from human disposal and removed from areas of *manufacture* and *use;* may result from either one-time refuse disposal or long-term disposal resulting in *stratification*. (Chapter 4)

migration   Movement of human populations from one area to another, usually resulting in cultural contact. (Chapter 9)

model   A theoretical scheme constructed to understand a specific set of data or phenomena; descriptive models deal with the form and structure of phenomena, while explanatory models seek underlying causes for phenomena; models may also be *diachronic* or *synchronic*. (Chapters 1 and 2)

multilinear cultural evolution   A theory of *cultural evolution* that sees each society pursuing an individual evolutionary career shaped by accumulated specific *cultural adaptations*, rather than seeing all societies as pursuing the same course (compare with *unilinear cultural evolution*). (Chapters 2 and 9)

multiple working hypotheses   The simultaneous testing of alternative *hypotheses* to minimize bias and maximize the chances of finding the best available choice. (Chapter 3)

multivariate strategy   A class of *models* of *multilinear cultural evolution* that see major cultural changes as the result of multiple, relatively small adaptive adjustments (compare with *prime movers*). (Chapter 9)

negative feedback   A response to changing conditions that acts to dampen or stop a *system*'s reaction. (Chapter 9)

nonarbitrary sample unit   A unit of archaeological investigation; a subdivision of the *data universe* with cultural relevance, such as rooms or houses (compare with *arbitrary sample unit*). (Chapter 4)

nongovernmental organization (NGO)   A group acting independently of national or other governments, and usually not-for-profit. In archaeology, these include organizations working to protect cultural heritage in the U.S. and/or internationally.

nonprobabilistic sampling   Gathering of sample data based on informal criteria or personal judgment; it does not allow evaluation of how representative the sample is with respect to the *population* (compare with *probabilistic sampling*). (Chapter 4)

norms   Rules that govern behavior in a particular society. (Chapter 3)

obsidian hydration   Adsorption of water on exposed surfaces of obsidian; if the local hydration rate is known and constant, this phenomenon can be used as a *relative dating* technique through measurement of the thickness of the hydration layer. (Chapter 7)

oral history   Spoken accounts about the past that maintain historical traditions without reliance on written documents. (Chapter 1)

organic artifacts   *Artifacts* made of organic materials, including products of the wood, bone, horn, fiber, ivory, or hide *industries*. (Chapter 6)

penetrating excavations   *Excavations* that reveal the vertical dimensions of archaeological deposits to define the depth, sequence, and composition of buried data (compare with *clearing excavations*). (Chapter 5)

period   A broad and general chronological unit defined for a *site* or *region* based on combined data, such as sets of contemporary *artifact* types (see also *time-space grid*). (Chapter 3)

phytoliths   Microscopic silica bodies that form in living plants and provide a durable floral *ecofact* that allows the identification of plant remains in archaeological deposits. (Chapter 6)

population   The aggregate of all *sample units* within a *data universe*. (Chapter 4)

positive feedback   A response to changing conditions that acts to stimulate further reactions within a *system*. (Chapter 9)

postprocessual archaeology   Archaeological *interpretation* aimed at understanding the past by reconstructing the point of view of past peoples who produced the *archaeological record*. (Chapters 3 and 9)

potassium-argon dating   A *radiometric dating* technique based on the *half-life* of the radioactive isotope of potassium (^{40}K) that decays to form argon (^{40}Ar). (Chapter 7)

pottery   A class of *ceramic artifacts* in which clay is formed into containers by hand or in molds or with a potter's wheel, often decorated, and fired. (Chapter 6)

prehistoric archaeology   The area of *archaeology* concerned with preliterate or nonliterate societies. In the United States, both prehistoric archaeology and *historical archaeology* are considered a part of *anthropology*. (Chapter 1)

pressure flaking   A technique for manufacturing chipped-stone *artifacts* in which *flakes* or *blades* are produced by applying pressure against a *core* with a punch usually made of wood or bone (compare with *direct percussion* and *indirect percussion*). (Chapter 6)

primary context   The condition that results when *provenience*, *association*, and *matrix* have not been disturbed since the original *deposition* of archaeological data (compare with *secondary context*). (Chapter 4)

prime movers   Factors crucial to stimulating major cultural change; they are emphasized in some *models* of *multilinear cultural evolution* (compare with *multivariate strategy*). (Chapter 9)

probabilistic sampling   *Sample data gathering* based on formal statistical criteria in selecting *sample units* to be investigated; it allows evaluation of how representative the sample is with respect to the data *population* (compare with *nonprobabilistic sampling*). (Chapter 4)

processual archaeology   See *cultural process approach.*

provenience   The three-dimensional location of archaeological data within or on the *matrix* at the time of discovery. (Chapter 4)

pseudoarchaeology   Use of real or imagined archaeological evidence to justify nonscientific accounts about the past. (Chapter 1)

publication   The final stage of archaeological *research design*, providing reports of the data and *interpretations* resulting from archaeological research. (Chapter 4)

quern   A common Old World term for ground-stone basins used to process grains (see also *metate*). (Chapter 6)

radiocarbon dating   A *radiometric dating* technique based on measuring the decay of the radioactive isotope of carbon (^{14}C) to stable nitrogen (^{14}N). (Chapter 7)

radiometric dating   A variety of *absolute dating* techniques based on the transformation of unstable radioactive isotopes into stable elements (see *potassium-argon dating* and *radiocarbon dating*). (Chapter 7)

reflexive method   A method that emphasizes constant and continuous *interpretation* and reinterpretation, based on the premise that evidence does not exist apart from interpretation and theory. (Chapter 3)

region   A geographically defined area containing a series of interrelated human communities sharing a single cultural-ecological *system*. (Chapter 4)

relative dating   Determining chronological sequence without reference to a fixed time scale (compare with *absolute dating*). (Chapter 7)

remote sensing   *Archaeological survey* methods involving aerial or subsurface detection of archaeological data. (Chapter 5)

research design   A systematic plan to coordinate archaeological research to ensure the efficient use of resources and to guide the research according to the *scientific method* (see *formulation, implementation, data gathering, data processing, analysis, interpretation,* and *publication*). (Chapter 4)

resistivity detector   An instrument used in *subsurface survey* that measures differences in the conductivity of electrical current and thus may identify archaeological *features*. (Chapter 5)

retouch   A technique of chipped-stone *artifact manufacture* in which *pressure flaking* is used to remove small, steep *flakes* to modify the edges of flake tools. (Chapter 6)

sample data gathering   Investigation of only a portion of the *sample units* in a *population* using either *probabilistic* or *nonprobabilistic sampling* (compare with *total data gathering*). (Chapter 4)

sample unit   The basic unit of archaeological investigation; a subdivision of the *data universe*, defined by either arbitrary or nonarbitrary criteria (see *arbitrary sample unit* and *nonarbitrary sample unit*). (Chapter 4)

science   The systematic pursuit of knowledge about natural phenomena (in contrast to the nonnatural or supernatural) by a continually self-correcting method of testing and refining the conclusions resulting from observation (see *scientific method*). (Chapters 1 and 9)

scientific method   The operational means of *science*, by which natural phenomena are observed and conclusions drawn. (Chapter 1)

secondary context   The condition where *provenience, association,* and *matrix* have been wholly or partially altered by *transformational* processes after original *deposition* of archaeological data (compare with *primary context*). (Chapter 4)

sequence comparison   A *relative dating* technique based on the presence of similar sequences of *artifacts* at two or more *sites*. (Chapter 7)

seriation   Techniques used to order materials in a *relative dating* sequence in such a way that adjacent items in the series are more similar to each other than to items farther apart in the series (see *frequency seriation* and *stylistic seriation*). (Chapter 7)

settlement archaeology   The study of the spatial distribution of ancient activities, from remains of single activity areas to those of entire *regions*. (Chapter 8)

shovel testing   A *subsurface survey* technique using either posthole diggers or shovels to make a rapid determination of the density and distribution of archaeological remains. (Chapter 5)

simple random sampling   A *probabilistic sampling* technique in which each *sample unit* has a statistically equal chance for selection. (Chapter 4)

site   A spatial clustering of archaeological data, comprising *artifacts*, *ecofacts*, and *features* in any combination. (Chapter 4)

slip   A solution of clay and water applied to *pottery* to provide color and a smooth and uniform surface (see also *glaze*). (Chapter 6)

smelting   Application of heat to ores to extract metals prior to the manufacture of metal *artifacts* (see *metallurgy*). (Chapter 6)

social systems   One of the three basic components of *culture;* the means by which human societies organize themselves and their interactions with other societies (see also *technology* and *ideology*). (Chapter 8)

specific analogy   An *analogy* used in archaeological *interpretation* based on specific comparisons that are documented within a single cultural *tradition*. (Chapter 8)

strata   The definable layers of archaeological *matrix* or *features* revealed by *excavation* (see *stratification*). (Chapters 2 and 5)

stratification   Multiple *strata* whose order of deposition reflects the *law of superposition* (see *stratigraphy*). (Chapter 5)

stratified sampling   A *probabilistic sampling* technique in which *sample units* are drawn from two or more sampling *strata*. (Chapter 4)

stratigraphy   The archaeological evaluation of the significance of *stratification* to determine the temporal sequence of data within stratified deposits by using both the *law of superposition* and *context* evaluations; also a *relative dating* technique. (Chapters 2, 5, and 7)

stylistic attributes   *Attributes* defined by the surface characteristics of *artifacts*—color, texture, decoration, and so forth—leading to stylistic *classifications*. (Chapter 5)

stylistic seriation   A *relative dating* technique in which *artifacts* or other data are ordered chronologically according to stylistic similarities (see *seriation*). (Chapter 7)

stylistic types   *Artifact* classes based on *stylistic attributes*. (Chapter 5)

subassemblage   A grouping of *artifact* classes based on form and function that is assumed to represent a single occupational group within an ancient community (see *assemblage* and *archaeological culture*). (Chapter 5)

subsurface survey   *Remote sensing* techniques of area below ground carried out at ground level; includes *auguring, coring, shovel testing,* and use of a *magnetometer, resistivity detector,* and similar means. (Chapter 5)

surface survey   An *archaeological survey* technique using direct observation to discover and gather archaeological data present on the ground surface; includes mapping and surface collection. (Chapter 5)

synchronic   Pertaining to phenomena at one point in time; a concurrent perspective (compare with *diachronic*). (Chapter 1)

system   An organization that functions through the interdependence of its parts. (Chapters 3, 8, and 9)

systematic sampling   A *probabilistic sampling* technique in which the first *sample unit* is selected at random and all other units are selected by a predetermined interval from the first. (Chapter 4)

taphonomy   Study of the *transformational processes* affecting organic *ecofacts* after the death of the original organisms. (Chapter 4)

technological attributes   *Attributes* related to the characteristics of raw materials and *manufacturing* methods; lead to technological *classifications*. (Chapter 5)

technological types   *Artifact* classes based on *technological attributes*. (Chapter 5)

technology   One of the three basic components of *culture;* the means used by human societies to interact directly with and adapt to the environment (see *ideology* and *social systems*). (Chapter 8)

three-age system   A traditional *diachronic model* describing the sequence of technological *periods* in the Old World, each period characterized by predominant use of stone, bronze, or iron tools. (Chapter 2)

time-space grids   A synthesis of temporal and spatial distributions of data used in the *culture history approach* based on *period* sequences within *culture areas*. (Chapter 3)

total data gathering   Investigation of all *sample units* in a *population* (compare with *sample data gathering*). (Chapter 4)

trade   Transmission of material objects from one society to another; a descriptive cultural *model* used in the *culture history approach* (see *exchange systems*). (Chapter 9)

tradition   Cultural continuity through time; the temporal basis of the New World *culture history approach* synthesis proposed by Willey and Phillips (1958) (compare with *horizon*). (Chapter 3)

transformational processes   Conditions and events that affect archaeological data from the time of *deposition* to the time of recovery (compare with *behavioral processes;* see also *taphonomy*). (Chapter 4)

type   A class of data defined by a consistent clustering of *attributes* (see *classification*). (Chapter 5)

unilinear cultural evolution   A 19th-century version of *cultural evolution* holding that all human societies change according to a single fixed evolutionary course, passing through the same stages, described as savagery, barbarism, and civilization by Lewis Henry Morgan (compare *multilinear cultural evolution*). (Chapter 2)

uranium-series dating   A *radiometric dating* technique based on uranium isotopes with short *half-lives* used to date calcite and similar samples. (Chapter 7)

use   The third stage of *behavioral processes*, in which *artifacts* are utilized (see *acquisition, manufacture*, and *deposition*). (Chapter 4)

vitrification   Melting and fusion of glassy minerals within clay during high-temperature firing of *pottery* (above 1000°C), resulting in loss of porosity. (Chapter 6)

Index